THE FEAST NEARBY

THE *Feast Nearby*

How I lost my job, buried a marriage, and found my way by keeping chickens, foraging, preserving, bartering, and eating locally (all on forty dollars a week)

ROBIN MATHER

TEN SPEED PRESS
Berkeley

For my mother, Jane Bobby Hughes Mather (1921–1999),
who taught me well and truly about everything that matters;
and for Boon, who was a Good Dog.

Copyright © 2011 by Robin Mather
Illustrations copyright © 2011 by Barry Fitzgerald

All rights reserved.
Published in the United States by Ten Speed Press, an imprint of
the Crown Publishing Group, a division of Random House, Inc., New York.
www.crownpublishing.com
www.tenspeed.com

Ten Speed Press and the Ten Speed Press colophon are
registered trademarks of Random House, Inc.

Library of Congress Cataloging-in-Publication Data

Mather, Robin.
  The feast nearby : how I lost my job, buried a marriage, and found my
way by keeping chickens, foraging, preserving, bartering, and eating
locally (all on $40 a week) / Robin Mather.
      p. cm.
  Includes index.
  Summary: "A charming ode (with recipes) to eating well and locally, on
$40 per week, from a recently unemployed food-journalism
veteran"—Provided by publisher.
  1. Low budget cooking. 2. Cookbooks. I. Title.
  TX652.M2958 2011
  641.5'52—dc22
                              2010045085

ISBN 978-1-58008-558-8

Printed in the United States of America

Design by Nancy Austin

10 9 8 7 6 5 4 3 2 1

First Edition

CONTENTS

WINTER

INTRODUCTION

In April 2009, my husband of twelve years told me that he wanted a divorce. Less than a week later, the *Chicago Tribune*, where I worked as a staff reporter for the food section, laid me off, effectively ending my lifelong career as a newspaper reporter. Equipped with skills the imploding newspaper industry no longer needed, I was too old for hiring managers to consider me seriously, at a difficult age to launch an entirely new career, and too young to simply give up. I found myself without income, heartbroken, and terrified.

Battered by life storms, I retreated to my lakeside cottage in western Michigan. I hoped that the contact with so much native beauty—a life embedded in the rhythms of the natural world—would salve my spirit. There I settled with my standard poodle, Boon, and Pippin, an African Grey parrot. The animals are a very large part of my life; they are as much a part of this story as the weather or my acts.

Of necessity, I had to live on a very strict budget, limiting myself to just forty dollars a week for food—all food, including spices and coffee—because as a freelancer, I couldn't count on a guaranteed income.

For more than twenty-five years, I'd sampled the finest foods and wines the world has to offer. The late Julia Child prepared lunch for me at her Cambridge, Massachusetts, home. I ate foie gras five days in a row while spending a week at Paul Bocuse's culinary academy just outside Lyons, France. I had insider access to the exhibitors' booths and their samples of spectacular specialty foods and fine wines at the biennial Slow Food gathering in Turin, Italy. My work took me to South Korea, where I tasted food all day, every day, for more than a week with Korea-born chef Bill Kim, and to Chiapas, Mexico, where I traveled with Mexican food authority and restaurateur Rick Bayless. I won national prizes for a story that followed a "silverbrite"—a shrewd marketing term for chum, or dog, salmon—from its home waters in remote western Alaska to a Kroger market in suburban Detroit and was a two-time James Beard journalism award finalist for feature writing.

1

Those days were gone. Still, eating well had become my habit. I was unwilling to compromise on that matter.

So, following the conclusions I drew in writing my first book, *A Garden of Unearthly Delights: Bioengineering and the Future of Food*, I determined to spend as many of those precious food dollars as I could with the people who grew my food.

This book reflects what I did over the course of a year in following that disciplined regimen. You will find recipes for the foods I ate, together with essays that follow my thinking as I lived out that year. The book begins in spring, because spring is the beginning of the growing season and because spring is the season of rebirth; this recounting is also about a season of rebirth in my own life. It may be read as a cookbook, as a collection of gastronomic writing, or as a history, a peek into the heart and mind of a middle-aged woman determined to resurrect her life. The recipes are all kitchen-tested by me, an experienced but not professionally trained home cook, using simple kitchen equipment. The recipes are not gourmet or high-end, but rather the kind of food that satisfies the spirit and nurtures the body. They draw inspiration from my twenty-five-plus years of food writing and travel and are grounded in sound nutritional principle. Although I live alone, the recipes are geared to serve four to six people. Sometimes I froze surplus servings or ate leftovers for a day or two, but more typically, I invited someone to share my table. Having enough to share is one definition of wealth for me.

❋ ❋ ❋

The concept of eating locally and sustainably has gained broad interest since I advocated for it in my first book in 1995. It put Michael Pollan's books on the bestseller lists and has catapulted Barbara Kingsolver into wider audiences than just those of us who love her fiction.

It's relatively easy to be a locavore if you live in a major urban area like Chicago. There, farmers' markets operate nearly year-round and are prosperous enough to draw growers from four states. But critics of locavore subsistence often snipe about its cost. Throw in budget constraints, and the prospect of eating locally looks much tougher. A weekly budget of forty dollars for a woman my age falls a little more than halfway between the United States Department of Agriculture's "thrifty" food budget of $34.80 per person and its "low-cost" budget of $43.20. But the USDA's suggested shopping lists for those budgets involve a lot of squishy white bread and peanut butter sandwiches for dinner, powdered milk, and instant orange drinks. Menus like that may provide enough calories to sustain life but there's little there to please the inner woman. I wanted to look forward to meals, to have enough good food at hand to keep my spirits high. Because I live six miles from the nearest village and more than ten miles from the nearest town of any size, I needed to keep a well-stocked pantry; the several times I was snowed in for two or more days at a time proved the wisdom of doing so.

Eating locally requires, almost by definition, some compromises. Coffee doesn't grow in the Great Lakes region and neither do chocolate nor olives for oil or table. Eating locally meant more work: I'd have to commit to canning, freezing, and dehydrating the surpluses of the season. It meant prowling farmers' markets for bargains and figuring out what to do with them once I got them home. With no sunny spot in my shady lake-lot yard for a garden, I couldn't grow much myself.

I decided early on that I couldn't limit myself to organically grown foods. In some cases, it turned out not to be an option, and with my budget, I couldn't always afford to seek out organic produce. Moreover, some of the growers I befriended through weekly purchases were still transitioning to organic, or were unable or unwilling to do so; I wanted to support those growers who are my neighbors. I considered joining a community-supported agriculture, or CSA, endeavor, but couldn't afford the up-front costs and needed more produce—to can and freeze—than a weekly share would bring me.

Cues from the natural world guided my food choices. The last big snowstorm blew in just as maple sugaring started. When the forsythia marking old farmsteads bloomed, asparagus and rhubarb were on their way. When a snapping turtle as big as a galvanized washtub laid her eggs in my driveway, it was time for early strawberries. When the white-tail bucks left their mixed herds in August, their antlers shedding velvet as they prepared for the rut, I dug out the corn cutter for sweet corn.

Along the way, my journalistic curiosity caused me to investigate why finding local milk is difficult, but not impossible, and why dairy products—butter, cream, sour cream, and yogurt—may pose one of the locavore's biggest challenges. I gave thought to reasonable compromise—surely I couldn't live without chocolate!—and to when spending money on expensive specialty goods, like imported Parmigiano-Reggiano cheese, was a sound value for me. I taught myself some new skills because I needed them, and I discarded some old ways of thinking about food. I pondered whether buying locally made staples at a locally owned supermarket fits into the locavore mindset. The answers I reached may not echo those you might make. That's fine with me.

In the end, my decisions were shaped by several philosophies. There is fundamental importance in living well even in hard times. By "living well," I mean finding a way to live that rings true to you and your values and that brings pleasure to your life.

I have chosen to live as simply as possible. Some of that decision was made for me; I live so far out in the woods that no cable television is available to me, and my heavily treed lake lot makes a satellite dish unworkable. Daily newspapers in the closest cities will not deliver to me, out here in the woods. So I take my news from the radio and from the Internet. In the interests of using my resources wisely, I go into the village once a week, combining several chores at once; and I go into the nearest town once a week, too.

That way of thinking extends into my kitchen. I have a small indoor electric composter, but since chickens came into my life, they get almost all of my kitchen scraps. The coffee grounds, egg shells, and other stuff the chickens don't want go into the composter. Bones from roasts and whole poultry go into the stockpot. Prepared food leftovers go into the freezer, or occasionally to the chickens; if something "gets away from me," as my mother used to say about food wasted by spoilage, the composter takes care of that. I think through cooking so that when I cook rice for dinner one night, I cook enough extra to make rice pudding, or I plan to eat congee for breakfast the next morning. Little is wasted in my intentional kitchen.

Finding and shopping with local growers has deepened my sense of place in my small corner of the world. It pleases me deeply to look over a table ringed with friends and realize that Tom Otto, too, is here, having provided one of his fine turkeys. Steve's kale and winter greens bring him to dinner. Wally has joined us, in the form of the pickled tomatoes and "everything sauce" that I made from the riches of his garden. The roasted butternut squash that Tom Robertson grew makes him a welcome addition. The Northern Spy and Gala apples from Cotant's orchard make an especially fine pie for dessert, although we could just as well enjoy blueberry buckle, thanks to the Kendalls, or strawberry shortcake with Nathaniel's berries. These are all people that I didn't know a year ago. They enrich my life and its pleasures.

Eating this way has had some unexpected benefits. My meat consumption has fallen significantly, because much of the protein in my diet comes from my chickens' rich eggs. Though we have been schooled that eggs are too high in saturated fat and cholesterol to eat every day, my research indicates that my chickens' good free-range eggs are actually one-third lower in cholesterol and saturated fat than conventional store-bought eggs. I eat two eggs almost every day without qualm. Though I prepare and eat three meals a day at home, by fall my weekly grocery shopping had been reduced to a gallon of local milk, a few staples, and food for the animals that share my life. Knowing that I need so little pleases me. It means that my hungers don't take food from the mouths of others who may need it more. And certainly eating lower on the food chain has improved my carbon footprint, reducing my consumption of costly and irreplaceable fossil fuels.

In the year set out in the following pages, you will see how committing to eat as much locally grown food as possible helped me bring my life closer to the principles that are important to me. That, in my eyes, is the most profound definition of living well.

SPRING

1

On settling in and making maple

THE SNOW MELTED IN PATCHES, making the dirt road muddy and slippery. The curvy road's steep hills made me glad for my old Subaru's all-wheel drive. Where the snow was not melted, it was crusted and rotten. The shadows lay long as the daylight dwindled.

We were, all three of us, tired. On a good day, it's a three-and-a-half hour drive from Chicago, but this wasn't a good day. Traffic was unusually heavy, and I was battered emotionally, devastated by the pain of losing a marriage and a career within the span of a week. As I eased the car down the lakeward-sloping drive to park close to the cottage, Boon sat up alertly in the passenger seat. He remembered the scents of this place and his wagging pom-pom tail told me he associated it with pleasure. In the back seat, Pippin, in his carrier, gave a long, low whistle—a sound that he makes only when pleased. The dog, the parrot, and I had arrived.

The cottage was chilly. It stood unoccupied over the winter, although we kept the furnace running at its lowest setting to keep the pipes from freezing. Bumping the thermostat up to sixty-five degrees, I heard the ancient oil-fired furnace kick in reassuringly. Because the cottage is so small—just 650 square feet, encompassing an L-shaped living room, a good-sized kitchen, a modest bedroom, and bathroom—I knew it would be warm in short order.

Boon, big even for a standard poodle, sniffed around for a few minutes. Finally, he settled under the kitchen table. After putting the kettle on to boil for a mug of dripped coffee, I uncovered Pippin's carrier and invited him to step onto my hand. He stretched first the wing and leg on one side, then the other; a quick shake of his ruffled feathers and the flippant wag of his crimson tail signaled his contentment. "Pip," I said, "there's a whole lot of stuff in the car that needs unloading, but it can wait for a while." He bobbed his head in the quick up-and-down that told me this was good news to him. While we waited for the kettle to whistle, Pip and I crooned to each other for a bit. Although African Greys are known as standoffish parrots, Pippin is very cuddly and sweet-tempered.

The hot coffee, sweet and milky, provided instant comfort. I leaned back against the counter, trying to prioritize. Dinner first, I thought; something simple like scrambled eggs or soup. Then dishes. Then an early bedtime. Do the simplest things first. Save the hard thinking for when you're fresh and stronger.

I wondered when that would be, when I'd feel fresh and stronger.

❦ ❦ ❦

The cottage was bought as a retirement place two years ago, when my husband and I were earning good money. Because of its size, it wasn't expensive. Now, having returned to my native Michigan, it was to be my full-time home, as I figured out the next steps in my life.

The cottage sits on eighty-acre Stewart Lake, nestled in more than twenty-two thousand acres of state game and recreation land in Barry County. The far side of the lake is owned by an old cooperative camp; its nearly three hundred acres of land means that my northwest view—of a horizon of hardwood trees following a ridge line, undulating in gentle curves—will never change.

The camp, Circle Pines Center, has an interesting history. It was formed in 1940, when a group from the Central States Cooperative League bought the old Stewart farm. Through the 1940s and 1950s, Circle Pines flourished as a family camp and folk school; blues musician Big Bill Broonzy was on staff for a while, and perhaps that's why folksinger Pete Seeger came to visit. During the turbulent 1960s and 1970s, Circle Pines members were active in antiwar and antinuclear-power demonstrations, and some were active in the civil rights movement. These days, the center continues to espouse a mission of building a sense of cooperation, community, and peace.

Stewart Lake has no public access. Because it is a "no-wake" lake, boaters can use only small electric trolling motors to move their crafts. It is refreshingly quiet. Of the forty or so houses on the lake, only a handful are year-round homes. The rest are empty most of the year, save the three long summer weekends of Memorial Day, Fourth of July, and Labor Day. My nearest year-round neighbor to the west is Jim, a retired submariner, four houses away; to the east, three houses away, it's eight-year-old Dakota, his mom, and her parents. The lake's peaceful nature was another big draw for us when we bought the cottage.

As is true with most lake properties, my lot is small. But the property owners' association owns fourteen acres across the road, behind me, so that land, too, will never be developed. And with thousands of acres of state land at my doorstep, there is no sense of feeling cramped. Boon and I can walk for miles on trails or just through woods.

Wildlife is shockingly abundant here. White-tailed deer, wild turkey, coyotes, rabbits, woodchucks, squirrels, otters, weasels, marten, and mink fill the woods; there are rumors that cougars have made Barry County home. The lake is home to several turtle species, Canada geese, lots of different kinds of ducks, swans, owls, hawks, and even an occasional bald eagle. A loon, solitary, stops by to rest each spring for a couple of weeks on his way north for the summer. Fishermen pull bluegill, sunfish, perch, crappie, and bass—as well as the occasional dogfish and walleye—from the lake. Hummingbirds, cardinals, chickadees, nuthatches, slate juncos, downy woodpeckers, flickers, bluejays, and Baltimore orioles visit my feeders.

I was counting on the lake's beauty, its wealth of natural riches, to provide sustenance as I rebuilt myself and learned how to live in this small corner of the world.

※ ※ ※

The sun shone brightly the next morning as I finished breakfast. The car still needed unloading, but I was drawn to go for a walk with Boon first. On that first day we just walked up to the nearest stop sign, about a half-mile away; the road's hills gave us both an energizing work-out.

As is typical in early April in Michigan, it was raw and blustery, but it felt good to be outside. Boon romped ahead as I trudged along, eyes down to plot my steps carefully, to keep from slipping and falling on the muddy, rutted road. At the top of the steep hill where the stop sign is, I paused to catch my breath. I lifted my eyes to scan the maples and oaks, looking at the tips of the branches, checking to see if the buds had begun to swell. They had not. It was still sugar season.

We make a lot of maple syrup here in Michigan, where old-timers call it "making maple." The relatively warmer days—with temperatures above freezing—and the still-cold nights of March and April cause the sap to rise in the sugar and black maples that are best for tapping. Fewer than 1 percent of the possible trees for sugaring in Michigan are tapped, and that's probably because sugaring is a lot of work. First you have to find and tap the trees, which means walking through cold, slushy, muddy woods; then you have to drill the hole, drive in the spile (the little tube that lets the sap drop into a bucket), and attach the bucket. Then you have to come back every day to collect the sap you've gathered, and then boil it down to evaporate the water until you get a single gallon of syrup from every forty or so gallons of sap you collected. If your evaporator is wood-fired, you can figure you'll burn a cord of wood a day for every twenty-five gallons of syrup you make, and all that wood had to be cut, split, and stacked.

There have been some minor technological improvements in how the sap is heated to boil off the water—some sugarers use oil or gas now, instead of wood—and some use vacuum tubing to draw the sap for collection. But otherwise, the process is the same as it was when the Ojibway, the Ottawa, and the Potawatomi made syrup in bygone years.

When I was growing up, my mother always gave us Michigan maple syrup on pancakes, waffles, and French toast. She disliked the maple-flavored sugar syrup found on supermarket shelves—the Mrs. Butterworth and Log Cabin sort of stuff—and wouldn't buy it, so I grew up knowing the flavor of real maple syrup. Mom also used maple syrup—sparingly, because it was expensive then as now—on baked ham and in baked beans.

She was right to feed us the real thing. Maple syrup has some trace minerals: calcium, phosphorus, iron, potassium. It also has some trace vitamins: B_2 (riboflavin), B_5 (pantothenic acid), B_6 (pyridoxine), niacin, biotin, and folic acid. Today's maple-flavored syrups, besides being empty of nutrients, are generally made with high-fructose corn syrup, which I strive to avoid.

As I stood at the road's junction, thinking about maple syrup, I realized that I had most of a half-gallon I bought last summer, still in the refrigerator in the cabin. It was Grade B, which is darker than Grade A, but which I prefer because it seems to have more maple flavor and is perhaps slightly thicker. Mine came from Shane Hickey's Hill Top Maples in Vermontville, about thirty-five miles from the cottage, where a maple syrup festival is held in late April each year. Kept refrigerated, maple syrup will last a long, long time; if it develops any mold, which has never happened to me, it can be heated, skimmed, and returned to its jug for further storage with little change in flavor.

So perhaps that would be Step One on my road to rebuilding my life: Remembering the good foods that my mother gave me and finding my own sources for them.

Boon was restless, ready to return to the warm house. So was I. My heart felt lighter; my mood lifted. On the way, I thought about which maple-infused delicacy I wanted to prepare to please myself. Should it be maple-oatmeal cookies or baked acorn squash with sausage and maple syrup?

I'd figure that out later, I guessed. Right then, I had a car to unload.

baked acorn squash with sausage and maple syrup

MAKES 4 SERVINGS

This simple dinner is easy and delicious. My mother usually served Waldorf salad with baked squash—the crunchy apple-celery-nut salad was a good companion to the baked squash's silky richness, and its cool-weather flavors seemed to go well, too. My father especially loved this dish; I can see him rubbing his hands together in gleeful, greedy anticipation of one of his favorite dinners.

+-+

2 acorn squash

1 pound bulk sage pork breakfast sausage

1/2 cup pure maple syrup

Preheat the oven to 350°F.

Using a very sharp knife, prepare the squash by cutting them in half from stem end to stern. Scoop out and discard the seeds and fibers. Turn the squash over; cut a small flat slice from the bottom of each squash half so it will sit squarely in a baking dish. Place the squash halves in a baking dish large enough to hold them.

Divide the pork sausage into four portions. Pack the cavity of each squash half with pork sausage. Drizzle 2 tablespoons of the maple syrup over the pork sausage in each squash half. Add 1 inch of water to the baking dish around the squash halves. Cover the dish with aluminum foil.

Bake for 1 hour, or until the squash is tender when pierced with a knife. Serve immediately.

maple and sherry vinegar–glazed pork loin

MAKES ABOUT 6 SERVINGS

Maple's sweetness complements roast pork; adding a little sherry vinegar and powdered mustard to the glaze lends complexity. I usually serve this with a simple dressing of stale torn bread pieces with lots of onion, celery, sage, and black pepper, moistened with chicken broth. Add a green vegetable or a salad and you're good to go.

1 (4¹/₂- to 5¹/₂-pound) bone-in pork loin roast

Salt and freshly ground black pepper

¹/₄ cup pure maple syrup

¹/₄ cup sherry vinegar

2 teaspoons cornstarch

1 tablespoon powdered mustard

2 large cloves garlic, smashed and minced

Preheat the oven to 325°F.

Place the roast, fat side up, on a rack in a roasting pan; season with salt and pepper.

Roast the pork, uncovered, for about 2 hours.

Combine the maple syrup, vinegar, cornstarch, powdered mustard, and garlic in a blender or food processor. Blend until the mixture is combined. Transfer to a small saucepan on medium heat and bring the mixture to a boil. Decrease the heat and simmer until thickened, about 5 minutes. Remove from the heat and brush the glaze over the roast. Continue roasting, basting once or twice, for 30 to 45 minutes, until the roast registers about 155°F on a meat thermometer inserted into the center of the roast.

Let the roast rest for 10 minutes before slicing and serving.

oatmeal–maple syrup drop cookies

MAKES ABOUT 2 DOZEN COOKIES

This is a humble, homey cookie that tastes good with a glass of milk or a cup of coffee. I usually substitute dried cherries, dried cranberries, or dried blueberries for the traditional raisins because I'm more likely to have them on hand. Use walnuts if you have them, but if you don't, feel free to use chopped cashews, almonds, pecans, or peanuts. These cookies keep well, but usually don't last long enough for that to be a concern.

1/2 cup (1 stick) salted butter, at room temperature

1 cup pure maple syrup

1 egg

1 1/2 cups whole wheat flour

2 teaspoons baking powder

1/2 teaspoon salt

1/2 teaspoon ground cinnamon

1/4 teaspoon ground cloves

1/4 cup whole milk

1 1/2 cups rolled oats

1/2 cup dried cherries

1/2 cup chopped walnuts

Preheat the oven to 350°F. Prepare two cookie sheets by greasing lightly or lining with parchment paper.

In a large bowl, beat the butter, maple syrup, and egg until the mixture is light and fluffy. Set aside.

Sift together the flour, baking powder, salt, cinnamon, and cloves. Add to syrup mixture alternately with milk. Mix well. Stir in the oats, cherries, and nuts. Drop by rounded tablespoonfuls onto the prepared cookie sheets, leaving 1 inch between each cookie. Flatten the mounds with your fingers or the oiled bottom of a drinking glass.

Bake for 15 to 20 minutes, one sheet at a time, until the cookies are golden and look dry. Cool on the cookie sheets for 5 minutes, then transfer to a wire rack to finish cooling.

maple-walnut pie

If you like pecan pie, you ought to like this, a traditional New England dessert made with "Yankee" ingredients. It's not as tooth-achingly sweet as pecan pie, which makes it a winner in my book. I'm also happy that it doesn't use corn syrup, which I dislike.

Pastry for a single-crust 9-inch pie

$1/4$ cup ($1/2$ stick) salted butter

$1/2$ cup sugar

$1/2$ teaspoon salt

1 cup pure maple syrup

3 large eggs

1 cup walnut pieces

Preheat the oven to 375°F. Line a 9-inch pie pan with the pastry; crimp the edges, and set aside.

In a small saucepan over medium heat, melt the butter. Pour the butter into a mixing bowl. Add the sugar, salt, maple syrup, and eggs. Beat the mixture until well-blended. Add the walnuts. Pour the filling into the unbaked pie shell.

Bake for about 35 minutes, or until a knife inserted in the filling comes out clean. Cool completely on a wire rack before serving.

2

On snapping turtles
and strawberries

ONE DAY BOON AND I took a bag of trash up to the dumpster. When we turned to go back to the house, I noticed a snapping turtle just finishing laying her eggs in the sandy soil. I have a deep affection for turtles and tortoises, so I was drawn to inspect her.

It was easily the biggest snapper I'd ever seen. Her mossy shell, chipped around the edges, was as big around as a Hummer hubcap. Her sharp claws, still soiled from digging, were as long as my index finger. Her jaws could have taken off my thumb without pause. The turtle peered at me myopically and decided I posed a threat to her just-laid eggs. Hissing, she advanced. Hastily, I retreated.

I raced into the house for my camera, knowing that no one would believe the size of the turtle without a photograph. Boon, thinking we were playing, ran ahead of me to the door. I was glad. He hadn't bothered the turtle, perhaps hadn't even noticed her, but I didn't want him to fool with her—or she, him. Snatching my camera from the kitchen table, I told Boon to stay and rushed back up the driveway.

The turtle was still there. As I focused the camera, she began to advance again. Again, I stepped back to give her plenty of space. Eventually, satisfied that I was benign, she raised herself up on surprisingly long legs and began her 150-yard walk down the hill to the lake. Much to my astonishment, she chose to clamber down the wooden steps that lead to the parking area, rather than simply walking around the small fence that defines it.

As I watched, she stepped down, paused, pushed herself off the first step and tumbled to the second, landing hard on her chin. After a moment's rest, she rose and repeated her push, tumbling down the next step, and again landing hard on her chin. Another rest, one last tumble down the third step, and she was on the ground.

The trip down the hill took the turtle nearly twenty minutes. She stopped to rest periodically, but her drive to return to the safety of the water was impressive. I knew as I watched that it was unlikely that I would ever see anything like this again. It was a perfect moment in a life that hadn't seemed so perfect just lately.

As I drove to the farmers' market later that day, I noticed turtles in and alongside the road every few yards. All must have been motivated by the same drive that obsessed the snapping turtle I'd spent so long observing. On a whim, I popped into the Department of Natural Resources' office to show the photos to a DNR officer. He told me that he thought the turtle's size indicated that she was sixty to eighty years old. I was astonished: her age meant she had been laying her eggs since before any of the houses on my small lake were built. For more than sixty years, she had been banking on the future by laying her eggs in that very spot each spring.

At the farmers' market, the Mennonite farmer, Nathaniel, who sold me two quarts of fat, crimson strawberries told me that his were Honeoyes, a cultivar developed in New York State. They're popular with commercial growers because they produce a lot of berries, and the plants continue to produce for several seasons, making them a little less work for the farmer. The berries are firm and richly fragrant with that lovely strawberry scent; they retain their color with freezing or in preserves.

So then I knew: When turtles begin to move, it's strawberry season.

There are three families of cultivated strawberries: June-bearing, day-neutral, and everbearing. The Honeoyes that Nathaniel sold me are a June-bearing variety; in general, June-bearing strawberries are better for jams and preserves, freezing, and dehydrating. Everbearing and day-neutral varieties produce berries over a longer period of time, but in some cultivars, the berries tend to be smaller. Most commercial growers grow a June-bearing cultivar of one type or another because the crop is ready all at once and requires just one or two harvestings. It's worth asking the grower you like best which variety or varieties he or she grows, and which ones they prefer for which purposes.

Strawberry season used to be a moment of some excitement in my house. They are my husband's favorite fruit, so I usually made it a point to make more than a dozen jars of strawberry preserves to please him. Strawberry preserves aren't my favorite, however, and with him no longer a part of my life, there was little reason to make so much. But I did make some, because I like the process and I like having the preserves to eat with yogurt, in granola, and over ice cream or pound cake in the winter.

The preserves I make are by an old French method, which does not use added pectin. The preserves are soupier than most, but I cherish them for their intensely fruity flavor. I don't like adding pectin because it's too easy to get a rubbery result. If firm preserves are your preference, my recipe won't please you.

Once during each strawberry season, my husband and I had a supper of strawberry shortcake—just strawberry shortcake, as much as we could eat— in the tradition that my mother started. Even my father, a hearty eater with a big appetite who liked a square meal, loved the once-a-year treat of dessert for dinner. Like my mother, or perhaps because of her, I prefer a sweetened biscuit kind of shortcake, rather than the spongy angel food rounds sold at the grocery store. When my mother made shortcake for a family of seven, she made one big round of shortcake, split it while still hot, buttered it lavishly, and sloshed sugared sliced strawberries over the bottom half before replacing the top, buttering it and adding another sluice of strawberries. We were invited to spoon more strawberries over our portions and to dress the shortcake with slightly sweetened whipped cream—made from heavy cream, not the kind that comes in a tub. These days, when I make shortcake, I generally cut out individual shortcakes with a three-inch biscuit cutter; after they bake, I treat them the same way she did. It is a merry moment, strawberry-shortcake-for-dinner night.

To please myself alone, I made a small batch of shortcakes and enjoyed my strawberry-shortcake-for-dinner in solitude. And rather than remember the years I shared that dinner with my husband, and the many jars of strawberry preserves I put up for him, I thought instead of those meals with my family—and looked forward to the years to come when I'll have the pleasure of eating strawberry shortcake for supper with someone else.

Like the snapping turtle who laid her eggs in my driveway, I would invest my energy in the future, not the past.

French-method strawberry preserves

MAKES ABOUT 6 HALF PINTS

Because these preserves do not have added pectin, they are runni
may be used to. But the two-step method of adding the berries to the boiling syrup preserves the berries' bright color, and their delicate flavor is not
cooked away, as in some other jam recipes. I think of these as "jewels in a
jar." Note that the berries are not sliced in this method. A candy thermometer is definitely helpful here. I usually preserve this jam under a $1/2$-inch layer
of melted paraffin, rather than use the boiling water bath to seal the jars,
though the USDA frowns on that method. The USDA no longer recommends
paraffin sealing because it is prone to mold, although I have never had a jar
of preserves get moldy under paraffin. The boiling water bath further cooks
the berries, which I don't want to do. If you prefer to use the boiling water
bath method, see page 253 for instructions.

◆-◆

5 pounds strawberries, rinsed and hulled

5 cups vanilla sugar (see Note, page 22)

$1/4$ cup fresh lemon juice

In a large, shallow pan, sprinkle half the strawberries with 1 cup of the
sugar. Add the remaining berries and another 1 cup of the sugar. Cover the
berries and allow to stand at room temperature overnight.

Prepare 6 half-pint jars by washing in hot soapy water. Immerse the jars
in a boiling water bath and boil for 10 minutes to sterilize. Place them on a
shallow towel-lined baking sheet and keep in a preheated 200°F oven until
you are ready to fill them. Prepare the lids by setting them in hot water for
at least 5 minutes. They do not have to be boiled.

Transfer the berries to a colander set over the pot you'll use to make the
preserves. Let the juices drain into the pot, reserving the berries. Stir the
remaining 3 cups sugar into the pot and cook over low heat, stirring frequently, until the sugar is dissolved.

Increase the heat to high and bring the mixture to a hard, rolling boil
that cannot be stirred down. Add the reserved strawberries and lemon juice.

continued

Bring the mixture back to a hard, rolling boil and cook, stirring constantly, for exactly 5 minutes. Remove the berries with a slotted spoon to the colander, set over a bowl.

Boil the remaining syrup for exactly 5 minutes. Add any juices that have accumulated in the bowl and continue boiling to reduce the mixture slightly, about 10 minutes.

Prepare the paraffin for sealing the jars, if you use this method, by melting the paraffin in a well-washed can or an old liquid measuring cup set into a pan of warm water on low heat. Return the berries to the syrup and boil again for 5 minutes, or until mixture reaches 220°F on a candy thermometer. Remove the pan from the heat and skim off any foam; allow the jam to stand for 10 minutes.

Spoon the jam into the warm sterilized half-pint jars, leaving room for the paraffin, and seal by pouring a 1/2-inch layer of melted paraffin over the hot preserves, tilting the jar to be sure the paraffin contacts all of the inside of the jar.

Or skip the paraffin entirely, and process the half-pint jars in a boiling water bath canner for 10 minutes, according to the instructions on page 253. You can also forgo both the paraffin and boiling water bath methods: simply refrigerate the filled half-pint jars immediately, and use within 2 months.

> *Note: While vanilla beans are expensive, they are powerful and just a couple will easily flavor the sugar. Simply add 1 or 2 vanilla beans, split lengthwise, to a pound of sugar and let stand, closely covered, for a couple of weeks before using.*

HOW TO DEHYDRATE STRAWBERRIES

I dehydrate several quarts of strawberries during the growing season to use in cookies, granola, and on top of oatmeal in the winter. Strawberries dry easily and the resulting quality is excellent. Each quart of fresh strawberries will yield 1 to 2 cups of dried strawberries, depending on how big the fresh berries were.

Choose deep red, sweet varieties for dehydrating. Wash in cold water, a quart at a time. Drain the berries well in a colander. Remove and discard the cap from each berry and cut into $1/2$-inch slices or, if the berries are quite small, in half. If the slices are too thin, they will stick to the drying surface, so err on the side of generosity when slicing them. Where possible, lay the slices skin side down. Arrange the berries in a single layer on the dryer racks of a thermostatically controlled dehydrator or on baking sheets lined with waxed paper or parchment paper.

In the dehydrator, dry the racks of berries at 150°F for 1 to 2 hours. Then decrease the temperature to 130°F and continue drying until the berries are pliable and leathery, 10 to 12 hours. Let them cool before tumbling them into zip-top plastic bags or glass canning jars with tight-fitting lids. Store at room temperature for up to a year.

To dry the berries in an oven, turn the oven to its lowest setting. Slide the baking sheets into the oven, propping the oven door ajar with a wooden spoon. Dry the berries, checking them every 3 to 4 hours and turning the slices once or twice, for 12 to 24 hours, until the slices are pliable but leathery. Let the berries cool before storage, just as above.

whole strawberries in balsamic–black pepper syrup

MAKES ABOUT 6 HALF PINTS

These sweet-savory preserves are a boon alongside plain roasted meats, as well as a surprising filling for a layer cake or a topping spooned over pound cake. They are also delicious, of course, straight from the jar on toasted brioche or rustic bread with good butter.

5 pounds strawberries, rinsed and hulled

5 cups vanilla sugar (see Note, page 22)

3 cups good-quality balsamic vinegar

2 tablespoons coarsely cracked black peppercorns (see Note, page 25)

Sort the berries, leaving small ones whole and slicing large ones in half. Spread half the berries in a shallow pan and sprinkle with 1 cup of the sugar. Repeat with the remaining berries and another 1 cup of sugar. Cover and let stand overnight at room temperature.

The next day, transfer the berries to a colander set over the pot you'll use to make the preserves. Let the berries drain. Set the colander with the berries over a bowl while you prepare the balsamic–black pepper syrup and prepare the jars and canner (see page 253).

Add the remaining 3 cups sugar, balsamic vinegar, and black peppercorns to the preserving pot that holds the strawberry juice. Over high heat, bring the mixture to a hard, rolling boil that can't be stirred down. Cook, stirring often, until the mixture thickens and reaches 220°F on a candy thermometer, about 10 minutes.

Add the strawberries and any additional juice to the preserving pot. Return the mixture to a hard boil and cook, stirring constantly, until mixture returns to 220°F.

Remove the preserves from the heat. Skim off and discard any foam. Let stand for 10 minutes, then fill the warm sterilized half-pint jars and seal with the prepared lids. Process in a boiling water bath canner for 10 minutes, according to the instructions on page 253. Store the jars in a cool, dry place.

Note: To crack whole peppercorns, place the peppercorns in a heavy-duty zip-top bag and run a rolling pin over them several times until they are coarsely cracked.

HOW TO FREEZE STRAWBERRIES

I freeze whole strawberries by the gallon in zip-top bags to use in smoothies and desserts all winter long. Rinse and hull the strawberries and let them drain thoroughly. Arrange the berries in a single layer on a rimmed baking sheet or jelly roll pan and place in the freezer. When the berries are frozen solid, transfer to zip-top bags.

Sliced berries in sugar syrup also freeze perfectly. Hull and slice the berries and sugar them at a ratio of 1 cup of sugar to every 2 pounds of berries. Let the berries stand, covered, at room temperature for 24 hours. Spoon the berries into pint- or quart-size freezer bags and divide the juices among them. Seal the bags carefully, lay them flat on a rimmed baking sheet or jelly roll pan, and place them in the freezer. When they have frozen solid, the bags stack easily in the freezer.

favorite granola

Back when I was in college in the early 1970s, everyone made their own granola, and it was so ubiquitous that it was a cliché. The recipes from that era, however, called for lots of oil to help carry flavor, and they were always sticky with honey. It was a great day for me when I figured out that granola doesn't need any oil at all; dry-toasting the oats and the nuts in a moderate oven builds flavor without fat. I think it stores better without the fat, too— although a batch never lasts long enough to go rancid.

---

10 cups rolled oats (quick-cooking is okay, but don't use instant)

1/2 cup each of two kinds of nuts (cashews, almonds, walnuts, peanuts, pistachios, or hazelnuts)

1/2 cup each of two kinds of seeds or grain (hulled sesame seeds, sunflower seeds, pumpkin seeds, or millet)

1/2 cup each of two kinds of dried fruit (apples, pears, peaches, apricots, strawberries, dates, cherries, blueberries, raisins, or currants), coarsely chopped if large

1/4 cup shredded coconut (optional)

1/4 cup sweetener (pure maple syrup, brown sugar, honey, or agave nectar)

2 teaspoons liquid flavoring (vanilla, almond, orange, lemon, coconut, rum, or butterscotch extract)

1/2 teaspoon coarse salt, such as kosher salt

Preheat the oven to 350°F.

In a large, deep baking dish or roasting pan, spread out the oats so they are no more than 1/2 inch deep. Toast in the oven, stirring occasionally, for 10 to 15 minutes, until the oats are golden brown. Remove from the oven and transfer to a large bowl.

Spread out the nuts in the baking dish and toast them in the oven, stirring often, for 5 to 10 minutes, until they are fragrant and darkened slightly.

Allow the nuts to cool. Transfer to a food processor and chop coarsely, or use a knife on a cutting board to chop. Add the chopped nuts to the oats.

Add the seeds, dried fruit, coconut, sweetener, extract, and salt to the bowl. Stir to combine. When the mixture is completely cool, transfer to a storage container with a tight-fitting lid. Store at room temperature for up to 1 month.

sweet-biscuit strawberry shortcake

MAKES ABOUT 6 SERVINGS

Shortcake is nothing more than sweetened biscuit dough made "short," or rich, with extra butter. Given how toothsome it is, and how easy to make, I can't understand the appeal of those little sponge cake rounds, which go sodden and soggy at the first touch of sugared berries. I use self-rising flour for biscuits for several reasons. It's easier, of course, because it already contains leavening, but it also is usually made from "softer," lower-protein wheat. That means it doesn't form the elastic, stringy gluten so easily, which in turn means a tender, light biscuit. See the Note (at right) if you wish to use regular flour.

2 quarts strawberries, washed, hulled, and sliced (about 4 cups)

1 cup plus 2 tablespoons sugar

2 cups self-rising flour, plus more for dusting

5 tablespoons salted butter, plus more for serving

3/4 to 1 cup heavy cream or whole milk

Whipped cream or sweetened yogurt, for serving

Preheat the oven to 450°F. Lightly grease a 10½-inch cast-iron skillet or heavy baking griddle.

In a large bowl, combine the strawberries and 1 cup of the sugar. Stir well. Set aside while you prepare and bake the shortcakes, about 30 minutes.

In a large bowl, whisk together the flour and the remaining 2 tablespoons sugar. Using your fingers or a fork, cut in the butter until the mixture is coarse and crumbly; the largest pieces of butter should be about pea-sized.

Using a fork, stir in 3/4 cup of the cream. Toss the mixture with the fork, adding additional cream until the mixture holds together and is slightly sticky to the touch.

Dust a cutting board generously with flour. Scrape out the dough, sprinkle its top with flour and, with floured hands, knead the dough two or three times. Pat out the dough to make a round about 1/2 inch thick. Transfer whole to the prepared skillet or use a 3-inch biscuit cutter to cut into individual shortcakes. Place the individual biscuits in the skillet or on the griddle with sides touching. Reroll the scraps and cut again, if you are making individual shortcakes; discard the remaining scraps.

Bake for 12 to 14 minutes, or until golden brown. If the top begins to brown too quickly, decrease the oven temperature to 400°F after the first 10 minutes of baking.

To serve, split the biscuit(s) while still warm and butter generously. Place the buttered bottom round(s) on a serving platter or individual plates. Generously spoon the sugared berries over the biscuit bottom(s). Replace the top(s); add additional berries. Garnish each serving with a dollop of whipped cream and pass the remaining strawberries and whipped cream at the table.

> *Note: If you don't have self-rising flour on hand, use 2 cups all-purpose flour, 2¹/₂ teaspoons double-acting baking powder, and 1¹/₄ teaspoons salt. Whisk the baking powder, salt, and sugar into the flour before cutting in the butter.*

3

On asparagus and
the all-too-brief window

WITH SUCH DELIGHT do we Michiganders greet the first asparagus of the season! It is among the earliest crops here in the Great Lakes region, and when asparagus arrives, we can be sure that it really is, truly is, spring. April's fits and starts, clotty snows and mucky mud, can deter the belief that winter is over. But asparagus? Well, asparagus does not lie.

Old-time Michigan rural folks called asparagus "speary-grass," a nickname that makes sense when you consider its growth habits. (In the same way, they called sumac, the shrubby nonpoisonous kind, "shoe-mac," which also makes sense: its tannin-rich red berries can be used in leather tanning and dyeing.)

The grassy herbaciousness of asparagus was surely welcome after a long winter of mostly preserved vegetables, a kind of spring tonic that provided much-needed nutrients. Asparagus is high in folic acid and is a good source of potassium, fiber, vitamins A, B_6, C, and thiamine. So perhaps that instinctive yearning for the fresh, tender spears is based on intuitive body knowledge.

My father was a true asparagus aficionado, although we didn't eat it often when I was growing up. When I was about ten years old, my father used asparagus as part of an object lesson in reading a person's character. He told the story of how, when he was a student at Lake Forest College outside Chicago and living in a fraternity house, fresh asparagus was on the menu one night. One of his fraternity brothers picked up the platter on the community table, smiled broadly, and said, "Oh, I love asparagus!" With that, he cut off all the tender tips and served them to himself, leaving only the decapitated stalks for the rest of the diners. "That guy," my father said, still angry those many years later, "was a selfish prig. You can tell a lot about a person by the way he eats. He didn't take a second to think about anyone else. Make sure you never do that." At ten, I wasn't clear about what, exactly, it was that I shouldn't do: cut off all the tender asparagus tips or selfishly think only of myself. Later, of course, I figured it out. In my father's name, I have never done the former, and work hard not to do the latter.

The loose, sandy soil of west Michigan's Lake Michigan counties, especially Oceana County, makes ideal asparagus growing fields, and Michigan grows as much as twenty-five million pounds of asparagus each year, making us the third-largest asparagus growing state. Growers plant the spidery crowns a foot or so below the soil's surface. A newly planted field usually can't be harvested for the first three years, to give the crowns plenty of time to develop strong roots, but a carefully tended bed will provide a good harvest for as long as fifteen years. When the gods smile, asparagus can grow ten inches in a day, and the crowns will send up spears for about six weeks—six lovely, brief weeks.

Young beds provide big spears, the sturdy, thumb-thick spears that may need to have a little tough skin scraped away at their bottoms. Gourmands say the bigger the spear's diameter, the better the asparagus—based, I think, on the ratio of tender flesh to crisper outer skin. But I actually prefer the thinner spears, as do many people, because I like that crisp texture. And though I admire *Los Angeles Times* food writer and editor Russ Parsons immensely, I disagree with him—politely, of course—about how to deal with those woody bottom ends. He says cut off the bottom inch or so; I say bend the spear until it breaks naturally, and sometimes you don't even have to do that if the asparagus is extremely fresh. Here in Michigan, growers hand-snap the spears at harvest, rather than cutting them below the soil as growers do in other states, which means there's less likely to be a woody part in the first place. Do whatever makes you happy.

Only about a quarter of the crop is sold fresh, to grocery stores, farm stands, and at roadside markets. Most of Michigan's harvest used to be sold to processors, who froze more than a third as cuts and tips or spears, and canned the rest.

I learned some of the above from a fascinating documentary called *Asparagus! Stalking the American Life*, which filmmakers Kirsten Kelly and Ann de Mare released in 2006 after spending more than two years on the project. Although the documentary has won prize after prize and has aired on

PBS, I've yet to meet anyone else who has seen it. When the federal government launched its ill-conceived War on Drugs program, persuading Peruvian farmers to grow asparagus instead of the coca that is turned into cocaine, Michigan growers couldn't compete with the cheap imported stuff. It's true that Peru's harvest of coca dropped by 61 percent in the ten years after the trade program began. It's also true, as the documentary points out, that coca production rose by 74 percent in neighboring Colombia, and Peruvian coca growing has resumed its steady rise. And when NAFTA opened the doors for corporations to move their manufacturing and processing plants into Mexico and South America, where labor is ruinously underpaid—who can live on twenty dollars a week in wages, even when the cost of living is low?—the companies that pack American asparagus flew south like vultures.

Fortunately, freezing or canning asparagus is simple.

To freeze whole asparagus spears, snap the spears, if needed. Bring a large, shallow pan of water to a boil over high heat and add the asparagus. Cook just until the color changes to bright green, perhaps two to three minutes. Then shock the spears by dropping them into a sink of cold water to stop the cooking. The asparagus is nowhere near cooked at this stage. What you just did is called "blanching," and you do that to stop the enzyme activity in fruits and vegetables that would cause the quality to deteriorate, even while frozen.

When the asparagus has cooled, pat it dry with paper towels or cloth ones—I use my oldest kitchen towels for projects like this—then arrange the spears in a single layer on a baking sheet and freeze. Once they're frozen solid, transfer them to a zip-top gallon-size bag and place in the freezer. Now you have individually frozen spears, ready to remove as needed throughout the rest of the year.

To cook that frozen asparagus, the best method is to microwave it, according to the Michigan Asparagus Commission. Place the frozen spears on a microwave-safe plate or shallow dish with the tips in the center. Add two tablespoons water and cover tightly. Microwave at 100 percent power for four to seven minutes, depending on the quantity cooked. Stir or rearrange the asparagus halfway through the cooking time.

Sometimes I don't even bother to cook the frozen spears. I just thaw them by running them under warm water, then cut them into pieces to add to omelets, stir-fries, frittatas, sandwiches, soups, and other dishes.

I don't can much asparagus, because I don't make a lot of the casserole-type dishes for which canned asparagus seems best suited. Instead, I make a half-dozen or so jars of pickled asparagus, which requires some trimming so the stalks fit neatly into the jars. Whatever is trimmed goes into the food processor with some water for asparagus puree, which I freeze by the tablespoon, dolloped onto a waxed paper–lined baking sheet. After the dollops are frozen, I move them into a zip-top freezer bag. That puree, stirred into some hot pasta or made into soup, keeps the bright green flavor of asparagus fresh on my palate deep into winter. If, however, you'd like to can asparagus, you need a pressure canner. Like all low-acid foods, asparagus must be pressure-canned to remain safe.

Only in season and on feast days—Thanksgiving, Christmas, Easter—do I treat asparagus as a vegetable side dish, usually by grilling or broiling it. The rest of the year, I treat it as an ingredient in some dish or another. Because its season is so short, and because my budget is so limited, I simply can't buy enough to make it less than a luxury.

So each week during asparagus season, I buy three pounds of asparagus for about five dollars. I eat a little with dinner the night I buy it, and blanch the rest for the freezer after dinner. The next morning, as I'm drinking my coffee, I'll pull that baking sheet out of the freezer and move the frozen spears to storage bags. When I have ten or twelve pounds in the freezer, I start making pickled asparagus and asparagus puree. Experience has taught me that ten pounds of asparagus will see me through the year, though I'll be missing it and really ready for asparagus again when it comes into season the next year.

Learning to appreciate a fleeting pleasure for itself is part of life, I guess. I am working on cultivating my delight in a season's riches without longing for them when they have passed. Like the seasons in my own life, they will march along, whether I am ready for their changing or not.

asparagus bread pudding

MAKES 6 TO 8 SERVINGS

Savory bread puddings make an easy, delicious brunch, lunch, or dinner, but they require a little forethought since they should sit refrigerated for at least 6 hours (up to 12 won't hurt) before baking. If you don't have stale bread on hand, lay out the slices on the counter overnight to stale or dry them in a 300°F oven for a few minutes.

➤—•—•—◄—•—•—➤—•—◄—•—➤—•—•—◄—•—➤—•—•—◄—•—➤—•—•—◄—•—➤—•—•—◄—•—➤—•—◄—•—➤—•—•—◄—•—➤—•—◄

$1^1/_2$ pounds fresh asparagus, tough ends removed, spears cut into 1-inch pieces

$2^3/_4$ cups whole milk

8 large eggs

1 teaspoon powdered mustard

$^1/_4$ teaspoon grated nutmeg

$^1/_2$ teaspoon salt

$^1/_4$ teaspoon freshly ground black pepper

3 scallions, white and tender green parts, finely chopped

12 slices sturdy bread, the staler the better

3 cups shredded Swiss cheese

1 cup freshly grated Parmigiano-Reggiano cheese

Butter a 12-cup baking dish or casserole.

Cook the asparagus in lightly salted boiling water just until tender, 2 to 3 minutes; drain.

In a bowl, whisk together the milk, eggs, powdered mustard, nutmeg, salt, and pepper until well blended; add the scallions.

Place four slices of bread in the bottom of the baking dish, overlapping if necessary.

Layer one-third of the asparagus and one-third of the Swiss cheese over the bread. Repeat the layers two more times. Pour the egg mixture over the top. Cover and refrigerate for at least 6 hours, or overnight.

When you are ready to bake, preheat the oven to 350°F. Sprinkle the Parmigiano-Reggiano over the casserole.

Bake for 50 to 60 minutes, until the center is set and the top is golden. Serve hot.

spring risotto

MAKES 4 SERVINGS

A dish of risotto provides supreme comfort on a still-chilly spring night.
I use homemade chicken broth in mine, but commercial broth will also
give a nice result. If you are "in funds," as the British say, by all means use
proscuitto, although I prefer tiny cubes of the good smoked ham that I buy
locally. The simplicity of this dish demands true Parmigiano-Reggiano.
Leftovers make good croquettes, shaped into patties and cooked in a skillet
in olive oil until crisp and brown on both sides.

5 cups chicken broth

1 tablespoon olive oil

2 tablespoons salted butter

$1/4$ cup minced scallions, white
and tender green parts

$1^1/4$ cups short-grained risotto
rice, such as Arborio

1 pound fresh asparagus, tough
ends removed, spears cut into
1-inch pieces

$1/2$ cup finely diced smoked ham

$1/2$ cup freshly grated
Parmigiano-Reggiano cheese

Salt

In a large, heavy saucepan, bring the broth to a simmer over medium heat.
Combine the oil and 1 tablespoon of the butter in a heavy saucepan over
medium heat. Add the scallions and cook, stirring frequently, for 5 minutes,
until softened and fragrant. Add the rice and cook for 5 minutes, stirring
to coat well, until the grains of rice have become translucent with a pearly
"eye." Add 1 cup of the broth; cook, stirring constantly, until absorbed.
Continue adding broth by small ladlefuls, stirring constantly and allowing
each addition to be absorbed before adding more, until the rice is creamy
and tender but still firm to the bite, 20 to 25 minutes in all. Add the asparagus and diced ham during last 5 minutes of cooking.

Remove from the heat and stir in the Parmigiano-Reggiano, the remaining 1 tablespoon of butter, and the salt. Divide the risotto among four pasta
bowls. Serve immediately.

pickled asparagus with lemon, tarragon, and garlic

MAKES 4 PINT JARS

These crunchy pickles are good in their own right on a dark winter night; they also make terrific "stirrers" for Bloody Marys, if that cocktail happens to be on your agenda. They are not powerfully puckery, as some pickles can be. Try them tucked into a winter sandwich for an unexpected crisp contrast in texture. I like to use wide-mouth canning jars for this—trimming the asparagus to fit into the jars is the time-consuming part (see page 33). Save the trimmings! Pickling salt, available where canning supplies are sold, has no additives to cloud the pickling liquid.

3 pounds fresh asparagus, tough ends removed

2 cups white wine vinegar

1¹/₂ cups white vinegar

1 cup water

¹/₄ cup sugar

1 teaspoon pickling salt

4 sprigs fresh tarragon

4 large cloves garlic, peeled and left whole

4 (¹/₂-inch by 3-inch) strips lemon zest

Prepare the jars for canning (see page 253); they do not have to be sterilized. Prepare a boiling water bath for canning.

Wash the asparagus and trim each spear to a 4¹/₄-inch length, or long enough to fit into a wide-mouthed pint jar, leaving ³/₄ inch headspace.

Combine the wine vinegar, white vinegar, water, sugar, and salt in a nonreactive saucepan over high heat. Bring to a boil.

Fill the hot jars with asparagus, tips down. Tuck the tarragon, garlic, and lemon zest among the spears in each jar. Pour the vinegar mixture over the asparagus spears to within ¹/₂ inch of the jar rim. Seal. Process in a boiling water bath canner for 15 minutes, according to the instructions on page 253. Store in a cool, dry place. The pickles will keep for up to 1 year.

4

On early beets and solar hoop houses

THE EARLY MAY MORNING dawned clear and cool, a delight after the first night of the year of sleeping with opened windows. A neighbor's lilac endowed the late-spring air with its intoxicating scent of the season. The lake, still and mirrorlike, reflected both the brilliant chartreuse of newly unfurled leaves on the trees across from the cottage and the Parrish-blue sky dotted with poufy clouds. The mourning doves' soft cooing was the only sound. I took my coffee on the deck to enjoy the vista.

The local free newspaper had told me that a new farmers' market would open in Middleville. There might be slim pickings at this market, but if that were the case, I could skip down to the long-established Kalamazoo Farmers' Market on Saturday. So after coffee, I pulled on a pair of jeans and a light sweater, loaded Boon into the car, and set out on the twelve-mile trip to the market.

Indeed, the new market was small, with just a handful of vendors. So early in the season, few had much to offer in the way of food; most of the vendors offered plant starts of herbs, tomatoes and other vegetables, and ornamentals, although I knew we still had a couple of weeks before our frost-free date, when it would be safe to set out the tender plants like tomatoes and basil.

To my surprise, however, one of the vendors had beets on offer, generous bunches of six to eight three- to four-inch diameter beets, with greens attached. I happen to love beets, adore the earthy scent of them, revel in their jeweled color. Their aroma reminds me of the way the dry earth smells after a rain, which makes sense because an organic compound in beets, geosmin, is responsible for the odor in both beets and newly wetted soil. Humans are uncommonly sensitive to the smell of geosmin. But beets, so early in May? It seemed unlikely.

"Did you grow these?" I asked. I know that in some markets, vendors can buy and bring in items that they didn't grow. Although I have no issue with that, I feel that vendors should be clear about the origins of what they're selling. Besides, I would prefer to spend my dollars with someone who's done the work of growing. Buying beets from a vendor who picked them up from a wholesaler who imported them from California or elsewhere would defeat my purposes.

"Sure did," the vendor said. "I have a hoop house, solar heated, with solar-operated vents to regulate the temperature."

"What variety are they?" Someone who bought them from a wholesaler would pause before answering, not knowing what variety they were, I thought.

"Detroit Dark Red," the grower said immediately. "It's an old variety, developed in 1892, a longtime standard."

Having grown beets myself in other times and places, I knew that he was right. The variety was developed by Detroit seedsman D. M. Ferry. His company, now known as Ferry-Morse, still sells seeds today, although the company is owned by a French agricultural conglomerate. Detroit Dark Reds are ready to harvest fifty-eight days after they're planted. Since they can be sown in the ground six to eight weeks before our frost-free date of May 15—so, around March 15 here in western Michigan—he clearly could have started them in early February in his sun-powered hoop house. Beets like warm weather, but not too hot, for growing, so they are traditionally a fall crop, the seeds planted in late August for October harvest. But the hoop house makes a spring crop possible, even here in Michigan.

"I'll have four bunches, please," I said. The grower reached for a knife to lop off the greens. "No! Please leave the greens!" I fairly shouted. "I'll braise those for dinner."

"Most people don't want the greens, so I save them and my wife cooks them up for us," he said.

"They're mighty good eating," I said. "Sorry to take food from your mouth."

He laughed, pointing to a nearly full brown paper bag on the ground behind his counter. "Well, the price includes the greens. We have plenty. Enjoy them."

I exchanged a few more pleasantries with the grower as I selected salad and breakfast radishes, lettuces, kale, and chard.

Was he having a good market today? Yes, he said; he was doing well enough to want to come back.

What else would he have in the coming weeks? Carrots next week, he said, and more beets. The peas would be ready in a few more weeks, the green beans, summer squash and zucchini, broccoli, cabbage, and greens were coming on and he'd have tomatoes by mid-June.

"Oh my!" I said. "Tomatoes so soon?"

"The plants have already started to set fruit," he said. "I'll have Early Girls first, then some heirloom and beefsteak varieties a little later." He turned to tend to another customer.

Because the market was a new one, I wanted to spend a little money with every vendor I could. I bought a dozen beautiful large eggs of mixed brown, blues, greens, and pale ivory from a very friendly woman. "You're keeping Ameraucanas," I said, looking at those delicately tinted blue and green eggs. "Yes," she said. "I call them 'Easter eggers,' though, because they're not true Ameraucanas—they just have the gene for laying blue eggs. They're good laying hens, and people really seem to like those colored eggs."

At the baker's stand, I was surprised to find a loaf of salt-rising bread, an old-time bread with a dense crumb that few people make. It's time-consuming and a little fussy to prepare, and some people object to the cheesy aroma as the starter "works." Salt-rising bread, or SRB as some of its fans call it, relies on the bacterium *Clostridum perfringens* rather than yeast for its leavening. Although *C. perfringens* can sometimes be responsible for food poisoning, usually in badly cooked food, the baking of salt-rising bread kills it so it poses no danger. Making salt-rising bread requires a dozen hours or more to start the sponge, which requires a constant temperature of around 100°F. Finding a way to incubate the starter can be problematic. Then there's a slow rising for the sponge and another slow rising for the shaped loaves. I've made salt-rising bread and love it, but don't always have the time to tend it. I snapped up the only loaf the baker offered.

At another booth, a friendly woman vendor sold mixed dried herb packets for seasoning, as well as some dried lavender, which I like to put in sachets for my dresser drawers and to tuck into my pillowcase; it seems to help me sleep well and deeply. At two dollars for a pint-size zip-top bag, her lavender buds were a bargain, so I grabbed one of those.

The next booth over had a woman selling goat's milk soaps, which I make and use myself. But she had a very nicely scented bay rum bar—that cologne reminds me of my father, who wore it on special occasions—and to remember him, I bought a bar from her.

Back at home, in the kitchen, I trimmed the greens from the beets and put them in a sink full of cold water while I attended to the beets themselves. I thought I would roast them first, then dice some to freeze, and slice the rest to prepare a couple of pint jars of pickled beets with onion. I arranged the foil-wrapped beets on a baking sheet and put them into a 400°F oven to roast.

As I swished the greens around in the water to rinse them, I thought about the marvel of a sun-powered hoop house bringing food to market so early in the season. It wasn't a new idea, of course.

Hannah Glasse, the eighteenth-century British author of *The Art of Cookery*, wrote about how to grow winter endives in a box of compost by the open-hearth kitchen fire. The English colonists who settled New England knew of Glasse's book, a docent at Greenfield Village in Dearborn, Michigan, told me years ago. They followed her suggestions and ate very well, it seems, judging from the recipes in *The Art of Cookery*. Glasse, married to a spendthrift and suffering from financial problems throughout most of her life, published *The Art of Cookery* in 1747, after shrewdly noting that the market lacked books of that type, as a way to raise money to feed her family. She meant for the book to be useful to the literate servant-cooks of the rising middle class, she said, and provided recipes with French, German, Dutch, Portuguese, Spanish, Indian, and other ethnic influences—considerably broader than most of us might credit to a mid-eighteenth-century cook. My copy of *The Art of Cookery* is a facsimile of the original. I consult it sometimes out of curiosity, but Glasse's directions are clear even now to a reasonably able cook. "All things green should have a little crispness," wrote Glasse, "for if they are over-boiled, they neither have any sweetness or beauty." That stands as good advice today, more than 250 years after she penned it.

Here is Glasse, for example, on how to pickle "beet-root." The punctuation and language are Glasse's, although I have added a couple of words for clarity:

> Set a pot of spring-water on the fire; when it boils, put in your beets, and let them boil till they are tender, then peel [by rubbing] them with a cloth, and lay them in a stone jar; take three quarts of vinegar, two of spring-water, and so do until you think you have enough to cover your beets [In other words, combine three parts vinegar to two parts water, enough to cover the beets in the crock]. Put your vinegar and water in a pan and salt it to your taste; stir it

well together till the salt is all melted, then pour them on the beets and cover it with a bladder [a tight-fitting lid], do not boil the pickle.

Now we have come full-circle, it seems, returning to learn anew many of the old ways that Glasse and her contemporaries knew. Figuring out how to grow things outside their regular season vanished from our way of thinking about food over the last century; my guess is that when first rail, then air shipping made it possible to move fresh produce from sunnier climes to the winter-bound northern reaches of this country, the need to think that way disappeared.

Lately, however, we have the estimable Eliot Coleman, among others, to thank for resurrecting the hoop house idea for locally grown year-round produce. Coleman, who lives in Harborside, Maine, is the author of *Four-Season Harvest* and *The Winter Harvest Handbook*. In *Four-Season Harvest*, Coleman notes that his Maine organic farm is on the forty-fouth parallel, the same latitude as the southern part of France, and introduces ideas to use cold frames, unheated tunnel greenhouses, and root cellars to extend the growing season and its harvest. In *The Winter Harvest Handbook*, Coleman expands on that notion, giving information on how to build and maintain unheated or minimally heated, relatively inexpensive greenhouses in which good food can grow in even the harshest winters. At Four Season farm, where Coleman lives with equally esteemed gardening and food writer Barbara Damrosch, Coleman grows more than thirty crops year-round, including artichokes—not normally thought of as a cold-climate crop.

The grower who sold me my beets had proved himself an inventive and resourceful man. Even with Michigan's cloudy winter skies, he knew that with warmth and the bright light made possible from daylight reflected by snow, his early crops could get a good start in his hoop houses.

Perhaps he had even taken one of Adam Montri's courses in hoop house growing. Montri is a teacher of those methods, through his affiliation with the nonprofit Michigan Food and Farming Systems and the Michigan State University Student Organic Farm, operated under the auspices of MSU's Department of Horticulture. In his workshops, Montri distributes a cropping schedule for hoop-house growing, which is available online. The schedule tells growers what varieties to plant in winter and late summer—my farmer's Detroit Dark Red beets are one of the three recommended beet varieties for seeding February 1. Montri's handout is like a roadmap for a beginning hoop-house grower, explaining when to plant, when to transplant, and how long each crop needs to grow before harvest.

I swished the beet greens through the water again, on the off chance there were bugs or sand on them, rolled them into a cloth dish towel, and stashed them in the refrigerator. By the time I finished a few other small chores, the beets were done roasting. I gave Pippin, who had been keeping me company in the kitchen on his play stand, a couple of slices of still-warm beets. Research has shown that African Greys are as intelligent as six-year-olds and that they use language as appropriately as a child, so I speak to Pip as I would to a smart little kid. His responses to my conversation are often eerily correct, and Grey companions tell dozens of stories about their birds' smarts. But Greys are often wary of new foods and need a little coaxing. "Try that," I said, putting a couple of sliced beets in his dish and letting him see me eat one, too. "See if you like it. That's beets. They're good! I like them."

Pippin regarded me mistrustfully for a moment, then sank his gleaming black beak into one of the slices. He patted the tip of his anvil-shaped tongue on the slice, to taste it without commitment.

"Mmmmmmm!," he said. "That's good!" With that, he picked up the slice in his one of his dextrous claws and began to nibble around its edges. Soon his beak was covered in red beet juice. He ate all the first slice and most of the second before he began to wipe the juice away by rubbing his beak on his perch.

Dividing the batch of beets in two, I diced the first half and sliced the second. I measured the diced beets into two-cup servings—enough for dinner for me and leftovers for lunch with a little for Pip the next day—put each serving in a zip-top freezer bag, pressed out the air, and carried them down to the big freezer in the cellar. Then I sliced onions for the pickled beets and filled the jars, poured over them the hot seasoned vinegar and put them in the canner. By dinnertime, I had three batches of diced beets in the freezer and four ruby pint jars of pickled beets cooling on the kitchen table. Dinner would be something light—a salad, perhaps—to end a productive day. I yawned.

After dinner, as I carried Pippin to his night cage, he cooed, the sweet sound he makes when he is happy and tired. "Want a peanut before bed?" I said, reaching for the bag of unsalted, roasted peanuts in the shell that I keep on hand as a treat for him.

"No," he said, in his squeaky, funny, little-old-man voice. "Want a beets."

moroccan-style roasted beets with cumin and olive oil

MAKES 4 TO 6 SERVINGS

The cumin in these good beets plays up their earthiness. They improve by standing at room temperature, covered, for up to 24 hours. After that, if there are any left, refrigerate them.

–·–

2 pounds beets

2 tablespoons extra-virgin olive oil

2 cloves garlic, smashed and minced

1 teaspoon ground cumin

Juice of 1/2 lemon

A pinch of coarse salt, such as kosher salt

Preheat the oven to 400°F.

Wash the beets and prepare them by trimming away all but 1/2 inch of greens if they still have their leaves, and leaving them untrimmed if they don't. Don't worry about their root-end tails. Wrap the beets in heavy-duty aluminum foil and place the package on a rimmed baking sheet. Roast the beets for 1 to 2 hours, until they are completely tender when pierced with a knife. Remove the beets from the oven; allow to cool.

Skin the beets with a paring knife. Cut the beets into 1/2-inch dice and put into a bowl.

Heat the oil in a small skillet over medium-high heat. Add the garlic and cook, stirring, for 1 minute, or until the garlic is fragrant but not yet brown. Add the cumin and continue to cook for 1 minute longer. Pour the hot oil over the beets. Toss the beets to coat them with the oil; add the lemon juice and salt and toss again.

Let the salad stand for at least 30 minutes to allow the flavors to blend. Serve at room temperature.

pickled beets

Make sure your family likes beets before you bother to make these! Because I love beets, I make a couple of batches every year. While most recipes tell you to boil the beets in the first step, I prefer to roast them, whole, and slice or quarter them after they cool. Jars of sliced beets are ready to eat a little sooner than the quartered ones, which take longer to absorb the flavors of the brine.

---

3 pounds beets

3 tablespoons mixed pickling spice

1 tablespoon whole black peppercorns

10 whole cloves

2$^1/2$ cups white vinegar

1 cup water

1 cup sugar

3 cups sliced onions

Preheat the oven to 400°F.

Wash the beets, leaving $1/2$ inch of greens on their tops if they still have them, or leaving them untrimmed if they don't. Don't worry about the root-tail ends. Wrap the beets in heavy-duty aluminum foil and place the package on a rimmed baking sheet. Roast the beets for 1 to 2 hours, until they are tender when pierced with a knife. Remove the beets from the oven; allow to cool.

Prepare the pint jars, lids, and a boiling water bath canner as instructed on page 253.

Skin the beets with a paring knife and slice or quarter them. Tie the pickling spices, peppercorns, and cloves in a square of cheesecloth and place in a large nonreactive saucepan. Add the vinegar, water, and sugar. Bring to a boil over medium-high heat, stirring to dissolve the sugar. Decrease the heat and boil gently for 15 minutes. Discard the spice bag. Add the beets and onions and return the mixture to a boil.

Fill the hot canning jars with the beets and onions and ladle in liquid to cover, leaving a generous $1/2$-inch headspace. Seal the jars. Process in a boiling water bath for 30 minutes, according to the instructions on page 253. Store the jars in a cool, dry place. They will keep for up to a year.

salt-rising bread

MAKES THREE 9 BY 5-INCH LOAVES

Salt-rising bread is notoriously finicky, and it takes 2 to 3 days to make it. First you make the starter, then you make a sponge, then you make the bread itself, which rises much more slowly than yeast-risen bread. If that seems like a great deal of work for a loaf of bread, perhaps its dense crumb and fine flavor will change your mind. Be aware that some people find the "cheesy" aroma of the starter unappealing, although the finished bread will not have that smell. Salt-rising bread will stay fresh for nearly a week, makes incredible toast, and freezes well.

◆-◆

STARTER

1 cup milk

1/2 cup stone-ground cornmeal

2 tablespoons sugar

1 teaspoon salt

SPONGE

2 cups warm water (110°F)

2 tablespoons sugar

3 tablespoons salted butter, melted and cooled

2 cups all-purpose flour

BREAD

1/2 teaspoon baking soda

1 tablespoon warm water (110°F)

6 cups all-purpose flour, plus more for the work surface

To make the starter, heat the milk just to steaming in a saucepan over medium heat. Remove from the heat and while still warm, stir in the cornmeal, sugar, and salt. Transfer the mixture to a jar or glass measuring cup and place in a slow cooker or electric skillet with a few inches of water in it. Cover the slow cooker or skillet, and, using the lowest setting on the slow cooker or placing the skillet in an oven set at its lowest temperature, maintain a starter temperature of 105° to 115°F for 7 to 12 hours, until the starter has begun to "work," releasing gas and the characteristic "cheesy" aroma and a bubbling foam forms on the surface. There's no rushing this step. Don't continue until the starter has fermented correctly.

When the starter is bubbly, make the sponge. Transfer the starter mixture to a bowl. Stir in the warm water, sugar, melted butter, and flour. Mix the sponge thoroughly. Put the bowl in the water in the skillet or slow cooker, cover, and maintain a temperature of 105° to 115°F. Let rise until light and full of bubbles, 2 1/2 to 3 hours.

To make the bread, grease three 9 by 5-inch loaf pans. Dissolve the baking soda in the warm water and combine it with the sponge. Stir 5 1/4 cups of the flour into the sponge; knead in more flour as necessary until the dough is no longer sticky. Transfer the dough to a floured work surface and knead for 10 minutes, or until smooth and manageable. Cut the dough into thirds. Shape each piece into a loaf and place each in a prepared loaf pan and cover with a clean kitchen towel. Place the covered pans in warm water or uncovered pans in a warm oven with a bowl of hot water, maintaining an ambient temperature of 85°F (note that the temperature in this step is not as high as for the starter and sponge). Allow the bread to rise to 2 1/2 times the original size, which may take 5 to 6 hours. The bread will round the top of the pans. Remove the bread from the oven.

Preheat the oven to 375°F.

Bake the bread for 10 minutes, decrease the oven temperature to 350°F, and bake for 20 minutes longer, or until the bread is light golden brown. Let cool in the pans for 15 minutes, then tip the loaves out of the pans onto a wire rack to finish cooling. Store in a zip-top plastic bag, or freeze after double-wrapping with heavy-duty aluminum foil for up to 3 months.

Note: Speed along your next batch by saving and dehydrating a bit of your successful sponge. Save 1/4 cup of the sponge, pour it into a saucer, cover with cheesecloth, and allow to dry at room temperature. Store the dried flakes in a glass or plastic jar in a cool, dry place or freeze. For your next batch, dissolve the flakes in the warm starter as in the first step above and continue as above. The dried sponge will help the starter begin working more quickly, which can save as much as 6 hours on the starter's working time. The flakes will keep indefinitely.

salade lyonnaise

MAKES 1 SERVING

This simple main-dish salad is perfect for lunch or a light supper. It pleased me the first time I ate it, at a cafe in Lyons, when the wonder of finally visiting France dazed me. The coddled egg, barely cooked, creates a creamy, rich dressing when tossed with a bit of hot bacon fat. Since I have no fear of contamination in locally grown chickens' eggs, I'm comfortable eating very lightly cooked eggs. If you're worried about egg safety, poach the egg instead.

2 cups torn romaine lettuce

2 strips bacon

1 large egg

1 tablespoon cider vinegar

Croutons

Salt and freshly ground black pepper

Wash the lettuce and spin it dry. Put it in a large mixing bowl. Set aside.

Cook the bacon in a heavy skillet over medium heat until it is brown and crisp on both sides, about 10 minutes. Transfer the bacon to paper towels to drain, then chop coarsely. Reserve the bacon drippings and keep warm.

Warm the egg by running it under hot water. Place the egg, still in its shell, in a glass measuring cup or small stainless steel bowl. Coddle the egg by pouring boiling water over it and letting it stand in the water for 1 minute. Remove the egg carefully, pat it dry, and break the egg over the lettuce. Add the chopped bacon, 1 tablespoon of the warm bacon drippings, and the vinegar. Toss to mix. Add the croutons, season to taste with salt and pepper, and toss again.

Serve immediately.

eggs baked on a bed of garlicky braised beet greens

MAKES 2 SERVINGS

If you don't have beet greens handy, make this easy, light supper dish with kale, Swiss chard, collards, mustard greens, or turnip greens. Serve with some good crusty bread, and dinner's done. When it's just me, I make this in a cast-iron skillet, but if I'm serving a guest, I usually braise the greens, then prepare individual gratin dishes of greens for each person.

Beet greens from 1 bunch beets

¹/₄ cup olive oil

2 cloves garlic, smashed and minced

Salt and freshly ground black pepper

4 large eggs

Wash the greens and chop them coarsely, both the leaves and stems. It's okay if water clings to them. You should have about 8 cups.

Preheat the oven to 350°F.

Heat the oil in a large, heavy skillet over medium-high heat. Add the garlic and cook, stirring, for 1 to 2 minutes, until the garlic is golden and fragrant. Add as many of the greens as you can fit into the skillet; cover with a close-fitting lid and cook for 5 minutes. Remove the cover and add any remaining greens; replace the cover and cook for an additional 5 to 10 minutes, stirring once or twice, until the greens are wilted. They will not be tender at this point. Season the greens with salt and pepper and stir them again.

Break the eggs over the greens. Cover the skillet and slide it into the oven. Bake for 10 minutes, remove the cover, and bake for 5 to 10 minutes longer, until the egg whites are set and the yolks are cooked through. Season the eggs with salt and pepper and serve.

5

On chooks and coffee

IN EARLY APRIL, soon after I fled to the lake, one of the brothers who own the house next door came by to visit. His name is Wally, but he's Wonder Wally in my mind, because he is so kind and does so many things for me. He and his wife live near Charlotte, about twenty miles away. Wally had heard the news about the divorce, he said, and wanted to make sure that I was all right. Over the next several hours, we talked and talked—about the divorce at first, but then, as the conversation went on, about other parts of our lives. I told him about the period, early in my marriage, when I had lived on a small rural property in my husband's native Mississippi. I was happy there, I told Wally, maybe the happiest I've ever been in my life. One of the things I missed most about that period in my life was my flock of Barred Rock laying hens. Everything about them pleased me.

It was just so perfectly Wonder Wally that he showed up a couple of days later with a large cheeping cardboard box. "I've brought you some chicks," he said, grinning. He'd also brought me a heat lamp, a bag of chick chow, a feeder, and a small plastic jug to supply the chicks with water. He'd heard me talking about something that made me happy and had taken steps to return some of that happiness to my life in a difficult time. It was certainly one of the kindest things anyone has ever done for me.

The chicks were a hybrid called Golden Comets. They're a sex-link hybrid, which means the day-old female chicks are dark rose colored, while the young males are as blond as Madonna. Because their colors are so different, it's easy to choose the sex you want.

For their first five weeks, they lived in their box in my kitchen. Every day, I removed the chicks, water dish, and feeder and put down fresh newspapers over the previous layers. Once a week, I bundled up the previous week's newspapers and burned them, starting over with fresh newspaper. It didn't take long each day, and each chick got soothing strokes and gently murmured encouragement. I liked their contented soft cheeping. But I was glad when they were ready to move to the coop: they generated a lot of dust as they preened away their down to make way for their feathers.

When they moved outside, I kept them cooped for a week 'round the clock; that trained them to return to the coop each night for safety. After that I let them out every morning around ten o'clock. The last thing before locking up for the night, I took the dog out and, and at the same time, closed the coop's chicken door after they were all in for the night.

Keeping chickens in the backyard has become rather trendy. A lot of cities have amended old ordinances prohibiting poultry in the city limits. I've read on Internet poultry bulletin boards about civil disobedience actions aimed at changing poultry-keeping laws. Residents of Atlanta, Chicago, and Los Angeles can keep chickens, at least at this moment; so can residents of Ann Arbor, Michigan; Fort Worth, Texas; and Miami, Florida. Most cities have rules about how many chickens, and how far the coop and pen must be from houses or neighbors. Some require paying for a permit. If you want to find out the law in your city, start with the city attorney's office. Police and other municipal officers may not actually know the law. Many, if not most, cities prohibit roosters, presumably because their crowing can be seen—or heard, I guess—as a nuisance.

The day-old chicks Wally gave me in April were two months old in June. Fully fledged, the chickens were remarkably beautiful: russet and white, with many of their white feathers edged in that rusty red. Because they hadn't started to lay, they were still officially pullets—they don't change into hens until that first egg is laid, which I estimated would be in early to mid-August.

The Australians call chickens "chooks," and that is how I call them as I scatter a handful or two of whole oats or cracked corn for them: "Chook, chook! Chook, chook!" They respond by running to me as fast as they can, knowing that call means something nice is in the offing. Galloping chickens never fail to make me laugh out loud.

At eight weeks, the chickens were both silly and sensible. I love the soft chirring they make when they find something tasty to eat and the creaky croak they utter when alarmed. They were gathering the strength in their wings at this point, so periodically one would rise to its toes and flap those wings hard for a couple of seconds. They sometimes leapt a couple of feet straight up in the air. Although the chickens wouldn't really fly much, they needed the lift to their night roost as they got older and to enter the nest boxes. When they were still young they slept in a heap in the corner of the coop. In general, the six traveled in a little herd, rarely more than a few feet apart. They usually came to scratch at my feet, but fled from anyone else.

Their coop is a handsome structure, compared to some I've seen that have been cobbled together from junk and chicken wire. The man who built it lives in a neighboring town and advertised his coops on Craigslist. Wally helped me fetch it home. It cost less than the wood used to build it, or so Wally said. It's made of half-inch marine-grade plywood and two-by-fours. If I had one more chicken, I would need a larger coop, but this one is just the right size for my six gals. The builder painted it barn red. Mind you, the chickens don't care what it looks like. But I thought the neighbors might, so I wanted something reasonably presentable. Tucked up against the back of my garden shed, it's not visible from the road, but my next-door neighbors on both sides certainly can see it.

My chickens are easy keepers, as people say about some horses. It takes less than ten minutes a day to give them fresh water and check their feeder, and to sprinkle fresh straw on the floor of the coop to keep odor and flies away. Before I scatter the straw, I dust the previous layer with a cup of a product called "Stable-Dry." It contains clay to absorb moisture and diatomaceous earth, a silica-based natural insect deterrent; its minute sharp-edged crystals cut the exoskeletons of flies and other pests, killing them without pesticides. It doesn't hurt the chickens.

A twenty-five pound bag of chow costs about twelve dollars and lasts for a couple of months; a bale of straw and some Stable-Dry costs a little more and lasts about the same length of time. There's no reason to supply grit to the girls, because they get plenty—but sometimes you have to add some crushed oyster shell once they start laying, to ensure sturdy shells on the eggs. I'm not raising chickens for eggs because it's cheaper, though; I'm doing it because I like chickens, and because I know the eggs will be so very good. I continued to pay three dollars a dozen for eggs at the farmers' market until the girls started to lay.

Once they're fully in the laying rotation, each hen will lay an egg a day, more or less. With six chickens, that's a dozen eggs every two days—way more than I can use as fresh eggs, that's for sure. But eggs freeze easily. I separate the eggs, place the white from each egg into a compartment of an ice cube tray, and then pop the frozen whites into zip-top freezer bags. They whip into frothy meringues and airy soufflés as well as fresh egg whites do. Egg yolks require a bit of extra treatment and will become unusable without it. They need $1/8$ teaspoon of salt, or $1^1/2$ teaspoons sugar, for every 4 yolks, lightly beaten. I freeze those in containers, labeled for sweet (with sugar) or savory (with salt) dishes. Both the whites and yolks will keep for up to a year. I may also freeze some containers that combine one whole egg and two whites, lightly beaten, for the health-conscious omelets I like, although some studies hint that the yolks from free-range eggs are lower in cholesterol and saturated fat than conventionally raised eggs.

I was glad when I came across a 1977 *Mother Earth News* article that tested various methods of keeping eggs. The article said the best results came from storing unwashed eggs—which still retain a protective covering on the shell called the "bloom"—in a covered, refrigerated container. "Even after seven months," the article said, eggs "stored in this manner smell good, taste good, have a good texture, and—in short—seem almost fresh."

So I watched the chooks every morning for a while as I drank a second cup of coffee and nibbled on a scone, a bit of shortbread, or a cookie, to make sure everyone's healthy and active, and to think about how interesting the world was when viewed from their perspective.

The coffee I drank was a chocolaty, fruity organic coffee from Chiapas, Mexico. The coffee doesn't grow here in the Great Lakes, of course, so I apply the notion of "acting locally" when selecting beans, even though the locality I'm acting in is many, many miles away. I like buying beans that come from farmers' cooperatives and small estates, because I know the growers get a fair price that way. "Farm gate" and "fair trade" are undefined terms, but still they imply an attitude of equity for the grower that I appreciate. I could buy cheaper coffee, that's for sure. But drinking this coffee means something specific to me. When I traveled in Chiapas, I saw coffee growers bringing their green coffee down to market from their mountain homes, their sturdy burros laden with burlap sacks of beans, having already walked for hours by the time the sun rose. It moved me to see that the growers, even with such a long journey ahead of them, dressed in their finest clothing: blindingly white shirts, bleached by the sun; intricately embroidered and richly embellished vests or jackets that identified them by their village. I thought of those growers every morning when I sipped the cup they worked so hard to grow and market for me, and I admired their tenacity and endurance. Each cup of coffee reminded me to cultivate those qualities in myself.

I started to roast my own beans about a year ago. The interest started, as do most of my interests, with a curiosity about how flavors develop in the things we eat and drink. That curiosity led me to learn how to make cheese, and to make fruit wines, meads, and hard ciders. But roasting my own coffee beans has wrought the most immediate change in my life, simply because I drink coffee every morning.

Coffee is an interesting crop. The shrubby tropical trees grow best as an understory species, but it's hard to mechanically harvest coffee in that habitat. So, many big coffee plantations have adopted varieties that can withstand the full sun and exposure that makes mechanical harvesting easier. The hitch in the get-along, as they say down South, is that planting those varieties means wholesale clear-cutting of the taller trees, which in turn deprives birds and animals of necessary habitat. Certified "shade-grown" or "bird-friendly" coffee beans command a premium price for those with an ecological bent. Other types of certified beans include organic beans, fair-trade, eco-OK, sustainable, and "partnership" or "relationship" coffees, in which grower and roaster agree to share some profit with a charity or organization. Many excellent beans meet those criteria, however, yet don't have certification of any kind. As an example, notes Kenneth Davids in *Home Coffee Roasting*, "Kenyan coffees are almost entirely produced by cooperatives of small-holding peasant growers, yet no Kenyan coffees are certified fair-trade. Chemicals of any kind are virtually unheard of in the Harrar region of Ethiopia and in Yemen, yet virtually no coffees from those regions are certified organic."

While I certainly understand—and appreciate—people who make the decision to pay premiums for those certifications, it hasn't become important to me. Perhaps one day it will.

A much more important decision for me was to buy only arabica beans. There are many different varieties of arabica—Bourbon, Catuai, Caturra, Maragogipe, Moka, and Typica, just for starters—but most coffee connoisseurs agree that arabica coffees are superior to robusta varieties. Robustas produce coffee that tastes "flatter," simpler, and less nuanced, than arabicas, but the beans are also considerably cheaper. Many supermarket coffees are a blend of the two types of beans—enough arabica to contribute bright flavor and a lot of robusta to keep costs down.

The language of coffee description shares a lot with the wine world. Coffees are described as "big" and "round," or "austere" and "bright," with varying degrees of acidity, fruitiness, and other flavors. I've done enough fine-wine tasting in my life to appreciate having the vocabulary, and even, to some extent, to use it correctly. But for me, in coffee and in wine, a good cuppa is instantly recognizable, with or without the descriptors. I don't give them too much weight, except as a guide when I'm trying to decide whether I'm interested in trying a new bean.

As with wine, the flavors of coffee begin with the soil and the climate where the fruit is grown. High-altitude coffees, grown in thin air and thin soil, taste different from lower-altitude coffees. But that's just the beginning. Coffee's flavor is also influenced by how the beans are processed, and, of course, how they are roasted.

What we think of as the coffee bean is actually the pit of the pulpy fruit of the tree, like the pit of a cherry; in fact, green coffee beans are just a little smaller than a cherry pit. How that pulp is removed is the first of many processes that affect the coffee's flavor. There are several methods. Wet-processing is the most common—and the most complex—method. The freshly picked beans are tumbled in a machine much like the stone-polishing gizmo I used to play with as a kid, to remove the outer skin of the fruit. Then the beans are fermented to remove the sticky, wet pulp. After a final washing, the beans are dried, sometimes by machine and sometimes by the sun. When the beans are completely dry, a machine tumbles off the paperlike parchment and silver skin. In some coffee-growing locales, the freshly picked coffee fruit is dried whole, and then the extraneous parts are rubbed away, in the dry method. Still another method, the semidry technique, combines part of the wet-processing steps with the final steps of the dry method. Wet-processed beans produce coffees with very consistent flavor profiles; they are also consistent in appearance. Dry-processed beans are often a mix of colors, and some of the beans may be broken. Coffee processing techniques are cultural and traditional; the idiosyncratic Yemeni coffees, dry-processed using centuries-old methods, gain much of their complex flavor from having dried in the sun on rooftops, in contact with the fruit. It's safe to assume, unless you are buying raw, or green, coffee beans from a reliable source that tells you otherwise, that most of the coffee you drink was wet-processed.

I roast my own coffee beans in small batches, enough for two days at a time, and grind the beans each morning, so my morning coffee is always freshly

ground and no more than forty-eight hours from the roaster. Coffe
benefit from standing for a while after roasting, although a cup ma
beans fresh and still hot from the roaster is a wonderful thing; the d
roast, in general, the longer the roasted beans should stand before grinding.
I buy most of my green coffee beans from Sweet Maria's (sweetmarias.com),
an Oakland, California, company that specializes in small-lot, often organic,
fair-trade, farm-gate or estate beans, or the Coffee Project (coffeeproject.com),
a similar California company. I bought my air-roaster from Sweet Maria's,
too; it cost about one hundred dollars and came with four one-pound bags of
green coffee. You can roast coffee beans in a covered cast-iron skillet if you're
strong—you have to keep the beans moving by shaking the skillet, not stirring
the beans—or even in a slightly modified popcorn air-popper or stove-top
popper. But as an absolute beginner, I found the reliability and ease of the
small air-roaster was a real draw. I usually roast coffee for the next couple of
days while I'm doing dishes after supper.

The beans cost, on average, five to seven dollars a pound; adding the shipping costs brings their price to about eight dollars a pound. For me, it's an
affordable luxury. I drink just two cups of coffee a day, so I want those cups
to be as delicious as I can make them. Fine wines are no longer within my
reach; artisan cheeses and specialty foods are too pricey for my budget, alas.
But a good cup of coffee? Yes, I can afford that.

Green coffee beans will keep almost indefinitely if stored properly—at
room temperature, kept dry. The gray-green beans are hard enough to crack
a tooth before roasting, with a grassy, herbaceous scent that gives no hint of
their eventual flavor after roasting.

In roasting, as their temperature rises, the beans' color changes, and that
color provides a clue to how the flavor is developing. The roasting goes quickly;
it takes just five to six minutes to roast a couple of ounces of beans at a time,
and the difference between a just-right roast and an overdone roast can be a
matter of seconds.

Roasting coffee beans enter a stage called "first crack." The beans start to
pop, just as popcorn does, as the moisture inside heats up, to just under 400°F.
But a coffee made from beans roasted only to first crack tastes thin and weak,
because the heat hasn't allowed the development of the flavors yet. The oils and
caramelized sugars that create coffee's flavors need higher heat to emerge.

The traditional and preferred roast in the eastern United States is a light,
medium brown, in which the beans have reached an internal temperature of

400° to 415°F—a few seconds after first crack. In many western states, the preference is for beans roasted to the next step, a medium brown with beans roasted to an internal temperature of 415° to 435°F. Some people call that an "American" or "regular city" roast. At 435° to 445°F, the beans enter "second crack," and if you stop the roast there, you'll have a "full-city" roast, the kind that's preferred in the Pacific Northwest. At that point, the beans are medium-dark brown and still look dry, although some might have faint patches of oil. I usually roast to city or full-city, depending on the beans.

Keep going past second crack, and you enter the espresso roasts, where the beans have become very dark and very oily: French, Italian, Turkish, Neapolitan, and Spanish roasts. At the darkest end, in a Spanish roast, the beans have risen to 475° to 480°F; at that temperature, most of the flavor compounds have burned away.

When beans are roasted black and oily, as some roasting companies do for all their coffees, and as coffee is traditionally roasted for French or Italian espresso, the brew is no longer about the bean: it changes into being about the roast. You don't need to spend extra money on fine beans if you want dark-roasted coffee, I realized, and paying a premium for over-roasted beans that claim national origin is just plain silly. If I was going to the trouble to buy beans from a specific origin, it defeated the point to over-roast them. I like my beans nut-brown, but not oily and certainly not blackened. By roasting only to that point, the coffee's specific attributes are preserved. My cup of organic Chiapas Priosh Cooperative tastes remarkably different from the Colombian estate coffee I drank last week, although each was a full-city roast.

I confess to a small amusement that I'm drinking "full-city roast" coffee here at the lake, where the nearest cities are more than twenty miles away. But the coffee-roasting tradition doesn't include a "smack-dab-in-the-middle-of-the-woods" roast, so full-city roast it is.

The chooks wandered into the hillside cinnamon ferns to scratch and peck, and they stayed there for an hour or more. By the time I stepped into the kitchen to see about lunch, they had come down the hill and dotted the flowerbed outside the kitchen window, doing my weeding for me and chirring in their quiet delight.

Their eggs would taste of home, quite literally. They would taste of my spot, here, on a Michigan lake. With a cup of tenacity and endurance grown in the mountains of Chiapas state, Mexico, they would nourish my spirit quite nicely.

gingered cornmeal shortbread

MAKES 1 DOZEN PIECES

Shortbread is so good and so easy that maybe it should be illegal. Really, who doesn't like butter and sugar? This gingery shortbread gets a little gritty crunch from a bit of cornmeal, perhaps because I think everything sweet in life should be balanced by a bit of reality. Of course, margarine is out of the question here.

+-+

1 cup (2 sticks) salted butter, at room temperature

1/2 cup superfine sugar (see Note below)

2 cups all-purpose flour, plus more for the work surface

1/2 cup coarse cornmeal

1/4 cup crystallized ginger, very finely chopped

Preheat the oven to 325°F.

Beat the butter and sugar in a stand mixer on medium speed for 10 minutes, no less. It should be very white.

Mix in the flour, cornmeal, and ginger with a rubber spatula. Transfer to a flour-dusted work surface, lightly knead the dough, and pat it into a square or rectangle to a thickness of 1/4 to 1/2 inch. Transfer to a baking sheet. Score the dough with a sharp knife into 12 pieces and prick each piece several times with the tines of a fork.

Bake for 15 to 20 minutes, or until lightly golden. Remove from the oven and cut the shortbread into pieces, following the score marks. Allow to cool fully before serving. The shortbread will keep in a tightly lidded container for up to 2 weeks.

Note: To make superfine sugar, simply whirl granulated sugar in a food processor or blender for 2 to 3 minutes.

espresso-walnut scones

MAKES 8 SCONES

I was once lucky enough to take a class taught by Shirley O. Corriher, the brilliant and generous food scientist whose books, *Cookwise* and *Bakewise*, are among the most dog-eared in my collection. In that class, she taught us that making a very wet biscuit dough leads to light, airy biscuits. Since scones are simply sweetened biscuits enriched with a bit of cream, I wondered, would the same logic apply? Sure enough, Shirley confirms that in *Bakewise*. As with biscuits, I prefer to use self-rising flour here, both for convenience and for its lower protein, which keeps the scones tender.

---

2 cups self-rising flour (see page 29), plus more for dusting

1/3 cup granulated sugar

1/2 teaspoon salt

1/4 cup (1/2 stick) salted butter, cold

2/3 cup heavy cream or whole milk

1 teaspoon vanilla extract

1 cup buttermilk or whole milk

2 teaspoons very finely ground espresso-roast coffee

1/2 cup chopped walnuts

3 tablespoons salted butter, melted

ICING

1 cup confectioners' sugar

1 teaspoon vanilla extract

1 to 2 tablespoons heavy cream

Preheat the oven to 425°F. Line an 8-inch round cake pan with parchment paper or grease it well.

In a large mixing bowl, stir together the flour, granulated sugar, and salt. Using your fingers or two knives, work in the cold butter until there are no large lumps. Gently stir in the cream, then the vanilla and some of the buttermilk. Continue to add the buttermilk until the mixture is very wet; it will resemble cottage cheese but should not be soupy. Stir in the ground coffee and the walnuts.

Flour a cutting board generously. Tip the dough out onto the floured board and flour it lightly. Without kneading, pat the dough into a round big enough to fill the cake pan. Transfer the round to the prepared pan. Using a floured table knife, score the dough in the cake pan into eighths.

Bake for 20 to 25 minutes, until lightly browned.

While the scones bake, prepare the icing. Combine the confectioners' sugar, vanilla, and 1 tablespoon of the cream in a large glass measuring cup. Add additional cream as needed to make a pourable glaze, but keep the consistency thick, like yogurt.

When the scones are done, remove them from the oven and brush the tops with the melted butter. Invert quickly onto a plate, then invert again on another plate so the scones are again right-side-up. Using the score marks as your guide, quickly cut the scones into eighths. Place the scones on a wire rack set over a baking sheet.

Drizzle the icing over the hot scones, allowing some to dribble down the sides of each scone. Be generous!

Eat warm, or allow to cool completely before placing on a plate and wrapping in plastic wrap. The scones will keep for up to 4 days.

the aunt gertrude cookie

MAKES ABOUT 2 DOZEN COOKIES

As kids, we were taught to call my grandmother's women friends "Aunt Friend's-first-name." Aunt Gertrude was Gertrude Ricketts, a tiny, cheery woman who kept a stoneware crock of these big fragrant, spicy cookies around for her young visitors. "You may have two," she would say, "one for each hand." These days, I'm more likely to have a cookie in one hand and a cup of coffee in the other.

* *

1 cup (2 sticks) salted butter, at room temperature (do not substitute margarine)

1 cup sugar

1 large egg

1 cup blackstrap molasses or sorghum syrup

4³/4 cups sifted all-purpose flour

1 tablespoon baking soda

1/2 teaspoon salt

2 teaspoons ground cinnamon

1 teaspoon ground ginger

1/2 teaspoon ground cloves

3/4 cup strong brewed coffee, cold

Raisins

Preheat the oven to 375°F. Lightly grease two baking sheets.

Beat the butter in a stand mixer at slow speed for about 5 minutes, or until light and fluffy. With the mixer running, gradually add the sugar and continue to beat until the mixture is light, about 5 minutes longer. Beat in the egg. Beat in the molasses, scraping down the sides of the bowl once or twice. The mixture will be thick, but light.

Sift together the flour, baking soda, salt, cinnamon, ginger, and cloves. Add half of the flour mixture to the butter mixture and beat for 30 seconds. Add the coffee and beat for about 30 seconds. Add the remaining flour mixture and beat for 30 seconds longer.

Drop the dough by heaping tablespoons about 2 inches apart on the prepared baking sheets. Press a raisin into the center of each cookie.

Bake the cookies, one sheet at a time, for 15 to 18 minutes, or until golden and a little dry around the edges. Cool the cookies on the baking sheets for 5 minutes, then remove to wire racks to finish cooling.

grandmother bates's oatmeal cookies

MAKES ABOUT 2¹/₂ DOZEN COOKIES

Georgia Smith Bates (1824–1903) was my great-great-grandmother. This
is her recipe for oatmeal cookies, passed down to her daughter, then to my
paternal grandmother, then to my mother, and finally to me. I have recast her
recipe in contemporary recipe style and added vanilla, but otherwise made
no changes. They are not as humble as traditional oatmeal cookies, nor as
sweet; the soda leavens them a little so they are light and airy. Bake them in
domed rounds, or use your fingers to flatten them a little before baking.

◆-•-◆-•-◆-•-◆-•-◆-•-◆-•-◆-•-◆-•-◆-•-◆-•-◆-•-◆-•-◆-•-◆-•-◆-•-◆-•-◆

*1 cup (2 sticks) salted butter,
at room temperature (do not
substitute margarine)*

1 cup sugar

2 large eggs

¹/₄ teaspoon baking soda

¹/₄ cup milk

1 teaspoon vanilla extract

*1 cup dried cherries, blueber-
ries, or raisins*

2 cups all-purpose flour

2 cups rolled oats (not instant)

¹/₂ teaspoon grated nutmeg

¹/₂ teaspoon salt

Preheat the oven to 350°F. Lightly grease two baking sheets or line with
parchment paper.

In a large mixing bowl, beat together the butter and sugar until light
and fluffy. Beat in the eggs one at a time, beating well after each addition.
Dissolve the baking soda in the milk, then add the vanilla. Add the milk
mixture to the butter-sugar mixture. Beat well to combine.

In another large mixing bowl, combine the dried cherries and flour. Toss
with a fork to lightly flour the cherries. Stir in the oats, nutmeg, and salt. Stir
well to combine. Add the flour mixture to the butter-sugar mixture. Beat just
until combined.

Drop the dough by the tablespoon 2 inches apart on the prepared baking
sheets.

Bake the cookies, one sheet at a time, for 18 to 20 minutes, until the
cookies are golden and set. Cool the cookies on the baking sheets for 5 minutes, then remove to wire racks to finish cooling.

6

On spring lamb and the butcher's headaches

MY PASSION FOR LAMB may have been the beginning of my interest in eating locally.

The Mather family loves lamb. We had butterflied leg of lamb, not ham, at Easter when I was growing up. My sister's time with the Peace Corps in Morocco, which introduced the family to the wonderful food she had learned about there, cemented this passion. We celebrated my younger brother's engagement with a party centered on grilled lamb, and when we buried my father, lamb was the only funeral meat. Indeed, lamb—grilled, roasted, or skewered—has figured in every important family gathering I can think of.

Back in the days when I had funds, I used to buy a whole lamb or two from a shepherd, first in Michigan and later in Illinois. The farmer took the lamb to a custom slaughterhouse, and by and by, I'd get a call from the butcher to find out how I wanted the carcass cut up. Then, within a week or so, I'd make the trek to the meat processor to pick up the lamb, now all cut up to my instructions and carefully wrapped and frozen. A lamb with a live weight of 125 pounds yielded about forty pounds of edible meat, once the skin and bone and other waste was subtracted; the meat fit into a couple of brown paper shopping bags or small boxes. I paid the shepherd for the live lamb; at the packing house, I paid for the cost of the slaughter and butchering and still came out ahead, saving a good bit of money over the retail price for lamb at the supermarket. Not only was I buying the lamb locally, but I also learned the breed of sheep; and I learned that I like a Corriedale lamb best of all. The Corriedale is a dual-purpose breed, bred for wool and meat— I learned to spin using Corriedale fleece—and it's big enough to provide a good-sized carcass, which in turns means a boned leg of about five to seven pounds. Smaller breeds, like Icelandics and Shetlands, have very good meat, indeed. But for my purposes, a Corriedale is the way to go.

Buying a whole animal meant learning how to use less familiar parts, like shoulder roasts and chops, riblets, and breast, as well as thinking about my own cooking style. I always asked for the scraps to be made into stew meat rather than ground meat, because I know I lean more to stew than to burgers. If I wanted ground lamb, perhaps to make kibbeh (page 72) as my Armenian-American friend Bob taught me to do, I could always grind it myself, either in the food processor or by using the grinding attachment on my KitchenAid mixer. But ground meat can never be made back into stew meat.

Of course, man does not live on lamb alone. Back in Michigan, I needed to find a source for locally raised pork and beef. My neighbor Jim told me about Geukes Market in nearby Middleville. Their bacon was especially good, he said, and I could buy lamb, beef, and pork there, too. For chicken, I would want to check out Otto's Chicken, also in Middleville, he said; and Tom Otto, kin to the chicken folks, raised turkeys nearby.

One Friday, after visiting the Middleville farmers' market, I made my way to Geukes Market, which is tucked away on the village's north side. When you walk into the retail shop, you enter a clean, brightly lit room with freezers along the walls and forming a center aisle, and a bank of coolers off to one side. Dozens of colorful, handmade thank-you notes from 4-H kids bedeck the walls, expressing their gratitude to Geukes's for buying the animals the youngsters raised to show at the Barry County Fair. There are a good many other awards and framed certificates showing Geukes's participation in all kinds of civic programs as well. This boded well, I thought.

The smoked ham and bacon filled one side of one cooler. The bacon came in vacuum-sealed packages of slices or packages of end cuts—little pieces of trim that were quite a lot cheaper than the sliced bacon, yet could easily work for seasoning in a pot of beans or soup. I picked up a package of each, then checked out the other half of the cooler, which featured "snack sticks," jerky, and cheeses from an Amish company just across the state line in Indiana. I meandered up and down among the freezer cases, checking the contents of each one. Ground beef, stew meat, roasts, and steaks filled one freezer, and I saw some cuts that are hard to find in the supermarkets here— flank and skirt steaks, bones for stock, and even dog bones. Pork cuts, from sausage and ground pork to chops to roasts, filled another freezer. Lamb and sausages filled another. I saw that bags of frozen fruit from a farm stand I liked in Coloma were tucked into the corner of the brats freezer. Everything was vacuum-sealed so freezer burn would never be a problem. Quite a selection, in other words. A white eraser board touted the week's specials. I was really very impressed.

I stepped up to the counter to pay for my bacon and a small bag of dog bones for Boon. The friendly woman cashier was happy to answer my questions. "Have you been here long?" I asked. "Oh, my, yes. Geukes has been in Middleville a long time," she said.

"Can you get me cuts that I don't see in the freezers, like oxtails and beef short ribs?"

"Sure, we can do that easily. You just tell us what you want, and we'll get it and call you when it's ready. It'll be frozen, so if you can't get here for a few days, that's okay."

"You do the slaughtering here?"

"Yes, we do custom-slaughtering for beef, pork, and lamb for farmers around here," she said. "We're the only USDA-inspected slaughterhouse in this area. But if you have more questions, you should probably talk to Don. He's the owner."

With a big, final smile, the woman behind the counter turned to check out the next customer, who had been waiting patiently behind me while I pelted the cashier with questions. "I'll do that," I said. "See you soon."

Back at the house, I was eager to taste this locally made, smoked bacon. I laid a quartet of strips—two for me, one for Pippin, and one for Boon—in my cherished 10¼-inch Lodge cast-iron skillet, a gift from Lodge for judging the tenth annual National Cornbread Cook-off in South Pittsburg, Tennessee, back in 2006.

As I laid the strips of bacon in the skillet, I noticed some keen differences. The slices were thicker than most store-bought bacon; they were about an eighth of an inch, instead of paper-thin. Far more interesting to me, though, was that the fat on the bacon was firm and white. It wasn't slick, almost slimy, as a lot of commercial bacon is. This was bacon from pigs that had eaten the kinds of foods that pigs are meant to eat.

As it sizzled in the skillet, the bacon told me something else. Four slices of bacon gave off very little grease, less than a tablespoon. It was well trimmed and well smoked; as it cooked, the aroma of smoked ham—a mouth-watering scent, in my opinion—filled the kitchen. When the strips were crisp and brown, they were still almost as big as they'd been when I put them in the skillet.

"Okay, you guys, let's see what all the fuss is about," I said to Pip and Boon. I handed each of them a strip of bacon after it had cooled a bit, and then leaned against the counter to sample my own ration.

Boon's, of course, was gone in a gulp. Pip nibbled his bacon delicately, his inky pupils flashing with pleasure. The crisp strips I kept for myself were richly smoky and meaty, with a firm heft and just the right amount of fat. I had to agree with the boys that this was some really, really good bacon, the best I could remember eating in a long time. I needed to talk to Don Geukes.

A few days later, I shook hands with Don in the back room at his store. He's affable and hale, looking far younger than his seventy-odd years. I settled at the employees' lunch table, while he, just a few feet away, eased into the chair at his desk. I wanted to talk to him about the miracle of a small-scale slaughterhouse prospering in a time when, according to the American Association of Meat Processors, such businesses have been failing at an alarming rate. Nearly 15 percent of small slaughterhouses closed in the decade between 1996 and 2006, according to AAMP.

"My grandfather Arthur started this business right here on this location," Don said. "That was back in 1929. They chose this location because it has water (a small creek and the Thornapple River) on two sides, which we needed for power and cooling. And of course, back in those days, rinse water and blood were sent into the river. We don't do that any more, of course. Haven't for years."

When his grandfather retired in 1945, he said, the business passed to Don's father, Chester, and his father's sister, Evelyn. The pair ran the business, both the slaughterhouse which was located where we now sat and the retail shop they opened on Middleville's main street, from 1945 until Don took it over in 1970. The retail shop in the village closed in the 1990s.

"We had state inspections twice a year back when I was working here while I was still in high school," Don said. "My father was instrumental in getting the state to begin inspections at the slaughterhouse level, in fact. But there came a time when Michigan could no longer fund the inspections, so the USDA, which is charged with overseeing meat packing companies, took over. That means there's a USDA inspector on the floor whenever we're slaughtering, which is usually three days a week."

The federal inspector is paid by the government, not the processor, but some small processors couldn't get comfortable with the presence of a federal inspector on their property, Don said. "It can be a little painful to see him in your business, I guess," he said. "So we saw a change—businesses like mine closing—when Michigan began inspecting, and then again when the USDA started to come in. Some old-timers couldn't take that. They weren't willing to make the changes they needed to make."

A slaughterhouse that wants to sell its meat at the retail level must be federally inspected, however. Strictly custom slaughterhouses, which butcher animals owned by their customers for their own consumption, must meet state requirements but don't have to be USDA inspected. If I buy a live animal—like the lambs I used to buy—from a farmer, it's then mine and a custom slaughterhouse can kill it and butcher it for my use. But they can't sell the meat from other animals to other customers.

In theory, the idea is to make sure that the animals are healthy before slaughter, and that the processing is done under clean, safe conditions. In practice, though, the federal rules have long favored the big packing houses like Tyson, Swift & Co. (now JBS), and Cargill, and those regulations have certainly played a role in the decline of small-scale meatpacking houses like Geukes's.

"Dealing with the USDA means a tremendous amount of paperwork," Don said. "They're really geared to the really big plants. There used to be a 'locker plant' [a kind of custom butcher that sold meat, usually by the quarter or half of an animal and provided freezer lockers for their customers in which to store the meat] in every town back when I was in high school. But slowly by slowly, they disappeared. Between the USDA requirements and the environmental requirements that changed disposal methods, a lot of guys just dropped out of the business. So now there are only about a quarter of the small meatpackers left that there once were."

Many sustainable agriculture advocates, including sustainable agriculture superstar Joel Salatin of Polyface Farm in Virginia's Shenandoah Valley, say the loss of small-scale meatpackers, together with the mountains of regulations that the remaining businesses must meet, is one of the key issues that the eat-local movement must address. Because employees work at slower speeds on fewer animals, those advocates say, they have time to do their best and safest work. Slaughter is likely to be more humane. And because a small packing house's market is so local, it's much easier to control and contain the outbreak of any foodborne illness. When a major packing house ships millions of pounds of meat all over the country, any contamination can quickly sicken people in many states, as we have seen repeatedly over the past two decades.

Don said he's never had any bacterial contamination, thank goodness. "We did a good job of producing a good product when I was back in high school, and we still do," he said. It may be because, as he said, "We're not small, we're very, very small by USDA standards." With just five employees— a full-time man to slaughter, "a couple more" for processing, and "a few more" for packaging—Geukes's employees can afford to take their time. Over the course of the year, Don said, they may slaughter about six hundred beef cows, eight hundred hogs, and five hundred lambs. The big meatpackers may handle many more animals than that, in just a single shift.

Small packing houses face other problems, Don said. One is that equipment used in packing and processing is designed for the big packing plants, not for a business that does only a few hundred animals a year. The owner of a small company can't afford to buy a piece of equipment that may cost hundreds of thousands of dollars, yet is only used a few days a week. But now, Don said, reaching into his desk drawer to pull out a catalog to show me, "There are companies that specialize just in smaller-scale processing equipment." And, he said, when he outgrows a piece of equipment, it can find a new home with another local company. "Tom Otto [the neighboring turkey farmer] called me last week about a piece of equipment he needs," Don said. "It's just the right size for his poultry packaging. There's a wealth of knowledge out there that didn't used to be there. One of the most exciting things happening is the availability of equipment for small-scale meatpackers."

For a long time, too, meatpacking houses with fewer than twenty-five employees couldn't ship meat across state lines, under federal regulations. That changed with the 2008 Farm Bill, which set aside 5 percent of the USDA's loan guarantee program for local food production, under the USDA's "Know your farm, know your food" initiative.

So Don is cheerful about the future for companies like his. "I think we're good on food safety issues," he said. "Everyone that's left in the business has to know what they're doing, and why. Everyone is striving for safe food.

"I'm optimistic about the future of a small-scale plant like this," he said. "I wish, in a way, that I was younger because there's some exciting things happening right now"—especially as the push for more locally produced food gains strength.

He sees some real stumbling blocks, though. "So many younger families used to buy half a beef, for example," he said. "But now they have no clue how to cook it. People seem only to know how to cook with ground beef or steaks. Seems like that could be changing, but the grandmothers need to be teaching their daughters and granddaughters how to cook those less-familiar, less-expensive cuts. And with both parents working, it seems like everyone feels like they don't have time to cook. It's easy to fill a slow cooker full of chili or stew or a pot roast, and it doesn't take much time. If people will learn to cook—even just a little—they can save a lot of money and still eat very well."

There's yet another problem, although Don is careful not to dwell on it. When he retires, he'll sell this business that's been in the family for almost a century. "My daughter has a family to raise, and my son is in agricultural finance, so probably neither of them will want to take on the business," he said. "But I think there'll be someone out there who wants to buy a business like this."

I knew that Don was busy, and I'd taken more than an hour of his time. He was involved in setting up for the Barry County Fair, where he served on the board. The weeks preceding the fair are always crazy-busy, as my friend and postal carrier Mary Guy, who works with the poultry exhibitors, has told me in the past. I thanked him for sitting with me and made my way to the front of the store to pick up a few things for my week's groceries.

"Did you enjoy talking with Don?" asked the cashier, as I fished my wallet out of my jeans.

"I did," I said. "He's a great guy. We are lucky to have him."

"Yes," she said. "We sure are."

My guess was that she was thinking of Don the man and the businessman, the benefactor in his community. And she was right: Middleville is lucky to have someone like Don Geukes in its midst.

But I was also thinking of Don as a representative of a special kind of local enterprise that big corporations want to drive out of business, that has nearly been made extinct. Those of us who want to put our money in our neighbors' pockets, who hope to live long enough to see the resurgence of vibrant local economies? We're lucky to have Don Geukes, too.

beef braised with dried tomatoes

MAKES ABOUT 8 SERVINGS

This is a robust dish, good on a cold winter night or a chilly spring one.
I can't think of anything better than mashed potatoes to accompany this,
perhaps made with roasted garlic and a little cream. If you haven't any dried
tomatoes on hand, you certainly could substitute 2 cups of diced tomatoes,
drained.

--+--

2 tablespoons olive oil

2 pounds beef chuck or round
steak, trimmed of fat and gristle,
cubed

2 onions, halved lengthwise
and sliced lengthwise about
1/4 inch thick

3 cloves garlic, smashed and
minced

1 tablespoon all-purpose flour

2 cups beef broth

1 (12-ounce) bottle dark beer

1 cup dried tomato halves, cut
into strips

2 tablespoons brown sugar

1 teaspoon dried rosemary

1 bay leaf, broken in half

Salt and freshly ground black
pepper

Heat the oil in a large Dutch oven over medium-high heat. Add the beef
and brown on all sides, about 4 minutes. Add the onions and cook until
softened, stirring occasionally, 7 to 10 minutes. Add the garlic and cook for
1 minute more. Stir in the flour and cook, stirring often, for 2 to 3 minutes
longer, until the flour has colored slightly.

Add the broth, beer, dried tomatoes, brown sugar, rosemary, and bay
leaf. Season to taste with salt and pepper. Decrease the heat to medium-low,
cover, and simmer for 1 hour. Remove the cover and simmer for 30 minutes
longer, or until the beef is tender. Discard the bay leaf halves. Spoon the beef
and sauce over a mound of mashed potatoes and serve.

machaca

MAKES 6 TO 8 SERVINGS

Machaca is Sonoran dry shredded beef, and I learned about it first on a working trip to Arizona, where it was offered at breakfast as an alternative to bacon, ham, or sausage. When I make a batch, I usually save a bit to heat in a dry skillet for breakfast over the next couple of days. But *machaca* is equally good as a filling for quesadillas, burritos, tacos, and enchiladas, so I generally freeze most of it in 2-cup containers to use later in that way. My friends enjoy a dinner of *machaca* with warm corn and flour tortillas, chopped onion, guacamole, chopped cilantro, chopped radishes, and other garnishes, so they can make their own soft tacos or little burritos. There's never any left when I offer it in this way.

2 onions, chopped

$1/2$ cup diced mild green chiles

1 teaspoon crushed red pepper flakes

$1/2$ teaspoon Tabasco sauce

$1/2$ teaspoon freshly ground black pepper

$1/2$ teaspoon ground cumin

2 cups canned diced tomatoes in juice or puree

2 pounds beef top round, trimmed of all visible fat and cut into 4 or 5 large pieces

In a large, heavy pan over medium heat, place the onions, red pepper flakes, Tabasco, black pepper, and cumin. Cook, stirring frequently, until the onion is tender and translucent, about 10 minutes, adding just a little water if needed to keep the mixture from sticking.

Add the tomatoes with their liquid and stir well. Cook for 3 to 5 minutes, until the tomatoes have darkened and most of the liquid has evaporated. Add the beef. Reduce the heat to a simmer, cover the pot, and cook, stirring occasionally and turning the pieces of beef once or twice, until the beef is thoroughly tender, about 2 hours. Remove from the heat and let cool. When the beef has cooled, refrigerate it in the cooking liquid overnight.

The next day, remove the beef from the cooking liquid and shred it, using your fingers or two forks. Skim any fat from the cooking juices. Moisten the shredded beef with some of the cooking juices, stopping before the mixture gets too wet; you don't want there to be juices in the bottom of the bowl, but you want all the shredded beef to have been wetted. Reheat over medium heat on the stovetop, covered, or in a covered casserole dish in a 325°F oven, until hot, about 30 minutes.

baked kibbeh

MAKES ABOUT 6 SERVINGS

Kibbeh is a classic Middle Eastern ground lamb dish, in which cracked
wheat lightens the texture and extends a little meat to feed more people.
I happen to love *kibbee nyee*, the raw version, which is very much like steak
tartare. This baked kibbeh is more guest-friendly and includes pine nuts
and onion to elevate it further. Traditionally, this dish is labor-intensive,
requiring more than an hour of pounding in a mortar and pestle to achieve
its silky texture. Today, it's simpler to whirl it in a food processor until the
smooth, soft consistency is reached.

1 pound very lean lamb, preferably leg, trimmed of all fat and
gristle, cubed

1 large onion, finely chopped

1/2 teaspoon coarse salt

1/4 teaspoon freshly ground
black pepper

1 cup fine bulgur

1/3 cup pine nuts

1/2 teaspoon ground cinnamon

1/4 cup (1/2 stick) salted butter,
melted

A few tablespoons of beef or
chicken broth

Preheat the oven to 375°F.

Combine the lamb, half of the chopped onion, salt, and pepper in a food
processor. Process continuously until the mixture is very finely chopped.

Rinse the bulgur in a strainer and quickly squeeze out the water. Add to
the meat and onion mixture. Add a tablespoon of cold water and process the
mixture again, this time continuing until it is smooth and soft.

Stir in the remaining onion, pine nuts, and cinnamon. Put the mixture in
an 8-inch square baking dish and pat to form an even layer. Score the top
with diagonal lines about 2 inches apart to create diamond shapes. Pour the
melted butter over the top of the kibbee.

Bake for 30 to 45 minutes, basting once or twice with the broth. The
kibbeh is done when the top is well browned and crisp. Cut along the scored
marks to separate the diamonds and transfer them to a platter to serve.

lamb and apricot tagine

MAKES 6 TO 8 SERVINGS

My sister's stint in the Peace Corps in Morocco introduced my family to the country's fascinating cuisine, and I have studied it ever since. A tagine is both a Moroccan cooking vessel—a round rimmed earthenware tray with a conical lid—and the stew that is traditionally cooked within it. Typically, a tagine is served with couscous, the steamed semolina beads, but you may certainly eat this by the bowlful as you would a stew. It is very Moroccan to mix fruit with meat, and to use honey and warm spices to make the dish complex. Orange-flower water is available in Middle Eastern and specialty food markets. It keeps indefinitely if tightly capped.

---

2 pounds lean lamb, preferably leg, well trimmed, cubed

2 tablespoons olive oil

1/2 teaspoon ground ginger

1/2 teaspoon coarse salt

1/4 teaspoon freshly ground black pepper

1/2 teaspoon ground coriander

1 teaspoon ground cinnamon

1 onion, finely chopped

8 ounces dried apricots, soaked in water overnight, drained, and chopped

2 tablespoons honey

Steamed rice or couscous, for serving

Orange-flower water (optional)

Put the lamb in a large saucepan, cover with water, and add the oil, ginger, salt and pepper, coriander, cinnamon, and onion. Cover and bring to a boil over medium-high heat. Decrease the heat and simmer gently until the meat is tender, about 2 hours.

Add the apricots and simmer for 20 minutes. Stir in the honey, blending it well, and cook for another 15 minutes.

To serve, spoon the tagine over the cooked rice or couscous and sprinkle with a teaspoon or two of orange-flower water.

marinated grilled leg of lamb

MAKES 6 TO 8 SERVINGS

When I worked at the *Detroit News*, my Greek-American friend Toula taught me how to make a lamb marinade. Over the years, it's evolved into something that is no longer hers and is certainly not authentically Greek. But it's very good, nonetheless, and I wouldn't dream of grilling lamb without it. It's nice to make a few small dishes of cumin-salt mixture—half ground cumin, half salt—and set them here and there on the table so people can sprinkle their meat with the mixture.

1¹/₂ cups olive oil

Juice of 3 lemons

¹/₂ cup dry red wine (cheap is okay for this, but it must be dry)

1 large onion, quartered

6 large cloves garlic, smashed and minced

¹/₄ cup Dijon mustard

1 tablespoon dried oregano

1 tablespoon dried basil

1 tablespoon dried rosemary, crumbled

2 teaspoons ground cumin

2 teaspoons coarse salt, such as kosher salt

2 teaspoons freshly ground black pepper

1 (7-pound) or 2 (3- to 4-pound) boneless legs of lamb

Combine the olive oil, lemon juice, wine, onion, garlic, mustard, oregano, basil, rosemary, cumin, salt, and pepper in a blender (preferably) or food processor. Blend until it's well combined and smooth—it will be thick and look almost like mayonnaise.

Untie the lamb, if the butcher tied it, and throw away the string. Place the lamb on a rimmed baking sheet and unroll it. Pour about half of the marinade on the cut side of the lamb and massage it well into the meat with your hands. Make sure you get marinade into every nook and cranny. Turn the lamb over and rub some marinade into the fatty side, too. Then fold the lamb in thirds, put it in a zip-top bag or a shallow pan, and pour the remaining marinade over it.

Cover and refrigerate for 8 to 24 hours, no longer—the acidity in the marinade will make the meat tough if you marinate it longer. (The 24-hour marinating time is just for your convenience; after a point, the marinade no longer penetrates the meat.) If it's in a zip-top bag, turn the bag every 8 hours or so; if it's in a pan, turn the lamb, re-cover the pan, and refrigerate again.

When it's time to grill, make a hot fire. Unfold the lamb and pat away the excess marinade from the fatty side with paper towels. Brush some of the marinade on the cut side. Discard the rest of the marinade.

Put the lamb on the grill cut side up, cover the grill, and cook for 9 minutes. Turn the lamb over and cook, covered, for 9 minutes longer. Transfer to a platter and let stand for 15 minutes before carving. You will have some well-done, some medium-rare, and some very, very rare meat, the way I like it.

SUMMER

7

On springing heifers and well-made cheese

EACH MORNING, when I tip a little milk into my coffee, I say a private thank-you to Doug and Louisa Westendorp and their children in Nashville, a village on the east side of my county.

For more than fifteen years, the Westendorps have milked about eighty Holsteins on their West-Vu farm, then bottled the milk in their on-farm plant under the Moo-ville Creamery label. I'm a huge fan of their cream-line milk and will go without milk rather than buy another brand. It's definitely more expensive, but this is one place where I won't compromise. When my husband and I were considering whether to buy the cottage, one of the things that sealed the deal for me was seeing Moo-ville milk in the local grocery.

Locavores often stumble on the issue of dairy products. Dairy laws, both state and federal, are among the most complex of all regulations regarding food. Finding local milk can be difficult, since milk is not labeled by its state of origin. Don Geukes told me that he regularly sees tanker trucks of Michigan milk headed to Florida for bottling there, yet I'm fairly confident that the milk cartons in Florida don't say, "farm-fresh Michigan milk." Finding local butter, cream, sour cream, yogurt, ice cream, and other such dairy products can be even more difficult, because most dairies don't have the facilities to make them. Locally produced cheeses, too, can be problematic, especially if you don't wish, or aren't able, to spend lots of money on artisan-quality local cheeses. If you just want a little grated cheddar to sprinkle on the enchiladas before sliding them into the oven, it seems witless to spend eighteen dollars a pound.

There are plenty of politics attached to milk, as well. A national brouhaha is brewing about consumers' rights to drink raw milk—that is, unpasteurized, unhomogenized milk, just as it comes from the cow. The federal government and many state governments say we have no right to choose to drink raw milk; many enthusiastic raw-milk supporters say we do. I'm not about to plunge into that battleground on either side, but it seems to me that people should be able to eat whatever they want, as long as they take responsibility for their risk-taking. If you choose to drink raw milk, you shouldn't be permitted to sue the farmer or anyone else if you get sick. I'm also not persuaded that the state and federal government needs to be involved in prohibiting the sale of raw milk, much less using Draconian enforcement tactics like raids on stores and dairies, with guns drawn—as happened in a 2010 California raid—in states where raw milk sales are legal. Beyond that battle, however, are other questions about milk: Is organic better than conventional? What about the use of Monsanto's injected recombinant bovine growth hormone, often called rBGH? Which dairying practices are humane, and which are not?

It seems like now's a good time to clarify a couple of terms. Milk in virtually all supermarkets is pasteurized, which means that it's been heat-treated to kill unwanted organisms. Some states permit the commercial sale of raw, or unpasteurized milk. Michigan was the first state to adopt a law—in 1948—requiring pasteurization and does not allow the sale of unpasteurized milk. Some folks can get around the laws that prohibit raw milk sales by buying directly from a farmer or joining a cow-share program, where you own a percentage of a cow and are, therefore, entitled to a portion of its milk. There are a couple of cow-share programs not far from me, but I can't afford them—neither the cost of the membership, nor the cost of the gas to drive the forty miles round-trip to pick up my weekly gallon of milk. Still, I think cow shares are an ingenious solution for people who want raw milk and are willing to go through the trouble.

Of course, the idea behind pasteurizing milk is to make it safer. Indeed, the United States has not seen epidemics caused by tainted milk—cholera, tuberculosis, diphtheria, typhoid fever—since pasteurization became the norm, and we hardly even think about those diseases any more. These days we're much more worried about campylobacter, E. coli, listeria, salmonella, yersinia, and brucellae. Pasteurization is meant to protect us from these, too, although some new strains of the bacterium that causes tuberculosis have surfaced that can survive pasteurization. Additionally, milk that has been sterilized by pasteurization may become contaminated farther down the processing line—by unsanitary equipment, for example—so pasteurization is not an automatic guarantee that milk will be bacteria-free by the time you buy it.

Milk is pasteurized in one of two ways. The first is by slow heating to a temperature of 160° to 165°F and holding the milk at that temperature for 15 to 30 seconds. Milk pasteurized in this way, often called "high temperature, short time" or HTST, is usually labeled "pasteurized." When you scald milk for a recipe by heating it just until it steams, you're essentially pasteurizing it in the HTST method.

The second way to pasteurize is by faster heating to a higher temperature of 275°F, where the milk is held for a shorter time, just a second or two. Dairy products pasteurized in this way are usually labelled "UHT pasteurized," where UHT stands for "ultrahigh temperature," or, less frequently, "ultra heat treatment." Both processes have their pros and cons. HTST temperature pasteurization certainly may make the milk "safe," but it doesn't prolong its shelf life by much. UHT dairy products may stay fresh longer, but they sometimes taste "cooked," since the higher temperature caramelizes some of the milk sugars, especially if the process is done carelessly. Some critics also say that UHT pasteurization isn't about safety for the consumer—that's you and me. It is, instead, about creating a dairy product that doesn't spoil, which in turn means more money for retailers. The longer the product can stay on the shelf, the better its chances of selling. UHT milk is shelf-stable at room temperature for six to nine months and is widely sold unrefrigerated in Europe. I used to keep a quart of Parmalat brand UHT milk in the pantry for emergency use, but I haven't seen Parmalat milk in a long time. Here in the States, shoppers weren't comfortable buying unrefrigerated milk. But if you've ever had milk on an airplane, or if you've had a McDonald's McFlurry, you've had UHT milk.

I've seen many recipes calling for "non-UHT heavy cream" from high-end chefs; yet even when I lived in Chicago and could find almost any foodstuff under the sun, it was hard to find heavy cream that *wasn't* UHT pasteurized. Now we live in a day when heavy cream is perceived as dangerous—"It's 30 percent fat! And it's all saturated fat!" cry the food-nervous, which most assuredly does not include me. Because of our current fat-phobia, heavy cream doesn't sell like it used to. So UHT pasteurization lets grocers offer heavy cream without assuming too much risk if it doesn't sell quickly.

Homogenization, on the other hand, isn't about safety. Homogenization is much more about creating a product that will keep longer—the cream doesn't separate from the milk to give away its age, and dairy processors have taught consumers to perceive it as creamier, richer somehow. Since homogenization has become the norm, most shoppers wouldn't know what to do with cream-line, or cream-top, milk. They'll pay extra for reduced-fat milk, when cream-top milk naturally separates into reduced-fat milk with the cream rising to the top.

Let me tell you why the Westendorps' Moo-ville cream-top milk pleases me so much. They pledged long ago not to use rBGH on their cattle, a practice I can't sanction as a lifelong lover of both milk and animals. The West-Vu cows have access to green pastures and plenty of sunshine. While I imagine the cows' ration is supplemented with additional feed, such as silage or some other high-calorie adjunct to the pasture to ensure the nutrition they need to provide lots of milk, the cows are not confined and can walk around, lay about, and do whatever else pleases their bovine hearts. Of course, the cows also have shelter on cold or wet days, and on hot summer days, they can walk through a cooling mister that helps keep them comfortable, much as little kids like to run through the sprinkler on a hot day. The sight of those big black-and-white Holsteins dotting a green field is an iconic image, and one I never tire of seeing.

Because the Westendorps' cream-top milk is not homogenized, the cream rises to the top of the jug; it amounts to a couple of tablespoons in each gallon, and it is ever so good in my coffee. Some important vitamins—thiamine, riboflavin, and B_{12}, as well as trace amounts of niacin, pantothenic acid, B_6, C, and folate—are found in milk, and its butterfat contains vitamins A, D, E, and K. Like all milk, the Westendorps' cream-top milk is a good source of calcium, too.

I prefer cream-top milk for a variety of reasons. First, homogenization is an unneeded step; it uses high pressure to shatter the fat molecules. I've read dozens of scientific studies about how homogenized milk affects our bodies. When milk's fat molecules are shattered in homogenization, an enzyme called xanthine oxidase is released, and it can move through our intestinal wall into our bloodstream. Xanthine oxidase scars the heart and arteries, which prompts the body to release cholesterol into the blood to protect the scarred areas. When I drink unhomogenized milk, its much smaller levels of xanthine oxidase move through my body without harm. (Of course, the milk industry will loudly and quickly counter that their science shows just the opposite. I choose to believe the scientists whose work wasn't funded by an industry that would benefit from their findings.) Second, I want milk in which the cream rises. We must have been drinking unhomogenized milk when I was a kid, because my mother taught me to shake the jug vigorously before pouring a glass of milk, and a glass of milk doesn't look right to me if it doesn't have the bubbles that come from a well-shaken jug. That's all it takes to mix the cream back into the milk. Alternatively, it's easy to skim the cream from the milk and set it aside for coffee, or freeze it to use to make butter or whipped cream.

Moo-ville milk keeps in my refrigerator for an especially long time. That's because the Westendorp cows are in such good condition; West-Vu dairy has won dozens of state and national prizes for their incredibly clean milk. Its low "somatic cell count" means that the milk comes from cows with healthy udders, which in turn means that the cows have been properly cared for and tended and haven't needed antibiotics to control infection. "Mastitis" is the name for the infection of udders, and it not only makes the milk unpalatable and unappealing, it's also painful for a cow who suffers from it.

The Westendorps do not claim their milk is organic, and that's fine with me. As far as I know, there are no organic dairies in Michigan that bottle their own milk, as the Westendorps do. The organic milk I see at my grocery stores comes from California and elsewhere, and some organic milk producers use the same production methods as their conventional-dairy counterparts: cows in confinement instead of on pasture, for example. For me, local trumps organic, and I want my food dollar to stay in my neighborhood. The Westendorps' Moo-ville Creamery milk is certainly local for me.

All in all, then, I am lucky to have the Westendorps as neighbors. Their care provides me with good, clean, local milk. I buy both cream-top whole milk, with about 3.5 percent butterfat, and cream-top reduced-fat milk, with about 2 percent butterfat. The choice is usually made for me at the grocery store because I check to see which type has the furthest expiration date that day. Either way, I know that I'm getting good milk from well-treated cows.

I also buy Moo-ville butter, which comes in one-pound blocks, but I have to drive to the dairy to get it. It's easy enough to cut it into quarters for my butter dish. Since I use mostly olive oil for cooking (occasionally, I use beef tallow for frying, especially for the rare times when I truly crave homemade fried french fries instead of my more usual baked ones), I don't use much butter. I've noticed that I use well less than a half-pound a month, which amounts to less than a teaspoon and a half a day, although, of course, several days' worth of butter goes into a batch of cookies or biscuits. But when I do use butter, I want it to be butter. I can't see any reason to switch to some heavily manufactured margarine when I eat such small amounts. Moreover, I think the fats in butter made from grass-fed cows' milk are healthier than those in margarines.

Whenever I go to the Moo-ville store to buy butter, I pick up three pounds and put two in the freezer. Butter freezes perfectly, but needs careful wrapping so it doesn't pick up off flavors; I wrap each block twice in aluminum foil, then put the wrapped blocks in a zip-top freezer bag. When I put the last quarter-pound stick in my butter dish, I fetch the next pound up from the freezer and stash it in the fridge. By the time I need it, it's thawed and ready. Going over to the store gives me a chance to enjoy some unusually pretty country scenery and an excuse to treat myself to an amazingly good ice cream cone in the bargain. Near the winter holidays, from around Thanksgiving to New Year's, Moo-ville also sells eggnog, which is mind-bogglingly delicious and so rich that just a jot is plenty.

It seems like whenever I visit the Moo-ville store, it's always hopping, abuzz with people of all ages. The dairy is open to tours by appointment, and a highlight of the tour is clearly an ice cream treat at the end. It's delightful to see the visitors, especially the little kids, gawping at the big black-and-white cows as they graze. It's fun to eavesdrop on the remarks people make as they look at the cows, calves, and other farm animals. I remain unendingly amused that people still wonder how much milk a bull gives, when a bull, being male, would not—could not!—be milked in the first place. But since most people didn't grow up around dairy farmers, it's not surprising that they no longer know dairy basics, or the names used to identify cows at different stages of their lives. A very young cow is a "calf." A castrated bull, usually being raised for meat, is a "steer." A young cow is called a "heifer" before she gives birth to her first calf, probably after having been made pregnant through artificial insemination since most dairy farms don't keep dangerous bulls any more. She remains a heifer through most of her first lactation, or milk-giving cycle, after giving birth. If she's ready to breed but hasn't yet gotten pregnant, she's an "open heifer." And, if she's just a week or two away from giving birth, or calving, she's a "springing heifer." Isn't that a lovely term? It conjures pictures of dancing cows in my prone-to-silliness imagination.

A dairy farmer knows the names for all the ages of the cows in his care, because one of his challenges is to keep a constant number of cows in milk. Some cows will naturally fall out of the milking rotation as they age. Some will never produce the amount of milk the farmer needs, so they will be sold or slaughtered—McDonald's remains the largest buyer of dairy-cow beef in the world. Still others will become sick or die. Some will move off the milking rolls briefly before and after they calve. So good dairy farmers—and to me that would include the Westendorps—will always need springing heifers to help keep their milk production consistent.

The Westendorps achieve their high yields by paying attention to their cows' needs. They take steps to reduce stresses on the animals—like providing the cows with green pasture and that cooling mister I mentioned earlier. They study their cows' nutritional needs, and I'm pleased to say, the Westendorps proudly announce that they do not give their herbivore-by-nature cows any animal products in their feed rations. I was astonished to learn, while researching my first book, that lots of dairy cows—animals designed as vegetarians—are fed rations made of ground poultry feathers, steamed bonemeal, and other dubious nutrients, even poultry manure. Since then, as we've learned more about mad cow disease and how it's spread, fewer dairy cows are fed the ground and processed remains of their sisters. But I can't even imagine a cow choosing to eat chicken droppings or feathers if it had its druthers.

Other dairy farmers are less finicky than the Westendorps about their animals' diets or care. Dairying is big business, or perhaps I should say Big Business, and Big Business is always concerned solely with the bottom line. Trimming pennies on food costs for the cows can amount to thousands of dollars of savings over the course of a year, especially at dairies that milk a thousand or more cows in three-shifts-a-day milking operations.

Another way to trim costs is to get more milk from each cow. That's why some dairy farmers in the United States started injecting their cows with Monsanto's recombinant bovine growth hormone (rBGH, marketed as Posilac) when it was introduced in the early 1990s.

I'm still furious that the federal Food and Drug Administration actually required dairymen testing Posilac for Monsanto to send that milk into the public food supply—long before scientists both public and private revealed that rBGH can be linked to some serious human health issues. It appears that rBGH milk contains significantly higher levels of a powerful tumor promoter called IGF-1, which stands for "insulin-like growth factor 1" and which is exactly the same in cows and humans. Elevated blood levels of IGF-1 are among the leading risk factors for breast cancer, and play a role in colon and prostate cancer and heart disease. Children are especially vulnerable, since their developing digestive systems have more IGF-1 receptors than adults have.

One Michigan dairy official I interviewed for my first book tried to ease my fury by telling me that the test milk "hadn't gone into the fluid milk supply. You didn't drink it." Well, then, I asked, where did it go? "It went into the cheesemaking supply chain," he said. "Cheese for the government to give away." My anger was doubled, not halved: the FDA thought it was fine to use cheese made from milk from rBGH-injected cows, later proven to be linked to ailments like cancer and heart disease, to give to the poorest and most vulnerable among us, including pregnant women and children.

The man in charge of making the decision to release that milk? The man who wrote the policy that requires non-rBGH milk to carry a label saying that it is not superior to milk from cows injected with the drug? Michael Taylor, then executive assistant to the commissioner of the FDA—and formerly a lawyer for Monsanto. (Taylor eventually left the FDA, went back to work for Monsanto, and then returned to the FDA in late 2009.)

One of the early rBGH testers in Michigan was dairyman Ken Nobis, whom I interviewed for my first book. We didn't really get along, Ken and I. The day I spent on his farm near Saint Johns was a painfully long, stressful day for both of us, although we both managed to stay polite and respectful.

Ken Nobis is now the president of the Michigan Milk Producers Association, by far the state's largest dairy co-op. MMPA serves more than 2,300 dairies in Michigan, Ohio, Indiana, and Wisconsin. I think it's safe to say that my state's largest dairy co-op is comfortable with milk from rBGH-injected cows, seeing as its president was among the first dairy farmers in the country to use it.

So when I see those shiny long tanker trucks stopping at dairy farms in my county, I know that the milk from a number of farms is blended in the truck before it arrives at the co-op. Some will come from cows injected with rBGH and some will not. Once the milk is tested for purity and quality, the co-op sells the milk to processors, who bottle it in plastic gallon jugs and cardboard quarts with labels promising just-off-the-farm freshness and purity. While some of the milk cartons I see in my nearest supermarkets promise they are rBGH-free, many—and almost always, the cheapest—make no such promises. When I buy Moo-ville Creamery milk, I don't have to even give it a thought: the Westendorps refused to use rBGH from the very beginning.

But Moo-ville's good milk, ice cream, and butter satisfy only part of my dairy desires. What about sour cream? That heavy whipping cream that's so hard to find? What about yogurt and cottage cheese and cream cheese and all the other cheeses?

I think there are several reasons why locally made versions of these products are scarce. While I could buy the balance of my dairy products from Michigan processors like Country Fresh, and you could, too, by doing a wee bit of research to find dairy processors in your state, I am disinclined to buy from them because they don't tell me where the milk they use comes from. Certainly, I have never seen a carton of sour cream labeled "Made from rBGH-free milk" in the conventional dairy section of my grocery stores. Organic sour cream is, by definition, made with rBGH-free milk, but I haven't found a local manufacturer of organic sour cream.

Most dairy farmers are in the business of milking cows, not in the business of bottling milk or making other dairy products. In this, the Westendorps are in the distinct minority. The regulations that govern processing milk into other dairy products are very different from those governing milk bottling. And, a small-scale processing plant for making cheese or sour cream or yogurt has to pay the same setup costs and follow the same laws as their gigantic Big Business brethren.

So I began to make my own yogurt—and taught myself some ways to use it. If I drain it for a few hours in a sieve lined with a coffee filter placed over a bowl, I have Greek-style yogurt, thick and creamy, or a lovely substitute for whipping cream. It doesn't whip to heavy cream's silky volume, of course, but lightened with a few strokes of a balloon whisk and sweetened with a little brown sugar, it stands in perfectly as a garnish for desserts and hot cocoa. Left to drain overnight, the yogurt turns into a mild, tangy spread called yogurt cheese (some people call it "quark"), which I use instead of cream cheese, as well as in dips and spreads. Sometimes I make *fromage blanc*, the very simple cultured fresh cow's milk cheese that is the bovine equivalent of the fresh goat's milk chèvre I love so much. The first thing I do when I bring home a gallon of Moo-ville Creamery milk is to set that week's yogurt to culture. A batch of yogurt requires about six cups of milk, so each seven-jar batch costs me less than $1.50, or a little over twenty cents a jar. So, with a little ingenuity and some yogurt on hand, I've taken care of sour cream, whipping cream, and cream cheese. But what about good aged cheese?

When I was a kid at the grocery store with my mother, I remember her buying the red-waxed Pinconning-style cheese called County Line from the butcher, who used his long keen knife to cut her order from a wheel on his countertop. It was a good Midwestern cheese, and I ate Pinconning cheese, a type of Colby, long before I ate Cheddar. But a conglomerate bought out the County Line company and closed the plant, and that was the end of County Line cheese for us. Later, when my late sister and her family moved to Oregon, I learned about Tillamook Cheddar, which I still think is the best American-made Cheddar, especially the creamery's black-waxed extra-sharp. For many years, she sent me two-pound blocks of Tillamook extra-sharp white cheddar for Christmas, and I miss those gifts almost as much as I miss her.

I am a big cheese eater. I use it in cooking, of course, and I need a couple of slices before bed or I can't settle to sleep, a habit that Boon cottoned onto very early in our life together. If I happen to forget to slice some cheese at bedtime, Boon will stare pointedly at me until I remember. That's because he gets one small slice to my two, and he, too, needs it to mark the day's end. So I needed to find some source of Michigan-made cheese.

Cheese is expensive because it takes a lot of milk to make it, and time and space to age it. I certainly don't begrudge the cheesemaker his cost, but on my budget, I needed to shop carefully to find the best value. One reason I prefer extra-sharp Cheddars and Colbys is that I can use far less cheese to achieve the same flavor. Knowing that, I mentally halve the amount of cheese needed in almost every recipe I look over, and I think most recipes call for much more cheese than is needed to give a good result. I wince when I see a casserole recipe that calls for three cups of grated cheese as a garnish to serve six: that's a half-cup of grated cheese per serving! On the extremely rare occasions when I order a pizza, I ask for half the usual amount of cheese. I will go out of my way to buy imported Parmigiano-Reggiano, because nothing tastes like it, because it keeps a long time, and because I use it sparingly. But for dishes like macaroni and cheese, for a little grated topping for something to go into the oven, or those bedtime nibbles, a sharp Colby or Cheddar would do me fine.

Luckily, I found the Williams Cheese Company of Linwood, near Saginaw. Williams Cheese Company was founded in 1945 and has been making Pinconning, Colby, Cheddar, Swiss, mozzarella, Havarti, pepper jack, Muenster, Limburger, and other cheeses under its own label and its Amish Country label ever since. Even better, I found that I could order the cheese trim, the odds-and-sods that result when the company cuts its forty-pound blocks into smaller sizes, at an incredibly reasonable price from the company's website, williamscheesecompany.com. Certainly I could order a pound-and-a-half chunk of Williams' sharp Pinconning for $6.35—even with shipping, that's a very good price, compared to the nearly ten dollars that a similar-sized block of sharp Cheddar costs at the grocery stores nearby. But I can also order *two pounds* of cheese trim, vacuum-sealed, for a dime less! Like the end cuts of Don Geukes' delicious bacon, the cheese trim made it affordable to me to add the good flavor of honest food to something I planned to cook.

I found other Michigan cheesemakers as well. Grassfields Cheese of Coopersville is noted for its cow's milk Edam, Gouda Leyden, and Faitgras Cheddar, the last an usually creamy version of the classic. Zingerman's Creamery in Ann Arbor makes a fine Great Lakes Cheshire; an excellent double-cream round called Bridgewater; the classically mold-ripened, soft-center Manchester; and some other varieties. I can find good goat cheeses, too, from places like Mattawan Artisan Creamery and Dancing Goat Creamery. If I wish to stretch my definition of local to include Wisconsin, my choices really multiply. At Christmas, I hope to find the money in my budget to place an order with Sid Cook's Carr Valley Cheese Co. in La Valle, Wisconsin, perhaps for his cave-aged goat's milk Cocoa Cardona, or the intense and fruity olive oil–cured Gran Canaria. Both award-winning cheeses are uncommonly good. Finding top-quality local cheeses is far less difficult than it was a decade ago, that's for sure. A good place to start if you'd like to find cheesemakers in your state is the American Cheese Society's website, cheesesociety.org. Its member directory includes an interactive map that helps you easily locate local cheese-makers. But the cost of many of these cheeses raises them to the level of very rare, special-occasion treats for me. For day-to-day snacking and cooking, I lean hard on Williams Cheese Co.'s cheese trim.

I believe we'll see more small-scale cheese plants and other dairy proces-sors in coming years, especially as the local foods movement gains strength. Bankers, state and federal regulators, and even federal loan programs have made it possible for small-scale cheese plants to reopen and prosper. For me, that's very important. Perhaps it is for you, too.

Until they do, however, we have to be creative in getting the dairy prod-ucts we need and want. If you can find a dairy like I'm lucky enough to have in Moo-ville Creamery, then you have what you need to get started. .

how to make fromage blanc or fresh chèvre

MAKES ABOUT 2 POUNDS

It's so easy to make *fromage blanc* (fresh cow's milk cheese) and chèvre (fresh goat's milk cheese) that I'm amazed more people don't do so. Both are mild, soft cheeses that can substitute for cream cheese or ricotta, fill ravioli, combine with hot pasta, or serve as the base for spreads to eat with bread or crackers. Neither requires aging.

The only equipment you will need is muslin or an old, clean pillowcase to drain the cheese, a squeaky-clean stainless steel stockpot, a thermometer, and some kind of stainless steel stirring thing. You'll also need milk, an ingredient to culture the milk, and rennet. Commercial cultures—the kind called "direct set" are easiest for the beginner—and rennet are available from cheesemaking.com, hoeggergoatsupply.com, and caprinesupply.com. You may also find rennet at health and natural food stores. Make sure the rennet you choose is right for cheesemaking and isn't the rennet used to make the nursery dessert called junket.

I haven't bought culture in years, however. Cultures come in two types—mesophilic, which can be thought of as room-temperature-loving, and thermophilic, which can be thought of as warmth-loving. Different cheeses require different types of starters; both *fromage blanc* and chèvre need mesophilic cultures. I use cultured buttermilk as a mesophilic starter and yogurt as a thermophilic starter.

When making *fromage blanc*, cow's milk will set to a firmer curd with a little calcium chloride—a kind of mineral salt—stirred in. It's also available from cheesemaking supply sources; follow the package directions to determine how much you should add. But you don't absolutely have to use it.

I highly recommend Michigander Mary Jane Toth's book *Goats Produce Too!*, volume 2 and Ricki Carroll's *Home Cheese Making* for more in-depth learning.

Here are the basic directions for both *fromage blanc* and chèvre.

+-+

2 gallons whole cow's or goat's milk

1/2 cup cultured buttermilk

3 drops liquid rennet diluted with 1/3 cup cool water

Coarse noniodized salt, such as kosher salt

Warm the milk to 85°F in a large, clean stainless steel stockpot over low heat. Remove from the heat, then stir in the buttermilk; mix well with a stainless steel spoon. Add 2 tablespoons of the diluted rennet; discard the rest. Stir well again and cover; let stand at room temperature (72° to 80°F) for 8 to 12 hours. The cheese is ready to drain when it looks like thickened yogurt; the curds may have a thin layer of whey floating on top.

Line a large bowl or colander with muslin or an old, clean pillowcase torn into a large square (about 24 by 24 inches). Pour the curds into the center of the cloth. Gather the corners of the cloth and use one corner to wrap around the remaining three, tucking the one end securely under the wraps. Hang to drip for 6 to 8 hours—I tie the remaining three corners around a heavy 1-inch dowel and let the cheese drip in my shower.

When the dripping stops, the cheese is ready. It should be the consistency of cream cheese. If you untie it and it is still too "wet" for your preference, use a rubber spatula to mix the cheese, retie it, and let it drip a little longer.

When the cheese has reached the consistency you like, scrape it into a bowl. You will have about 2 pounds (the yield will vary slightly depending on the creature, the season, and the proportion of milk solids in the milk). Add salt at the ratio of 2 teaspoons per pound (about 2 cups) of cheese and mix well.

The cheese will keep, refrigerated, for up to 2 weeks, although it will get tangier as it stands. I usually shape the cheese into 4-ounce logs, double-wrap them in waxed paper, freeze until solid, and then transfer the logs to zip-top plastic bags for longer storage (up to 6 months). Thaw in the refrigerator overnight. If you wish to flavor the cheese with herbs, spices, or vegetables, do so at serving time; flavorings don't freeze as well as unflavored cheeses.

Here are some suggestions for flavorings. To each 1 pound of cheese, add:

* 2 tablespoons minced fresh chives and 1 clove garlic, grated

* 1 tablespoon dried dill weed

* 3 tablespoons dried minced onion; shape the cheese into logs and roll the logs in cracked pepper

* 2 teaspoons sugar and 2^1/$_2$ tablespoons grated prepared horseradish (squeeze the juice from the horseradish before adding)

how to make cottage cheese

MAKES ABOUT 1 POUND

Once you've made *fromage blanc* or chèvre, you know the basics to make cottage cheese. It's easy and much better than the commercial stuff. Note the higher amount of rennet used here; it makes a firmer curd that you can cut.

- *1 gallon whole milk*
- *1/2 cup cultured buttermilk*
- *1/4 teaspoon liquid rennet*
- *1/4 cup cool water*
- *4 teaspoons coarse salt, such as kosher or sea salt*
- *Heavy cream or whole milk, to make cream style (optional)*

Warm the milk to 86°F in a large stainless steel stockpot over low heat. Remove from the heat, then stir in the buttermilk with a stainless steel spoon. Mix the rennet with the cool water in a small bowl and stir into the warmed milk. Cover and let stand at room temperature until curds form, about 1 hour. Use a spotlessly clean long knife to cut the curds into 1/2-inch curds by drawing the knife first from the top to bottom, then from side to side, and then at diagonals.

Place the stockpot into a larger pot partially filled with warm water and place the larger pot on the stovetop. Heat the pot of curds over medium heat until they reach 110°F. Hold at this temperature for 30 minutes. Stir often to keep the curds from matting.

When the curds are firm, drain into a cloth-lined colander. Drain for 20 minutes. Lift the curds, in the cloth, and wash them by dipping into a pot of cold water until the water draining from the curds runs clear and is no longer milky. Drain again in the colander until the curds stop dripping.

Transfer the curds to a large bowl; stir in salt at a ratio of 2 teaspoons per pound. Moisten the curds with cream or milk if you like cream-style cottage cheese. The cheese will keep, tightly covered, for up to a week in the refrigerator.

how to make yogurt

Yogurt, too, is so simple to make that I can no longer justify buying it.
I use some of the previous batch as a culture, but you'll either need to
buy yogurt culture or a little container of plain unflavored yogurt to get
started. Make sure it has living cultures; Dannon is a good brand for that.
Note that goat's milk alone makes a very loose yogurt; you probably want
to add some powdered milk to increase the milk solids, which will make it
firmer. Many commercial yogurts use gelatins and other thickeners for an
artificial texture.

I love my electric yogurt maker because it has seven 7-ounce glass jars
and it takes care of the constant 100°F temperature the yogurt needs as it
cultures. If you don't have one, I offer the method below that uses pint- or
quart-size canning jars and the warmth of a turned-off oven.

Flavor each serving as desired with fresh fruit, preserves, vanilla
extract, or extra-strong brewed coffee, as you wish. Yogurt is also good
instead of milk on granola and cereals.

+-+-+-+-+-+-+ +-+

8 cups cow's or goat's milk

*1 cup powdered milk (optional;
for goat's milk only)*

*2 teaspoons plain cultured
yogurt*

Warm the milk to 115°F in a pot over low heat. Stir in the powdered milk.
Add the cultured yogurt and stir well. Pour the mixture into pint- or quart-
size canning jars and set the jars into a roasting pan filled with 2 inches of
hot water.

Place the roasting pan in the oven with the light on if you have an electric
range or in a gas oven with a pilot light. Do not disturb the yogurt while it
cultures, 6 to 8 hours. The yogurt will be thickened when ready, but will
thicken more when it chills.

If you like thick Greek-style yogurt, as I do, pour the yogurt into a
muslin-lined colander and let it drain for 30 to 60 minutes. Yogurt will keep,
covered, for up to 2 weeks in the refrigerator.

continued

Note: Yogurt, like sour cream, will "break" or curdle in cooking. To stabilize yogurt for cooking, pour 4 cups of yogurt into a heavy saucepan. Whisk in either 1 egg white or 1 tablespoon cornstarch dissolved in a little cold milk. Heat the yogurt, uncovered, over low heat, stirring constantly, for about 10 minutes or until the yogurt has thickened. Remove from the heat. Refrigerate for later use after it has cooled, or use immediately in a recipe as a substitute for sour cream or in sauces.

how to make yogurt cheese

MAKES ABOUT 1/2 POUND

Yogurt cheese, or quark, is also easy to make and versatile in the kitchen. It can stand alone as a base for spreads or dips, or it can substitute for cream cheese in fillings for cookies, pastries, and so forth.

Pour 4 cups yogurt into a muslin-lined colander. Set the colander over a bowl and refrigerate until the yogurt stops draining, about 2 hours.

For a tangier version, let the yogurt drain, covered by a dish towel, at room temperature. Refrigerate for up to 2 weeks.

8

On fireflies, sweet cherries, and the hissing kettle

A FIREFLY, THE FIRST I'D SEEN ALL SUMMER, attached itself to the screen of my bedroom window one night. It was nearing midnight, so I turned out the reading lamp and arranged myself in bed just so, to watch the little beetle's lovesick light show. Had the bright white halogen bulb in my light convinced the lightning bug that some colossal lover with peerless genes waited inside?

The bug's glowing pattern was hypnotic. Some part of my analytical brain tried for a few minutes to figure out what it was saying in Morse code: a long . . . a long . . . a short. But I don't know Morse code, really, so the beetle's secret encoded message eluded me. There was something friendly, and yet a little sad, about the slow, rhythmic blinking. As one of the first of the season, the little bug's chances for romance seemed, if you'll pardon the pun, a bit dim. I wished the beetle good luck in finding a partner as sleep overtook me.

I was tired, having put in a long evening dealing with eight quarts of sweet cherries. Pitting them took time, not that I minded that—when I have such a repetitive task to do at the kitchen table, I usually fire up the laptop and plug into an instant-watch movie on Netflix. Occasionally, I listen to an audiobook or music on my iPod instead. If I'd had someone to talk to while I worked, that would have been even more pleasant.

These were ruby sweet Cavalier cherries, shiny and plump, good for eating but not so good for pies since pies want tart cherries. I had it in mind to dehydrate four quarts and put up a couple of pints of pickled cherries to eat as a condiment alongside roast pork or chicken during the winter. I like dried cherries instead of raisins in cookies and granola, and Pippin, who adores cherries, pounces on dried cherries when he finds them in his bowl.

Commercially dried cherries are usually the tart variety, with sugar added to sweeten them. And they are expensive! I skip the sugaring by drying sweet cherries instead. I know from long experience that a quart of cherries, pitted and split in half, will take a full rack in the dehydrator; and I know that two quarts of fresh cherries, dried, will yield about a pint jar of dried cherries for the pantry. When the cherries are dried and a little leathery, I pile them into pint-sized canning jars, screw on the lids, and keep them on the shelf with no further processing.

I use the dehydrated cherries in granola, muffins, quick breads, cookies, and other dishes. Cherries are so good for you, so rich in the valuable phytonutrients called anthocyanins that fend off heart disease, inflammation, and other physical woes, that I can feel a measure of virtue when I eat a couple of oatmeal-cherry cookies. A bit of cherry juice or a few cherries each day are said to ease joint pain and arthritis, and cherries are often prescribed to relieve the agony of gout. Cherries worked for the gout that plagued my mom; they were more effective, she said, than the drug that her doctor started her on, and of course, without the drug's side effects.

My late sister, Tamsen, was the cherry-lover in our family. When she still lived at home—I would have been ten or twelve years old then, she eighteen or twenty—she would buy herself a quart of cherries, wash them in a colander under cold running water, and then eat the whole quart by herself. Once I asked her to share. "If you want cherries," she growled, "buy them yourself." As the second of five children, Tam had learned early to protect her own interests. She was always generous with me, except when it came to cherries.

Many years later, when my husband and I lived in Birmingham, Alabama, a Russian violinist for the Alabama Symphony and his beautiful wife moved into the house next door to us. We became close to Alexander and Natalia and many of their friends, an international crew that included Ukrainians, Armenians, and Israelis. The day we met Alex and Natalia, I suggested that they come for dinner some time. Would they like that? I asked. "We are Russian," Alex said, patting himself on the chest. "We love to eat and drink!"

And so they did. It seemed that almost every weekend, their yard filled with people as the grill scented the air with the aroma of roasting lamb and beef. There was always enough food to feed an army, and all of it delicious, in the Russian style of the *zakuski* table with many dishes of different kinds of food, kind of like tapas. Many of the men we met seemed to share the first name of Alexander, with its diminutive nickname of Sasha. To keep them straight, we privately began to call them, for instance, "Sasha-with-the-pipe," whose fragrant pipe tobacco pleased me, or "Sasha-the-car-guy," who owned an auto repair shop.

Sasha-with-the-pipe, a Ukrainian, was one of my favorites, and I think he knew it. Every time we met, whether it had been days or just a couple of hours since we'd seen one another, he wrapped me in a big bear hug. His English was far better than my Ukrainian, to say the least, but it wasn't strong. Still, we managed somehow to talk about one of the great loves we shared: food and cooking. One evening, he told me about a way to pickle cherries as they had done back in the Ukraine: with kirsch, the cherry-flavored liqueur, and cider vinegar. He was careful, through pantomimed gestures and little carefully drawn pictures, to make sure that I understood each step. I could have kissed him for sharing that with me.

Although we later moved away and lost touch with the Russians, their warmth and affection has stayed with me even these many years later. When I think of the years we lived in Birmingham, the Russians top the list of the best parts of our time there.

Sasha-with-the-pipe was with me again when I saw those lovely sweet cherries at the market. So I'd spent the evening pitting and splitting cherries enough to fill six trays in the dehydrator, and then I pitted the remaining two quarts to pickle using Sasha-with-the-pipe's method. By the time I finished, my fingers were stained carmine red. Pippin, who can't seem to eat his fill of sweet cherries, had cherry juice all over his cream-colored cheeks and his black beak glistened.

If the season lasted long enough, I planned to pit some cherries for the freezer. As in years past, I planned to buy a couple of five-pound bags of frozen pitted tart pie cherries, too. I'd buy them fresh and pit them myself but that I had never yet seen fresh pie cherries in any of the markets I frequented.

Although most pickles, jams, preserves, and relishes—anything that's high-acid, like pickles, or high-sugar, like preserves—can be safely canned in a boiling water bath, I find I use my pressure canner for almost everything. Rather than keeping two canners on hand, I simply keep one: my trusty pressure canner. If, on occasion, I want to process something with a boiling water bath canner, I can do that in a pressure canner. But a boiling water bath canner can never substitute for a pressure canner.

The canner I use is a simple weighted-gauge pressure canner. In my dreams—sometimes literally—I use an All American heavy-duty aluminum canner, with its dial gauge and metal-to-metal closures. By all accounts, All American canners are the queen of pressure canners, and made in Wisconsin. I can't afford one, alas—they cost hundreds of dollars. So my Mirro canner, with its must-be-replaced-occasionally gaskets and its low-tech weighted gauge, stands in, and it does just fine. I store the removable gauge inside the dry canner when I'm not using it so it doesn't get lost.

Here's why a pressure canner cans low-acid or low-sugar foods safely. A boiling water bath canner, logically, can only raise the temperature inside the jars of food to the same temperature as boiling water: 212°F (assuming you're at sea level). By adding pressure to the mix, however, the temperature inside a pressure canner rises to 240°F or more, depending on how many pounds of pressure you're using. The lethally dangerous botulism organisms that thrive in low-acid foods are killed only at 240°F and above, so it's crucial to use a pressure canner for those foods.

It seems like everyone who cans goes through a period of fear about pressure canners. What if it explodes, we all say. I don't like that hissing, we all say. I'm not confident that I can get the temperature regulated properly, we all say. I know all these arguments because I had them with myself. But today's pressure canners—like pressure cookers, which can't be used for canning because they're not heavy enough—are designed to be completely safe. They have special valves that are designed to release steam if the pressure exceeds a safe level, instantly reducing the pressure build-up inside. Reading the instructions that come with the canner is a great start, too. I store those in the dry canner, also, so they're always handy when canning season begins. Now that I'm comfortable with my pressure canner, its hissing is a soothing sound: it tells me that I'm taking care of myself by preparing good food in a safe, healthy way.

You won't need a huge canner if, like me, you're only doing a few jars of something each week. But you will need proper canning jars. Trying to reuse glass jars from mayonnaise, spaghetti sauce, or other commercial products is a mug's game. Those jars aren't designed to be reused, so it's just a waste of your time and your hard work to use them; they may break in the canner, or they may not seal properly. Yard sales are a good source of canning jars, if you frequent them; check that the jars and rims aren't chipped before you buy them. Once you have a pantry full of canned goods, you'll have plenty of jars and screw bands for next year's efforts. Buying the lids is cheap enough.

The cherry-filled dehydrator's low thrumming provided a little white noise as I settled into bed and picked up my book. Not that I need white noise: it's so completely silent here that a sudden yip from a neighbor's dog will wake me from a sound sleep. The little firefly was back, telegraphing its romantic yearnings in luminescent chartreuse pulses. "It's just you and me, buddy," I said. "I'd help you out if I could, but I guess it wasn't planned that way." The firefly blinked again, sending its hope for a companion out into the universe.

We all have that, don't we? That hope for a companion? I wondered if I would blink my hopes into the ether if I were equipped with a glowing belly. Or was I, like the firefly, just a little out of synch with that season?

HOW TO DEHYDRATE CHERRIES

Use sweet cherries or tart cherries to dehydrate. Dried sweet cherries are good for snack mixes, granola, and eating out of hand. Dried tart cherries are better in cooking and baking, where other ingredients ease their puckery power, than for snacking.

Wash the cherries in cool water and let them drain well. When you are ready to dehydrate, remove any stems and pit the cherries. Using a cherry pitter is certainly easiest, but Donna Pierce, the longtime test-kitchen director at the *Chicago Tribune*, taught me that a plastic straw makes a good cherry pitter in a pinch: just punch the straw through the cherry to push out the pit. Use a paring knife to split the pitted cherries in half.

Some experts advise sulfurizing cherries before dehydrating to better preserve their color and flavor better, but I don't do that. Because I don't sulphurize, my cherries are very dark when dried and their flavor is slightly raisiny. I don't mind.

If you're using a dehydrator, arrange the cherries in a single layer on drying racks. Dry the cherries at 160°F for 2 to 3 hours, then turn the temperature down to 130°F until the cherries are dry and pliable, with no pockets of moisture. Let them cool before packing them for storage. I pile them into pint glass canning jars and put on a two-piece lid. They need no further treatment for storage at room temperature.

If you're using an oven to dry, turn the oven to its lowest setting and prop the door open slightly by placing a wooden spoon near the top of the oven door. Arrange the pitted, halved cherries cut side up on baking sheets in a single layer. You'll have to watch them and check them more frequently than you do in a temperature-controlled dehydrator. It will take 12 to 24 hours for the cherries to dry, depending on ambient humidity, your oven's lowest setting, and how big and moist the cherries were at the start. You shouldn't need to turn or stir them as they dry.

Most of the recipes in which I use dried cherries call for about $1/2$ cup. Each pint jar should hold about 2 cups of cherries, so a pint jar will take me through four batches of cookies, granola, or dressings. I use about 4 pint jars of dried cherries a year, although I would probably use more if I had them on hand.

Some other ways to use your dried cherries:

- Sprinkle a handful into a tossed salad.
- Mix one part cherries, one part nuts, and one part M&Ms or chocolate baking chips for a tasty trail mix.
- Add dried cherries to dressings and stuffings, especially for poultry and pork.
- Toss a few into the blender the next time you make a smoothie.
- Use in any recipe in place of raisins. Oatmeal-bran muffins studded with dried cherries are very good.
- Dried cherries may also be rehydrated by steeping them in boiling water to cover for a few minutes. Once they're rehydrated, use them anywhere you would use fresh cherries, except, perhaps in cherry pie.

sasha-with-the-pipe's Ukrainian pickled cherries

MAKES ABOUT 4 PINT JARS

These pickled cherries are tart and zesty, with a complex flavor profile that's delicious but seems unfamiliar to most Americans. Try serving them with roasted meats. Mace is the outer shell of the nutmeg, and its flavor is a little reminiscent of nutmeg. Cardamom pods are becoming easier to find, but if your market doesn't sell them, buy them from an online spice retailer like The Spice House (thespicehouse.com) or Penzey's (penzeys.com). Any well-stocked liquor store will have kirsch, a cherry-flavored brandy or eau-de-vie. This method does wonders for apricots, plums, and blueberries as well.

----

6 cups sweet cherries, stemmed

3 cups cider vinegar

1¹/₂ cups sugar

1 cup water

6 tablespoons kirsch

1 (3-inch) cinnamon stick

1¹/₂ teaspoons ground mace

3 whole allspice berries

Seeds from one cardamom pod, or ¹/₂ teaspoon ground cardamom

Put the cherries in a nonreactive bowl and cover with the vinegar. Cover the bowl with a towel and allow the cherries to stand at room temperature for at least 12 hours, and up to 16 hours.

Pour off the liquid from cherries into a stainless steel saucepan; set the cherries aside. Add the sugar and water to the cherry liquid, place over medium-high heat, and bring the mixture to a boil. Reduce the heat to a simmer and cook, stirring occasionally, for 12 to 15 minutes. Stir in the kirsch. Remove from the heat and allow to cool for 15 to 20 minutes. Pour the cooled brine over the cherries. Cover the cherries with a towel and allow to sit at room temperature for 3 days.

Prepare a boiling water canner, canning lids, and 5 pint jars according to the directions on page 253.

Drain the brine from the cherries into a stainless steel saucepan and bring to a boil over medium-high heat. Boil for 5 minutes. Remove the brine from the heat.

Pack the cherries into the hot jars. Pour the hot brine over the cherries, leaving a $^1/_2$-inch headspace. Place lids on jars and tighten to finger-tight (see page 253). Process in the boiling water bath canner for 10 minutes, according to the directions on page 253.

Store in a cool, dark place. The cherries will be ready to eat in 30 days and will keep for up to a year.

peppery cherry spoon bread

MAKES 6 TO 8 SERVINGS

Half soufflé, half easy casserole, spoon bread is a longtime Southern favorite. This lively version makes no claim to authenticity, but it's very good as a side dish with grilled or roasted chicken, pork, or fish. Try using other cheeses in this as well—grated Fontina, while completely different, gives an excellent result.

2 cups whole milk

2/3 cup cornmeal

2 tablespoons salted butter

2 tablespoons dry sherry

3/4 teaspoon coarse salt, such as kosher salt

1/4 teaspoon ground red pepper (cayenne)

2 teaspoons dried oregano, crumbled

1/2 cup shredded pepper jack cheese

1/3 cup finely chopped dried cherries

4 large eggs, separated

Preheat the oven to 350°F. Grease an 8-inch square baking dish.

Combine the milk, cornmeal, butter, sherry, salt, red pepper, and oregano in a saucepan and mix well. Bring just to a boil over medium heat. Decrease the heat to medium-low and simmer for 2 minutes, or until slightly thickened, stirring frequently. Remove from the heat. Stir in the cheese and cherries. Let stand for 10 to 15 minutes, until slightly cooled.

Beat the egg yolks in a small bowl. Stir them into the cornmeal mixture.

Beat the egg whites in a bowl with an electric mixer on high speed until soft peaks form. Stir one-third of the egg whites into the cornmeal mixture until well mixed. Gently fold in the remaining egg whites with a few quick strokes; some white streaks will remain. Pour into the prepared baking dish.

Bake for 25 to 30 minutes, until the top is browned and the center is slightly loose (a knife inserted into center should come out clean). Let stand for 5 minutes before serving.

9

On wild-crafting, bartering, and the very warm hat

WALLY POPPED IN ONE DAY to he'd say he was going to cut the grass at his place and would do mine as well. Since the yard had been looking tatty, I was thoroughly delighted. I didn't even own a lawn mower and sure didn't have the money to buy one.

I offered him a cup of coffee, and for what must have been the thirtieth time, Wally said, "Rob, I don't drink coffee." Why can't I ever remember that? Still, he said he'd stick his head in when he finished with the yard work. And sure enough, about an hour later, he was back at the kitchen door.

"Come on in, and I won't give you a cup of coffee," I teased. Boon wriggled his delight when Wally came in, and Wally, who also keeps a black standard poodle, fished a dog cookie out of his pocket. Boon sat instantly and delicately took the cookie from Wally's hand.

"So what have you been up to?" Wally asked. "Are you okay? The chickens look good."

He was asking how I was doing in coping with the divorce and the job loss. "I'm fine, surprisingly," I said. "Actually, I'm feeling quite merry lately. Jim and I went to pick raspberries the other day; that was fun. We picked enough for about eight jars of preserves, I guess. And I made some strawberry preserves a while back. Would you like some?"

Wally eased his ball cap off, scratched his forehead briefly, and resettled his cap. "I'm not much of a raspberry person," he said. "But I'd take a jar of strawberries, if you can spare them."

I looked at that kind man, his legs still spattered with grass clippings from cutting my grass, and said, "Just a second." I hopped downstairs and returned with two squat half-pint jars of strawberry preserves under paraffin. "Let me know how you like them," I said. "I have more." We chatted for a while, and then he had to go. Wally's always busy, I've noticed. He makes me think of a bumble bee, with lots of stops to make every day to make sure everyone is happily pollinated with Wally dust. We pollinees are left smiling in his wake.

When Wally rapped on the door again a few days later, I was a little surprised. Surely the grass didn't need cutting again already?

"I brought your jars back," he said, handing me two washed jars in a plastic bag. "Those strawberries were incredible! I ate them out of the jar with a spoon!"

I laughed. "All gone already? I still have more. I'll get you a couple more jars."

"If you'll keep giving me strawberries, I'll give you some stuff from my garden," he said. "How would that be?"

"I'd take every lick of stuff you can spare," I said. "And if you'll do that, I'll knit you a very warm hat to keep you warm when you're ice fishing this winter."

"Deal," Wally said. When he left, he had two more jars of strawberry preserves, one in each hand, and a big, big smile on his face.

Secretly, I was glad Wally didn't want my raspberry preserves. Raspberries are, far and away, my favorite fruit. I have vivid memories of growing up in a tiny village in rural Michigan. One of the best of those—the one I cite when people ask me what I liked about growing up in that way, in that place, in that time—was that my best friend and I knew all the places where the wild raspberries grew. I can still remember the two of us standing in a ditch along Grass Lake's South Street, bikes tossed off to the side, chucking wild raspberries into our mouths as fast as our hands could pick them. I think those days may have been the only time in my life when I ate my fill of raspberries.

All winter long, I look longingly at the clear plastic clamshells of fresh raspberries flown in from Chile or some other place far, far away. I can't justify buying them, not even as a special treat. You probably already understand why: the fuel costs of getting them to me, as well as the knowledge that the raspberry growers have taken land out of cultivation for growing food for people nearby. So I indulge my raspberry passion by eating them like candy when they're in season, and by making preserves.

When my neighbor Jim suggested that we go pick berries, I was tickled. He knew about a big berry patch on state land not far away, Jim said, and he'd show me where it was. I drove, and Jim gave me directions as we went. "Turn right here," he said, as we turned from one dirt road onto another, smaller, dirt road. "And left there," he said, pointing to a road that wasn't even dirt, but rather an overgrown two-track leading off into the woods. When at last we arrived, I was completely disoriented and totally awestruck: I was looking at about an acre—perhaps more—of berry brambles so heavily laden with fruit that they sagged under the weight.

It looked like heaven to me.

They were black raspberries. The drupe fruits—so called because each little "bubble" on the berry is a drupe, holding a seed—interbreed easily, so it can be hard to tell them apart. Raspberries, dewberries, loganberries, tayberries, boysenberries, olallaberries, marionberries: they're all related, in the prolific and amiable bramble berry clan. But blackberry canes grow each berry on its own stem, while raspberries fruit in a cluster.

As we picked, I thought about the riches in these state lands and remembered spring ramp digs on Marty and Kris Spence's farm in Fairbury, Illinois, back when I worked at the *Tribune*. The dig was a festive event each spring, with some of Chicago's best-known chefs and friends joining in a potluck after a ramble through the woods in the thin spring sunlight. Ramps are a kind of wild leek, a signature signal of spring. The ramps we dug at Spence Farm were all on private property, of course, but I knew that ramps grew wild in these woods by my new home as well. And spring also sent the morel hunters into the woods, all secretively seeking the delicious mushrooms. Morel hunters are almost religious in their protection of their favorite hunting grounds, and it's easy to see why. The mushrooms are hard to find and conditions must be just so for them to spawn. Morels like elms and old orchards, but even the best habitat doesn't guarantee that a hunter will find morels tucked into the leaf litter. A good mushrooming ground is hard to find, and a dedicated hunter wants to keep it private.

I remembered, too, an interesting jaunt I took in the woods near Ann Arbor one spring with naturalist and botanist Ellen Weatherbee of the University of Michigan. She was kind enough to squire me through the slushy snow and sharp wind that day, to show me the wild edibles in the woods for a story for the *Detroit News*. Ellen wanted to show me that Michigan's pioneers would have found plenty of wild food in the woods, even early in the spring, and that the tradition of the "spring tonic" came from just such foods. Nowadays, spoiled by foods flown in from thousands of miles away, we no longer seek out the wild foods in our own backyard.

These days, I wouldn't forage for wild edibles without someone considerably more knowledgeable than me. One of the things that Ellen showed me that day was how easy it is to confuse the lethal water hemlock with tasty wild watercress. The two plants grow in the same places, often "inter-twingled," a wonderful word my friend Colin coined. And just a little water hemlock can kill you. But I knew that wild berries like these couldn't be confused with anything unsafe.

The berry canes were taller than my head. Jim and I picked nearly a gallon of berries in about half an hour—berries as big as my thumbnail, sweet, juicy, and plump, of a deep, shiny ebony. I froze a few small bags, but most of the berries went into the jam pot, and after delivering some to Jim, the remaining jars occupied their own corner of my basement pantry shelves.

So Jim and I bartered—berries for jam—and now I was bartering with Wally: preserves and a hat in exchange for his garden's riches. The hat I planned to knit would take some time, so I started on it right away.

I used a kind of unspun wool called "pencil roving" for the hat I had in mind. By itself, the pencil roving is airy and delicate, easy to pull apart, like a cotton ball is. When knitted, though, it turns into a thick, windproof, warm fabric that's much sturdier than the roving itself. I'd seen Wally out on the lake ice fishing in all kinds of weather, and I wanted to give him a hat that would keep the wind from his ears and head.

So I cast on for Wally's hat and began knitting merrily away. Because the needles were good sized, the progress was fairly speedy. I think Wally thought me daft, actually. Really, he certainly could afford to buy a hat if he needed one. But the point of handmade gifts, like handmade quilts, isn't in their cost-efficiency or ease, is it? I wanted Wally to know that I was thinking of him, and of his comfort, as I worked along.

Wally was good at his word, as it turned out. He began showing up at my door every few days with bag after bag of stuff from his garden. Big, blocky bell peppers and slim dagger-shaped fiercely hot ones. Cucumbers both fat and bumpy and sleek and seedless. Tomatoes of all shapes and sizes, from little cherry and grape pop-in-your-mouths to massive, convoluted lovely globes that beg for mayonnaise in a drippy tomato sandwich. I put up jar after jar of diced tomatoes, tomato sauce, and crushed tomatoes, and the season was just beginning.

The very warm hat I was knitting will do its job to keep Wally's wonderful, thoughtful brain warm all through the long winter. And the strawberry preserves that he loves—I'm glad I took the time to make them after all, because I'll give them all to Wally—will nourish his wonderful bumblebee self.

Lucky I am, indeed, to have found myself on his pollination route.

wild black raspberry preserves

MAKES ABOUT 6 HALF-PINT JARS

If you're lucky enough to come into some wild black raspberries, this jam makes good use of them. Note that it has no added pectin. The jam must be watched carefully and stirred frequently to prevent scorching, especially near the end of the cooking time. Use any other berry in this method if you like, or combine berries to make a batch; I particularly like blueberry, black raspberry, and raspberries combined. Just be sure you keep the proportion of berries to sugar correct, and don't try to make double batches.

----

9 cups black raspberries, crushed

6 cups sugar

Prepare a boiling water bath canner, lids, and jars according to the directions on page 253.

In a large, deep stainless steel saucepan, combine the berries and sugar. Bring to a boil over medium heat, stirring constantly to help the sugar dissolve. Boil, stirring frequently to prevent scorching, until the mixture thickens, 10 to 15 minutes. Remove from the heat and test the gel by dipping a cold metal spoon into the mixture and lifting it to see if the preserves drop from the spoon in a sheet. Or, put a teaspoon of preserves on a chilled plate and set it in the freezer for 1 minute. Remove the plate and use your finger to push the edge of the jam. The surface should wrinkle when you push it and the jam should be set. If the jam has not reached the gel stage, return the pan to the heat, and continue to boil for 5 minutes longer. Retest and continue as needed.

Ladle the hot jam into the hot jars, leaving 1/4 inch headspace. Seal. Process in the boiling water bath canner for 10 minutes, according to the directions on page 253.

Store in a cool, dry place for up to 1 year.

raspberry fool

A "fool" is traditional English dessert of pureed cooked fruit and whipped cream. Here, I use sweetened, drained yogurt, whisked slightly to lighten it, to combine with the fruit. Almost any peak-of-the-season summer fruit will work here: peaches, apricots, cherries, blueberries, raspberries, gooseberries, currants, or what-have-you. I think melons and watermelons probably are too watery for a good fool.

+-+

2 cups raspberries

3/4 cup sugar

2 cups plain yogurt

1/2 teaspoon vanilla extract

In a heavy saucepan over medium heat, sprinkle the raspberries with 1/2 cup of the sugar. Cook, stirring, until the sugar dissolves and the berries release their juices, about 10 minutes. Mash the berries into a coarse puree. Remove from the heat; cool to room temperature.

While the berries cool, spoon the yogurt into a muslin-lined colander and drain the yogurt for 30 minutes. Transfer the yogurt to a bowl and whisk in the remaining 1/4 cup of sugar and vanilla.

Using a rubber spatula, fold the cooked berries into the yogurt, mixing quickly with just a few strokes. You want streaks of white showing.

Divide the mixture among four serving glasses. I like to use tall wine glasses with big bowls because the fruit-streaked yogurt is lovely to look at. Refrigerate until serving time, up to 2 hours.

how to knit a very warm hat

MAKES 1 HAT

This hat, warm and windproof, will please any recipient (including yourself!). I am presuming a certain amount of knitting skill for this "recipe," so if you are an absolute beginner, ask someone more knowledgeable to help you. Your favorite knitting store can order the pencil roving, which is unspun yarn, or enter "pencil roving" in your favorite Internet search engine. While most places sell pencil roving in natural colors—browns, creams, whites, and grays—some offer dyed rovings in intriguing colors. You'll need about 8 ounces for each hat. If you don't know how to do a provisional cast-on, your trusty Internet search engine can lead you to any number of how-to videos on the web.

1 (8-ounce) "cheese" pencil roving

Circular knitting needles, size 8

Double-pointed knitting needles, size 8

Large-eyed blunt-tipped needle

1. Measure, if possible, your intended recipient's head. If you can't because you're planning this hat as a gift, estimate. Most adults' heads are 21 to 22 inches around. Some people like snugger hats (including me); others like hats that are looser and don't hug the head. Use your discretion.

2. Using a provisional cast-on technique with 2 strands of pencil roving (the beginning and the end will both be accessible in the "cheese") and the circular needle, cast on enough stitches to go around your wearer's head. Two strands of pencil roving on size 8 needles work at a gauge of 4 stitches to the inch, so for my 21-inch head, this would be 84 stitches. Be sure you end up with an even number of stitches, divisible by 2.

3. Join the cast-on stitches, being careful not to twist them. Knit around once and place a marker on the needles to mark the beginning of the row.

continued

4. Work 6 inches of ribbing by knitting 1 stitch and purling 1 stitch, working around. When you have finished the ribbing, change to a stockinette stitch—knitting every stitch—and continue to work until the hat measures about 11 inches from the ribbing to the top of the work.

5. First decrease round: Knit 2, knit 2 stitches together for one round. Continue to knit in stockinette for 1 inch.

6. Second decrease round: You may need to switch to double-pointed needles here or on the next decrease round. Knit 2, knit 2 together for one round. Continue to knit in stockinette for 1 inch.

7. Third and fourth decrease rounds: Knit 2 stitches together around all the stitches for the third round; then do it again for fourth round. You'll be down to a dozen or fewer stitches. If you're not, knit one more round of knit 2 together.

8. Break the yarn, leaving a tail of about 12 inches, and thread both strands of pencil roving through the eye of a blunt-tipped needle. Twist the roving several times to make it more durable so it can take a little tugging. Thread the two twisted strands through the remaining stitches on the needles and pull them together. Go around through the remaining stitches again and pull up the stitches very tightly. Poke the needle through the center hole, take a few stitches to close it up, and darn the ends in.

9. Return to the provisional cast-on, pick up the stitches, and work steps 1 through 8 going in the other direction. When you are finished, you will have a big empty closed bag with curved ends. Tuck one end up inside the other, fold the cuffs up and try the hat on. You will find that you have a hat that is two layers thick, and the folded-up cuff provides four layers over your tender ears.

10

On dog days, a new arrival, and heretical thinking

OVERALL, IT HAD BEEN A COOL, DAMP SUMMER, the kind of unlikely weather that was a constant in every conversation I encountered. Not that anyone was complaining, I don't think. Michigan can be every bit as hot and as muggy as Mississippi ever was.

But now we had several days that were sticky and suffocatingly hot, with no break even after the sun settled behind the ridge across the lake. The bullfrog who must be as big as a dinner plate thrummed his jug-a-rum call all night long from the reeds at the base of my dock. The sugary nectar in the hummingbirds' feeders had to be changed every day or it fermented; the hummingbirds themselves, mamas and babies just off the nest, chittered and jousted impatiently, a half dozen at a time, waiting for me to wash and refill the hanging jug that quenched their thirst as well as fed them. The chickens stood as still as statues in the yard's deepest shadows, their beaks open and their wings held out from their sides, as they puffed away the afternoon. The relentless heat dazed Boon and Pip, too. Boon's pink tongue hung out the side of his mouth as he panted, until, exhausted, he fell into fitful sleep; Pip asked to go outside, to his big cage on the deck, where he dozed in the airless dappled shade.

Still, my spot provided some comfort. The deep woods exhaled their cooling breath, and the vista of the lake provided some psychological ease; without the concrete and asphalt of the village, it's always ten degrees cooler here than it is in town. That's reason in itself to stay put, even if the ninety-plus degree temperatures and 75 percent humidity didn't make me languorous and lazy.

It was time to make a batch of gazpacho.

In that kind of weather, I want cool, savory things for breakfast. On other mornings, the lightly sweet granola I made pleased me, and so, too, the steaming bowl of oatmeal, or two of my hens' good eggs, scrambled. But in that heat, I wanted gazpacho, with its crisp cucumber and crunchy bell pepper, its acidic tomato, and its coriander seed that smelled of new-mown hay.

I think, biologically, there must be a reason for this preference. Perhaps, as creatures made to move about in the fresh air, we instinctively sense that something light and cool serves us better in hot weather than something heavy and staid. At least, we *used to* sense that, back in the days before we all came to think air-conditioning was necessary to live. I well remember guests visiting me in Arizona many years ago, guests from New England who refused to surrender their habit of a huge, carbohydrate-heavy midday meal. I especially remember one day when Mama Guest insisted on preparing a lunch of iceberg lettuce slathered with thick, sweet Thousand Island dressing, fried breaded pork chops, gravy, mashed potatoes, bread dressing, buttered carrots, green beans, and pineapple upside-down cake. After eating, my guests lay around the living room, groaning about the one-hundred-plus degree heat. I could not persuade them that it might be better for their health—not to mention their happiness—to eat in the style of my Latino neighbors: gallons of unsweetened sun tea in sweating glasses tinkling with ice, basins of fresh pico de gallo and guacamole, big leafy salads clad with lemon-bright dressing and dappled with queso fresco, pencil-thin taquitos filled with shreds of beef. Because my guests would not change their eating pattern to match the place where they were, they spent each afternoon in a digestive torpor. They ended their visit still grumbling about the heat, never having come to see the severe beauty of the Sonora Desert and its manifold treasures. They might just have well stayed home, I always thought.

Have you ever linked the styles of cooking to the climes from which they come? I've noticed that in tropical climates, indigenous people eat light meals made fierce with the heat of chiles. Some speculate that fiery Indian curries and ferocious Mexican salsas promote a cooling sweat, the dampness on your forehead that a light breeze can tickle into a sense of comfort even in torrid heat. It makes perfect sense to me. So, in those dog days, I ate lightly and more frequently, eased up on the stodgy stuff, and reached instead for fruits and vegetables.

But of course breakfast is only part of the day's game, isn't it? The bowl of gazpacho I ate for breakfast carried me through a good part of the day, but eventually I was hungry again. Lunch was often a bit of cheese, a deviled egg or two, and perhaps some of the Kalamata or oil-cured olives that I'm lucky enough to find every now and again; or a few bites of leftover roast chicken, beef, or pork with a chunk of rustic bread with a crackling crust and a little fruit; or cool, creamy yogurt flavored with preserves. A meal of nibbles, in other words. Supper, when that time arrived, was pasta puttanesca, the chilled refresher of Rome's lazy long sun-pierced afternoons, or some sweet-tart "million bean" salad, or even a bowl of good old Midwestern macaroni salad with tuna or cheese.

Late at night when the day is at its coolest, or very early in the morning before the day has heated up, I did the modest cooking I needed to do to carry me through the next several days. Sometimes I pushed a chicken into the oven to roast at 10:00 p.m., and retreated to the deck with a glass of wine to sit in the night's softness for the hour or so it took to finish. Or, as the chicken sang in the oven, I could cook up a quadruple batch of pasta or macaroni for salad, suffering the steam because I knew I wouldn't need to endure it the next day in the heat of the day. When the pasta was done and tended to, I'd turn my hand to a batch of Welsh griddle cakes, the light, sweet half-scone, half-biscuits studded with dried cherries or blueberries that make an afternoon pick-me-up with a bit of butter and jam.

The gazpacho I could already taste required me to make a run to the market, whether I wanted to go or not.

At S and S, the farm stand I like between Hastings and Middleville, I bumped into Tom Robertson, the owner. His deeply tanned face was ruddy, his hands still honestly begrimed with the garden's dirt. We talked about the heat for a minute, commiserating about the discomfort it wrought.

"I'd have liked to go to the farmers' market, but I needed some things that couldn't wait until Friday," I said affably, stashing some ripe tomatoes into a bag, "and I'm always glad to shop with you."

To my surprise, Tom pulled a disgusted face.

"Don't talk to me about the farmers' market," he said. "I mean, I'm glad it's working out, and I think it's a good thing. Anything that gets people to think about where their food comes from is good. But it sure isn't benefiting me, or my business."

"Is it that competitive for you, Tom?" I said. "Does the market pull that much business from you?"

"No, no, it's not that. But those people who sell at the farmers' market? They don't have to pay utilities, like I do here. They don't have to come up with payroll, or pay for paving the parking lot, or come up with property taxes and all that. They get a tax-supported free ride to sell their stuff. I sure don't." He wasn't angry, not even one little bit. He was just offended, I think, that people didn't realize his own position.

I was, to use one of my favorite words, gobsmacked. I never, ever thought of the farmers' market from Tom's perspective. Here I have been, feeling so, well, smug about doing the right thing that I had failed to think about some other neighbors I wanted to support, about their challenges and their needs. I knew instantly that I would chew on that line of thinking just as surely as I would chew on the crisp vegetables in the soup I planned to make.

As I was driving back to the cottage, the Subaru virtually on autopilot as I rolled along the twisty, hilly country road, I saw a hand-lettered sign in someone's front yard. "Free kittens," it said. "We'll give you a week's worth of food." Almost unbidden, my car veered into the driveway.

I like cats and always had at least one—until my husband arrived in my life. He was allergic to cats, he said, couldn't abide one in the house. Now that he and his allergies no longer controlled my life, I suddenly realized, I could have a cat again if I wanted one. I knocked at the door, and in a minute, a friendly looking middle-aged woman answered.

"I'm interested in the kittens," I said apologetically. "Is this a good time?"

Yes, yes, she said, by all means, come in, come in. She showed me through the small living room to the glassed-in sunporch where four garden-variety kittens scampered about, their tails lifted in curlicued mischief. Seeing us standing there, the kittens paused for a moment, and then three of them went back to tussling skirmishes and leaping straight into the air like little helicopters. One of the four, however, sat stock-still, his tail curled around his four tiny, gleaming white feet, and regarded me seriously, blinking his eyes slowly.

"That's the little male," the woman said. "The rest are all females. They've all had their shots, they're litter-trained, and they're ready to go."

"May I pick him up?"

"Yes, sure," she said.

I bent to the kitten and picked him up in both hands. He immediately went boneless and limp, and his rumbling purr was surprisingly loud. He was a handsome little cuss, brown and black and white with a few licks of marmalade mixed in, a sort of raccoon-colored guy with a white belly and a tiny dot of an orange beauty mark on his muzzle.

"I'd like this one," I said, curling him into the curve of my arm, which he promptly gnawed before he settled himself and closed his eyes. I could feel his purring resonating in my chest. The woman gave me a little feeding dish and a zip-top bag of kitten chow to see me through the next couple of days, and we shook hands on the deal. I drove the short distance home with the sleepy kitten cuddled in my lap.

Boon was raised with cats and is protective of them, just as he is of the chickens, of Pip, of all the creatures he deems to be in his care. I wasn't worried about how Boon would take to the kitten, but I knew the kitten would fear this big, black creature in his new home. Pip, however, had never seen a cat, at least to my knowledge.

"What's that?" Pippin said, in astonishment, when I put the kitten on the kitchen table so the new kid could get a look around in relative safety. The kitten blinked a couple of times, then settled in for a nap. He was so small that he would have fit on one of my salad plates with room to spare.

"That's a cat, Pip," I said. "He's going to live with us now. He hasn't told me what his name is yet, though."

"Don't like it," Pip said. He laughed, and climbed his rope so he could look at the kitten from a higher vantage. "It's okay?"

It was my turn to laugh. "Yes, it's okay. He won't hurt you. He's just a baby."

"It's all right," Pip said. Then, more softly, to himself perhaps: "It's all right. It's all right."

Boon gave the kitten a single curious sniff and strolled off to find someplace comfortable to crash. I carried Pip to the deck for some time outside and set about making the gazpacho.

I was thinking, of course, about Tom's words.

One thing about the eat-local movement I have come to dislike is a sort of militancy about how to do it "properly," as if anyone really knows a "right way" to reinvent a system as complex as the way we get the food we eat. Some people who espouse eating locally insist that it's not "correct" if the food you choose isn't organic, isn't unprocessed, isn't this, or isn't that.

It's safe to say that some people come to the eat-local idea with a political agenda, just as some people come to it from an economic perspective or a quality perspective, or some combination of those things. For me, it's partly economic—as I've said, I want to give as much of my money to my neighbors as I can, and I want to reduce the energy costs associated with feeding myself—and partly about quality. I happen to think that food grown close to where I live is usually of higher quality than food that has traveled a long way to get to me. I've observed that people who bring a political agenda to eating locally tend to yell the loudest about the "right" way to do so—just as it seems that people with a political agenda yell the loudest on many issues.

Tom had made me think, quite hard, about another aspect of eating locally, one that doesn't get discussed much: the need to support local merchants, local bakers, local businesses like small supermarkets and specialty stores, as well as the farmers who grow our food.

Here's an example: The Chelsea Milling Company, which makes Jiffy Mix brand cake, cookie, baking, and muffin mixes, is headquartered less than twenty miles from the village where I grew up. My mom always bought Jiffy Mix, even when it cost more than Bisquick or a store brand of a similar product on sale. Since she was teaching me how to shop economically and wisely, I once asked her why. She said it was because the company was founded by a woman, Mabel White Holmes, to help support her family during the Great Depression; that it was nearby; and that Chelsea Milling provided jobs for people we knew—the fathers and brothers of the kids with whom I went to school. Suddenly her decision made perfect sense to me.

I don't buy much in the way of cake mixes or baking mix now that I know how to cook myself, but when I do, I still reach for Jiffy Mix. I have no idea how much, if any, of the wheat that Chelsea Milling makes into flour for its products is grown in Michigan. But whether that wheat comes from Michigan or Canada or anywhere else, I'd still buy Jiffy Mix every time. It's a Michigan-made product, and that makes Chelsea Milling a neighbor for me.

Here's another example. The farmers' markets where I buy most of my food can't provide me with olive oil, rice, light bulbs, or dish detergent, so I have to fill in those gaps in my groceries somehow. Two of the supermarkets I shop in most frequently are Michigan-owned, by a small chain called Spartan Foods. Sometimes, if my business takes me farther afield, I might shop at Harding's Market, another locally owned small supermarket chain, or Tom's Market in Hastings, an independent market. At each of those markets, I see employees who are raising their families in my corner of the world, high school kids who are saving for college, and differently-abled people who find a sense of worth and pride in their jobs at the market. I see shelves lined with hundreds, if not thousands, of products from around the world, from high-fructose corn syrup–laden Coke to pork and beef and chicken from concentrated animal feeding operations, or CAFOs, which I oppose. You've probably seen photos of CAFO operations—pens of animals crowded so densely that they can barely move. Yet here I also find peanut butter made less than thirty miles from my home—albeit with peanuts grown elsewhere—and corn and wheat tortillas from a mom-and-pop *tortilleria* even closer, though I'm betting they don't use Michigan corn in their masa or Michigan wheat in their flour tortillas.

Because my aim is to keep as much of my money with my neighbors as possible, it pleases me to spend the grocery money I must spend—on things my favorite farmers can't grow—in locally owned markets, buying locally made products whenever possible and providing work for my neighbors. So I spend a bit of time in shopping, to compare the choices by reading the labels to see where they're made and to choose the ones made closest to home.

This makes me a heretic in some eat-local circles, especially those who say that we should never, under any circumstances, support a food system that embraces industrial agriculture. I say there are plenty of times when we should support the businesses that haven't yet transitioned to more locally sourced materials for their products. Perhaps, with our support, they will make that transition; perhaps they never will. But they are my neighbors, nonetheless, and I wish to support them. And you know what? I don't care if I'm a heretic. I don't care if people criticize my choices, because the louder they yell, the more I know their criticism is about their politics, not my decisions.

My gazpacho would feature tomatoes, cucumbers, and bell peppers from Tom's market garden not a dozen miles from my house. But the coriander seed, the lemon juice, and red wine vinegar, even the olive oil? Definitely not locally produced, but local in the sense that they had come from one of my locally owned supermarkets.

Gazpacho is not difficult to make, but it does take a lot of chopping. I like the meditative "tok" of knife blade on cutting board, though, and find it helps me think through thorny questions. I was grateful that Tom made his points and planned to tell him so the next time I saw him. It's good to let people know that they've roused you to thought, I think.

With the gazpacho stashed in the refrigerator, I settled at the table and stroked the still-sleeping kitten. He stretched and yawned, his little pink tongue curling, and blinked at me.

"What is your name, little one?" I said, teasing his flank with one index finger. "You have to tell me your name."

The kitten regarded me thoughtfully, as if deciding whether to trust me with such valuable information about his deeply personal self. Then, as fast as a striking cobra, he snagged my finger with both of his front paws, claws fully embedded in my flesh, and used his back feet to rabbit-punch and rake the tender skin on the inside of my forearm. He gnawed furiously on my knuckle with his little needle teeth.

Although his sudden attack hurt, I couldn't help but laugh. Imagine being that brave, to fiercely attack something that is perhaps two thousand times your size and weight.

"Oh, tough guy! So you're going to give me some guff, then," I said, with mock severity. Instantly, the kitten stopped kicking, let go of my hand, and began to purr, ceasing his attack. "Guffy? Is that your name?"

The kitten rolled onto his back, baring his belly for me to stroke ever so gently. "Well, then, so it is," I said.

It had been a very nice day. Guffy had come to stay; a cool, refreshing soup would be ready in time for dinner; and my neighbor Tom had sharpened my understanding of my own philosophies. The three things will remain linked in my memory, so that every time I look at that pesky cat, I will remember the day, and the way that gazpacho and Tom set me to rights.

gazpacho

What I want in gazpacho is a tonic of a soup, one in which every brimming spoonful tastes of freshness and rich vitamin glory. To my mind, the crushed coriander seeds add an unexpected touch, lending a grassy aroma to an already delicious dish. Omit them if you wish.

6 to 8 very large, red-ripe globe tomatoes, cored

2 cucumbers

2 green or red bell peppers, finely chopped

1/2 cup finely chopped fresh cilantro, leaves and stems

1/4 cup finely chopped fresh flat-leaf parsley, leaves and stems

Juice of 1 lemon, or more to taste

2 tablespoons red wine vinegar, or more to taste

2 tablespoons extra-virgin olive oil

1 tablespoon coriander seeds, lightly crushed in a mortar and pestle or in a zip-top plastic bag with a rolling pin

Chicken broth, tomato juice, or water, if needed

Salt and freshly ground black pepper

Quarter the two largest tomatoes and whirl them in a blender or food processor until they are liquidized. Transfer the mixture to a large non-reactive bowl. Chop the remaining tomatoes coarsely; I don't bother to seed them, but you may if you like. Add the tomatoes to the bowl.

Cut off the tops and tails of the cucumbers. Taste a slice; if the peel is bitter or if it's waxed, peel the cucumbers. Split the cucumbers lengthwise and use a teaspoon to scoop out the seeds. Coarsely chop the cucumbers and add them to the bowl.

Seed the bell peppers; chop them coarsely and add to the bowl. Add the cilantro, parsley, lemon juice, vinegar, oil, and coriander seeds. If the soup is too thick, thin it with some broth. Once the consistency is correct, taste again. Does it need more lemony brightness? Does it want more vinegary tang? Adjust accordingly and season to taste with salt and pepper.

Refrigerate, covered, in the coldest part of the refrigerator for at least 4 hours or up to 8 hours before serving.

Danish cucumbers

MAKES ABOUT 2 CUPS

My mom used to make quart jars of these every few days all summer long because she knew my younger brother and I both love them. They are astonishingly good, considering how simple the ingredients are. As a "fresh pickle," they need to be eaten up within a couple of days. I'll eat Danish cucumbers at any meal—breakfast, lunch or dinner. I also find a bowl of them refreshing just before bed on a sticky, hot night.

＋－＋－＋－◄－＋－＋－＋－◄－＋－＋－＋－◄－＋－＋－＋－◄－＋－＋－＋－◄－＋－＋－＋－◄－＋－＋－＋

2 cucumbers

1 sweet onion, halved length-wise and thinly sliced lengthwise

1/2 cup cider vinegar, white vinegar, or white wine vinegar

1/2 cup water

2 tablespoons sugar

Freshly ground black pepper

Coarse salt, such as kosher salt

Cut off the tops and tails of the cucumbers. Taste a slice and peel if the skins are bitter or waxed. I prefer not to peel cucumbers whenever possible, but if the watering was uneven while they grew, the peel is sometimes bitter. Slice the cucumbers as thinly as you possibly can while keeping them in whole slices. Place the sliced cucumbers in a quart jar or nonreactive bowl and add the onion.

In a large glass measuring cup, combine the vinegar, water, and sugar. Stir until the sugar dissolves. Add as many grindings of fresh pepper as seems right to you; I generally end up with somewhere between 1 to 2 teaspoons of pepper. You want quite a lot here, so the pepper flavors the brine. Pour the mixture over the cucumbers and onion. Stir to combine (or cover the jar tightly and shake), then add a little salt. Refrigerate until serving time, at least 2 hours. These will be better the second day and best on the third day, if they last that long.

Welsh cakes

MAKES 12 TO 14 (3-INCH) CAKES

These little scone-like cakes bake like pancakes on top of the stove, so if it's a hot, hot day, the kitchen won't heat up because of the oven. Once you have the idea down, you'll find it easy to see that other flavoring options—grated lemon or orange zest, candied fruit, even cinnamon—would be good additions. I like a split and buttered Welsh cake with preserves in the late afternoon with iced tea, but they're also good as a post-dinner snack with cocoa on a cold night. Store them for a couple of days in a sealed plastic bag, or freeze for up to 4 months.

——

2 cups all-purpose flour, plus more for dusting

$1/3$ cup sugar, plus more for sprinkling

$2 1/4$ teaspoons baking powder

$1/4$ teaspoon salt

$1/4$ teaspoon ground mace

$1/2$ cup (1 stick) cold salted butter

$1/3$ cup dried cherries, blueberries, or cranberries

1 large egg, lightly beaten

1 teaspoon vanilla extract

2 to 4 tablespoons whole milk

In a large bowl, whisk together the flour, sugar, baking powder, salt and mace. Cut the butter into small pieces and use your fingers or a pastry blender to combine it with the flour mixture. The mixture should look like coarse crumbs. Stir in the dried fruit.

In a glass measuring cup, combine the egg, vanilla, and 2 tablespoons milk. Stir the mixture into the flour mixture and toss with a fork to combine. Add up to 2 tablespoons additional milk to make a light dough that is no longer crumbly and holds together well.

Tip the dough out onto a floured work surface and knead a few times, perhaps three to five quick licks. Roll out or pat to a thickness of about $1/2$ inch and cut into rounds using a 3-inch cookie cutter or a clean, empty tuna can. Re-roll the scraps and cut out additional cakes; discard scraps after the second cutting.

continued

Lightly butter a griddle, heavy frying pan, or electric skillet and heat to medium-hot. Cook the Welsh cakes for 5 to 6 minutes per side, until they are golden brown but still soft in the middle. Immediately after baking, sprinkle the cakes with sugar. Serve warm or at room temperature.

> Note: If you prefer, you can bake the Welsh cakes. Preheat the oven to 350°F. Bake the cakes on a parchment paper–lined baking sheet for 7 to 9 minutes per side. They won't brown as beautifully as griddled cakes, but they will still be very good. If you happen to have a baking stone, heat the stone in a 350°F oven and bake the cakes directly on the stone for 4 to 5 minutes on each side, until lightly browned.

savory cheese-chive biscuits

MAKES 12 TO 14 (3-INCH) BISCUITS

Biscuits come together easily and bake quickly, so they are a good choice in hot weather if you will have the oven on anyway. I find biscuits best when hot from the oven, but a later-day biscuit, several hours old, has its own charms. I also like my biscuits big—"cat head" biscuits, as they lyrically call them down South, because they are as big as a cat's head. If you don't have a heavy-duty 3-inch cookie cutter, a carefully washed empty tuna can stands in well.

---

2 cups self-rising flour (see page 29), plus more for dusting

5 tablespoons cold salted butter

1/2 cup shredded sharp Cheddar cheese

2 tablespoons snipped fresh chives or minced scallion, white and tender green parts

3/4 to 1 cup whole milk or buttermilk

Whole milk or melted butter, for brushing

Preheat the oven to 400°F. Lightly grease an ovensafe griddle or pie or cake pan.

In a large bowl, stir the flour with a fork or whisk to lighten it. Cut the butter into pieces and use your fingers or a pastry blender to gently work it into the flour until the mixture looks like coarse crumbs and the largest pieces are the size of peas. Stir in the cheese and chives.

Stir in 3/4 cup of the milk and work the dough, quickly and lightly, with a fork to combine. You may need to add a little more milk to make a dough that is not crumbly and holds together well.

Tip the dough out onto a floured work surface and knead it a few times, perhaps three to five quick licks. Roll or pat to a thickness of 1/2 inch and cut into rounds using a 3-inch cookie cutter or a clean, empty tuna can. Gently re-roll the scraps and cut out additional rounds. Discard any remaining scraps; the dough will toughen if you try to salvage every last scrap.

Arrange the biscuits, sides touching, on the griddle. Bake for 10 minutes; remove the biscuits from the oven and lightly brush their tops with milk or melted butter. Return the biscuits to the oven and bake for an additional 4 to 6 minutes, or until golden brown. Serve hot.

On dog days, a new arrival, and heretical thinking

million-bean salad

I happily eat a big bowl of bean salad for breakfast, lunch, or dinner—just bean salad, nothing else—in the deep heat of summer, because I know that beans are so incredibly good for me: protein-rich, full of fiber and other nutrients. It also keeps well for days in the refrigerator. On this salad, I like the traditional Midwestern sweet-tart sugar-vinegar dressing of the classic three-bean salad, but including just three kinds of beans seems stingy to me. Use canned beans if you like—drained and rinsed first, please—but if you have cooked and frozen beans on hand, as I often do, this is a great way to use them.

---

2 cups each of at least 4 different types of beans (chickpeas, kidney beans, small red beans, navy beans, pinto beans, cannellini, lima beans, black beans, adzuki, black-eyed peas, wax beans, or green beans)

1 sweet onion, chopped

2 ribs celery, chopped

1 green bell pepper, chopped

1/4 cup chopped roasted red pepper or pimientos

1/4 cup chopped fresh flat-leaf parsley

1/2 cup neutral vegetable oil, such as canola or soybean

1/2 cup cider vinegar

2 tablespoons sugar

Salt and freshly ground black pepper

Combine the beans in a very large bowl. Add the onion, celery, bell pepper, roasted red pepper, and parsley; toss to combine.

In a jar with a tight-fitting lid, combine the oil, vinegar, and sugar. Shake vigorously, until the sugar is dissolved and the dressing is thoroughly combined. Pour the dressing over the bean mixture; toss to combine. Season to taste with salt and pepper. Cover and refrigerate for at least 2 hours or up to 8 hours before serving. The salad will keep, refrigerated, for 4 to 5 days.

11

On cicadas, sweet corn, and the pleasure of a job well done

WHEN I WENT OUT TO COLLECT EGGS one morning, to let the chooks out of the coop so they could start their day, the still, sticky, hot air filled with the rising shrill whine of cicadas. Is there any sound more truly linked to high summer? Not in my life.

It was August, my younger brother's birth month. I've always thought that, somehow, all of August's wondrous stuff got put inside Steve. The month's brilliant sun, its healing warmth, is in his smile. The peppery scent of fields of sweet corn, the sweet intoxicating odor of new-mown alfalfa, the soapy sharp aroma of Queen Anne's lace—they were in the smell of his sun-warmed hair when he was a little boy who hadn't yet decided his big sister was "just a girl" and therefore no longer worthy of his time or interest. And August's expansive gifts, its amazing open-handed generosity—those, too, are in my younger brother's spirit.

I don't associate December's characteristics with my older brother, Chris. January's bleak days and long nights are not linked to my father, and March's blustery testiness was never part of my brother Mark's make-up. My sister and my mother both had September birthdays, yet I don't join that month with them in my imagination. It's only August and Steve who are so perfectly tied in my mind.

Because my brother's early August birthday kicks off sweet corn season—at least for me—I see Steve's mirthful self in every ear of sunny yellow corn I shuck for preserving.

I look hard for older, sometimes heirloom, varieties of corn, like Country Gentleman, Golden Bantam, and the venerable Trucker's Delight. But they are the very devil to find. As Americans have cultivated palates that prefer sugar over all other flavors, farmers find their customers prefer the supersweet and sugar-enhanced varieties like Mirai, So Sweet, Milk n' Honey, and Candy Store. These hybrids, conventionally bred so their sugars are high and take longer to convert into starch, ship better, too. The old rule of thumb about cooking sweet corn when I was a child was this: get the water on to boil before you pick the corn, and then sprint to the house with it, shucking it as you run. That's because those older varieties had sugars that turned to starch quickly, and it was necessary to get them into the pot fast to preserve their sweetness. Those older varieties tasted more like corn than sugar, and that's the flavor I want in my mouth. The ears of corn I see in my grocery store, whether in their green husks or already prepped in foam trays overwrapped with plastic wrap, didn't come in from the fields that morning, or even the day before. They arrived from fields in Florida or California, and they were picked days and days ago. Because of their genetics, they'll still taste sweet—too sweet for me, I should say—and their sugars may never convert to starch. I wonder sometimes which is the chicken and which is the egg in this situation: do we want sugary corn because we've trained our palates that way, or do the sugary versions of corn and other foods train us to want more sugar?

Each summer, I can some corn as whole kernels, and freeze a little loose, too, just so I can throw a handful into soups and stews without having to open a whole jar. I'll also put up a dozen or more half-pints of creamed corn, which I rarely use as a side dish in its own right; instead, I stir a half-pint into a batch of cornbread or a loaf of beer bread, to add richness and texture. And I'll also put up many half-pint jars of my great-great-grandmother Emery's corn relish. Her recipe is the real old-fashioned stuff, with cabbage, onions, celery, and sweet peppers bathed in a mustardy, turmeric-yellow sauce to brighten its flavors.

The farmers' markets tables groan with plenty more than just corn, though. Zucchini, crookneck and yellow squash, cucumbers, green beans, tomatoes, new potatoes, cabbages, edamame, and carrots jostle for space, sparring with all the summer fruits.

So green beans, too, find their way into my pressure canner. I truly love green beans; I know that I'll eat a pint jar at least twice a month, whether as an ingredient in soups and stews, as a side dish, or as the star in one of the many low-and-slow, Middle Eastern–style braises with lamb or beef. Of course, canned beans taste nothing like fresh green beans; that's okay with me because I think of canned beans as almost an entirely different vegetable from their fresh or blanched-and-frozen counterparts. I'll also make room, somehow, in my crowded freezer for a couple of gallon zip-top bags of green beans. I prepare those the same way I freeze asparagus. Usually, just to be sure I never suffer from a lack of green beans, I also dehydrate a couple of pounds. The shriveled, wrinkly little beans take little space, but go by the handful into the stew pot or into a mix of fruit and vegetables for Pippin, who likes their crunch. Like the other dehydrated foods, they store easily at room temperature in a capped canning jar.

Carrots, too, get the triple-method preservation of pressure canning, freezing, and dehydrating. I'll use far more of the dehydrated diced carrots—in soups and stews—than the sliced canned or frozen ones, but it's nice to have another vegetable option in the depths of winter.

Some of the vegetables that arrive in August don't really take well to canning. Certainly, I've never bothered to can zucchini or crookneck squash. Both may be frozen—I freeze them on trays, then transfer to zip-top bags. My Southern friends sometimes bread the slices in cornmeal before freezing, so they'll be ready to fry when they come out of the freezer. I did that for a couple of years, but found I never really wanted fried summer squash, so I quit.

My small dish garden yields a year's worth of basil, tarragon, oregano, summer savory, rosemary, sage, parsley, and thyme to dry for the winter, a little at a time. The dish garden sits on a small table carefully positioned in the only sunny spot on the little patio outside my kitchen door. Every tray of something that goes into the dehydrator has a few herb leaves tucked here and there. Once the leaves are dried, I crumble them into zip-top freezer bags and stash them in the freezer so they're handy when I need to refill the jars in the spice rack. Dried herbs don't have to be kept in the freezer if you know you'll use them soon, but I freeze dried herbs to add a measure of longevity to their fleeting aromatic oils.

Part of managing your own pantry is knowing how much of everything you'll need to eat, and that knowledge is well worth taking the trouble to learn. I sat down one night with a notebook and spent a couple of hours calculating how much of everything I need to go through a winter successfully with most of my food coming from my own pantry. First I made lists of the dishes I know I cook frequently and like very much; many of the recipes in this book appeared on that list. Then I detailed their ingredients, from the main requirements to the herbs, and tallied up their amounts. So, for example, in looking over my recipes, I saw that I needed a pint bag, or about four ounces, of dried basil, about the same of oregano, sage, and thyme. Although I love rosemary and savory, I use less of them; half of a pint bag of each would be plenty. Those are the herbs I use most frequently. Obviously, yours may be different.

I could see that I eat a good bit of chicken, probably a little less than one chicken a week. Over the course of the year, then, I would need forty-five to fifty chickens, best bought whole and cut into serving pieces if needed, because whole chickens always cost less than their parts. Most often, I simply roast the whole bird virtually naked; I eat a little that night, then shred or slice the rest of the meat from the bones for use in other dishes and make a stock the next day from the denuded carcass simmered with parsley, celery, carrots, and onions. (The broth can be safely pressure-canned or, of course, frozen if you have room. I do both, and to save room in the freezer, ladle the cooled, strained broth into pint-sized zip-top freezer bags, lay the sealed bags on jelly roll pans, and freeze until solid. Then the flat, frozen bags can be stacked in the freezer neatly in a relatively small space.)

Naturally, I didn't then rush out and buy fifty chickens. Instead, I realized that if I had three chickens in the freezer, that would probably last me about a month. So the next time I visited Otto's Chickens, I picked up three (three- to four-pound) fryers, frozen whole, and tucked them away. When I had just one left, I picked up a couple more.

Recipes that call for boneless skinless chicken breasts hardly ever appear in my repertoire. That's partly because they're expensive—why pay the butcher for something so easy to do yourself? If you don't know how to disjoint a chicken yet, there are step-by-step videos all over YouTube and photos in dozens of cookbooks that show you how. The larger reason is that I don't think about chicken that way anymore. I think of chicken as the whole bird and aim to make best use of all of its parts. Buying boneless skinless breasts and chicken tenders not only keeps you detached from what you're eating, it keeps you in an artificial mindset of convenience, rather than training your mind to use your resources wisely.

Turkey's not high on my list of favorite foods, and other than the obligatory Thanksgiving bird, I rarely cook it. One reason is that a turkey, even a small one, is mighty large for a one-person household; another is that chicken, to my lights, is more adaptable. But when I do hunger for turkey, I buy a whole small bird and roast it. I don't buy turkey ham or turkey deli meats or ground turkey, because I don't see the need for them in my life.

I reckoned that I needed some kind of beef each month—pot roast, shoulder roast, or chuck roast—big enough to give me leftovers to freeze and squirrel away for chili, stews, even pasta sauces, or to portion into stew beef and ground beef. I wanted bone-in cuts whenever possible so I could save the bones for making stock. That meant one four- to six-pound roast. The lamb I love could replace some or all of that beef, if the price were better, although it could be boneless since I don't make stock from lamb bones.

The same calculations with pork showed me that a pound of bacon— most of it used to season beans or other dishes—and four to six pounds of pork would see me through a month. I sometimes pick up pork loins at Geukes Market, because I can slice a few chops off each loin and still have a generous-size roast to go into the oven, again leaving plenty of leftovers to cube or shred for use in other dishes after roasting. But pork shoulders are usually much less expensive, so I'm more likely to choose one of those and then roast it, very slowly, in a covered Dutch oven at a low temperature. The leftovers shred easily for carnitas, enchiladas, tacos, pulled pork sandwiches, or any of a dozen more uses. Some weeks at Geukes, I spend my whole week's grocery budget on roasts and bacon or ham, but I know that in doing so, I'll have meat for a month or more.

So I calculated that, by the month, I was eating roughly the following amounts of meat:

4 pounds chicken (the edible weight from two $3^1/2$-pound fryers)

4 to 6 pounds beef and lamb

4 to 6 pounds pork, including bacon and ham

Some months I'll eat more chicken, some more beef or lamb or pork. Those numbers are a little on the low side, compared to the average American's diet, at least according to statistics from the United States Department of Agriculture. The USDA's economic research department reported these numbers as monthly averages for 2007:

$8^1/2$ pounds chicken or chicken and turkey

Nearly $5^1/2$ pounds beef and lamb

A little over 4 pounds pork

Of course, averages are deceiving. Some people eat more, some people eat less. But I was happy to see that my meat consumption was on the low side of average. While I doubt I would ever convert fully to a vegetarian diet, I do know that high meat consumption is linked to a lot of ailments. And high meat consumption requires resources and land that could be used for other food production, especially since a lot of American beef now comes from Mexico and South America, where land that used to provide food for its own residents has been taken out of cultivation to make grazing land. The flip side is that meat provides some nutrients—like the iron in beef—that may be hard to find elsewhere. So although one of my aims in setting out to live on a grocery budget of forty dollars a week was to reduce the amount of meat I eat, I knew I wouldn't eliminate it entirely.

In studying my cooking style, I saw that I use a lot of tomatoes—better than a pint of diced tomatoes a week, plus crushed tomatoes, sauce, paste, whole tomatoes, and dried tomatoes. I was surprised by how much of each I use. Fortunately, since Wally kept me in tomatoes from his garden, I had plenty to can, freeze, and dehydrate. When he brought me tomatoes, it was always a mix of whatever was ripe in his garden at the time: cherry and grape tomatoes, plum tomatoes for sauce or paste, and intricately corrugated or perfectly round slicing tomatoes in a rainbow of colors. I cheerfully ignored whatever their intended use was, and put all of them to use in whatever style I needed to put up that week.

Tomatoes may be canned in either a boiling water bath or pressure canner.

I can diced tomatoes in pint jars, knowing that each jar holds a little more than the 14$^{1}/_{2}$-ounce cans I used to buy. Diced tomatoes are a little finicky, because they take more time in prep than the other canned tomatoes. I wash the tomatoes, cut out their cores and stems, and slice them one-half inch thick. Then I cut the slices into dice. It's definitely messy. The next step is important because I wasn't using varieties especially meant for canning, but rather ones that were more juicy than the canning varieties: I piled the diced tomatoes into a colander and let them drain for a while before spooning them, raw, into pint jars already prepared with lemon juice and salt. Sometimes, when I pulled the jars from the canner, the tomatoes were all crowded up at the top of the jar, right under the lid, while the rest of the jar was filled with their juices. It was a happy day when I realized that a good shake after the jars cooled would redistribute the tomatoes in a more attractive way.

I canned diced tomatoes first, only turning to the other products when I had the forty to fifty pints I knew would last me until the fresh tomatoes arrived early next summer. Then I started on paste, sauce, and crushed tomatoes.

Last year I learned by happy experiment that washed, cored, and quartered tomatoes of all types, tumbled into a big slow cooker, will cook down perfectly into thick, aromatic sauces and paste with virtually no attention from me. I don't bother to skin the tomatoes or remove their seeds, because I don't see the need for it. For crushed tomatoes, I cooked the tomatoes for about twelve hours, then used a potato masher to break up any big pieces that remained. Tomato sauce cooked a little longer, say eighteen hours; and paste cooked even longer, twenty-four to thirty hours. I set the slow cooker on high and tipped the lid a bit so the juices evaporated. This slow-cooker method sure beat the daylights out of having to stand by the simmering pot of tomatoes, stirring it frequently. I canned sauce and crushed tomatoes in pint jars, but I froze dollops of about two tablespoons of tomato paste on a jelly roll pan and then transferred them to freezer bags.

The tomatoes destined for the dehydrator were sliced about one-half inch thick, laid on the racks, and sprinkled lightly with kosher salt. Once they were leathery and dry, I piled them into pint jars to store them as-is on the pantry shelves. If I wanted tomatoes packed in oil, I'd pour good olive oil over the tomatoes one jar at a time as I brought the jar into the kitchen. There's a very real risk of deadly botulism with tomatoes in oil, so the jar must be stored in the refrigerator, and it's best to use all those tomatoes within a week, two at most. But usually, I just pulled a few slices from the jar, snipped them into ribbons or bits with the kitchen shears, and sprinkled them into winter salads or pastas or rice. Pippin also likes these leathery little tidbits.

Toward the end of the harvest season, when I knew I had enough diced tomatoes, sauce, paste, and dried tomatoes to see me through, I pitched any additional tomatoes, washed and cored but with skins left on, into zip-top bags and added them to the freezer. Later, when I needed a couple of tomatoes, a quick rinse under cold water made their skins easy to remove. Those frozen tomatoes will never substitute for a freshly picked one in sandwiches or salads, of course; they really are only suited for cooking. I've made my peace with having fresh tomatoes only when they're in season and enjoying the heck out of them for those few fleet weeks. The decision was made long, long ago when I suddenly realized one day that out-of-season tomatoes never really taste the way I want them to and decided to stop wasting my money on them.

By the end of the month, my pantry shelves bulged with dozens of jars of carefully prepared food, and I had to spend some time rearranging the crowded freezer. It was a good time to take inventory in the freezer as well, moving the older things closer to the front so I could use them while they were still in good condition. Seeing all that food put by gave me a real sense of satisfaction and security. It far outweighed those long evenings listening to the pressure canner's hissing.

The phone rang, and it was my brother Steve.

"Obin-ray," he said, pitching his voice low, in the pig Latin we used as kids. I don't know anyone else in the world who still speaks pig Latin. Only silly Steve called me "obin-ray," or sometimes, "Nibor," my name spelled backwards. "Ut-way are-yay ooing-day?"

I laughed. "I'm canning tomatoes, eve-Stay. What are you doing?"

As I listened to him rattling about his chores for the day and sharing news about the far-flung second cousins of people I barely remembered from our hometown, I was grinning. It was August, and August's brilliant sun was shining, both outside my window and inside my beloved brother. I felt rich and happy in the world.

HOW TO CAN CORN

Sweet corn must be canned in a pressure canner. It can also, of course, be frozen or dehydrated.

- To can whole-kernel corn: You'll need about 4 ears of corn for each pint, or 8 ears per quart. Prepare the pressure canner, jars, and lids according to the directions on pages 253 and 254. Husk the corn and remove the silks. Cut the kernels from the cobs using a serrated knife. It's easiest to set the stalk end into the center of an angel food or Bundt cake pan so the kernels will fall into the pan as you cut. Loosely pack the kernels into the prepared hot jars to within a generous 1 inch of the top of the jar. Add salt, if desired ($1/2$ teaspoon per pint, 1 teaspoon per quart), and pour boiling water into the jar to cover the corn, leaving 1 inch headspace. Remove any bubbles and seal. Process pints for 55 minutes, quarts for 85 minutes at 10 pounds pressure, according to the directions on page 254. Store the jars in a cool, dry place.

- To can cream-style corn: You'll need 4 ears of corn for each pint. Don't process in jars larger than 1 pint for food-safety reasons. Prepare the pressure canner, pint jars, and lids according to the directions on pages 253 and 254. Husk the corn and remove the silks. Blanch the corn in a large pot of boiling water for 4 minutes. Drain, discarding the cooking liquid, and allow the corn to cool. Cut the kernels from the cob with a serrated knife; scrape the cob to extract pulp and milk. Measure the kernels, pulp, and milk together; for every 2 cups of corn, add 1 cup of boiling water. Transfer the corn mixture to a large stainless steel saucepan and bring to a boil over medium-high heat. Decrease the heat and boil gently for 3 minutes. Ladle the corn into the prepared hot jars; add $1/2$ teaspoon salt to each jar, if desired. Remove the bubbles and seal. Process in a pressure canner for 85 minutes at 10 pounds pressure, according to the directions on page 254. Store the jars in a cool, dry place for up to 1 year.

grandmother Emery's corn relish

Emily Frances Emery (1842–1923) was my great-great-grandmother on my father's side. Her corn relish includes cabbage, which more contemporary versions omit. I like its old-fashioned crunch and texture.

---

20 ears corn

4 large onions, peeled

3 green bell peppers, cored and seeded

1 head green cabbage, quartered and cored

4 cups cider vinegar

2 cups sugar

$^{1}/_{2}$ cup salt

$^{1}/_{2}$ cup all-purpose flour

$1^{1}/_{2}$ teaspoons powdered mustard

$^{1}/_{2}$ teaspoon ground turmeric

1 teaspoon celery seed

1 teaspoon mustard seed

Prepare the boiling water bath canner, half-pint jars, and lids, according to the directions on page 253. Shuck the corn and remove the silks. Cut the kernels from the cobs. Set the kernels aside, discarding the cobs.

In a food processor or blender, working in batches, chop the onions, peppers, and cabbage coarsely. Combine the corn and chopped vegetables in a large nonreactive pot. Pour 3 cups of the vinegar over the vegetables.

In a small bowl, combine the flour, mustard, and turmeric with the remaining 1 cup vinegar; stir to combine until no lumps remain. Add to the vegetable mixture.

Over medium-high heat, bring the mixture to a boil. Decrease the heat to a gentle boil and cook, stirring occasionally, for 30 minutes.

Ladle the corn relish into the prepared jars. Remove any air bubbles. Process in boiling water bath for 15 minutes, according to the directions on page 253. Store in a cool, dry place for up to 1 year.

HOW TO CAN TOMATOES

Tomatoes may be canned in either a boiling water bath canner or a pressure canner, in pints or quarts.

In both procedures, add bottled lemon juice to each jar (1 tablespoon per pint or 2 tablespoons per quart) and salt, if desired ($1/2$ teaspoon per pint, 1 teaspoon per quart). It takes 21 pounds of tomatoes to produce 14 pints or 7 quarts, and a bushel of tomatoes (53 pounds) will yield 30 to 40 pints or 15 to 21 quart jars. A pint jar of tomatoes holds just a little more than a $14^1/2$-ounce commercial can of tomatoes.

- To can tomatoes in a hot-water bath canner, prepare the canner, jars, and lids, according to the directions on page 253. Add lemon juice and optional salt to each jar. Pack raw tomatoes—quartered, halved, diced, or whole—into the jars, leaving a generous $1/2$ inch of headspace. Press down on the tomatoes in the jars until the spaces between them fills with juice, leaving $1/2$ inch headspace. Remove any air bubbles. Seal. Process jars both pints and quarts for 85 minutes, according to the directions on page 253. Store in a cool, dry place for up to 1 year.

- To can tomatoes in a pressure canner, prepare the pressure canner, jars, and lids according to the directions on pages 253 and 254. Add lemon juice and optional salt to the jars. Pack raw tomatoes—quartered, halved, diced, or whole—into the jars. Remove any air bubbles; add more tomatoes, if necessary, to leave a generous 1-inch headspace. Seal. Process pints and quarts for 25 minutes at 10 pounds pressure, according to the directions on page 254. Store in a cool, dry place.

fassoulia

MAKES 4 SERVINGS

Virtually all of the Mediterranean cultures have one kind of green bean stew or another. At the store, when I spy lamb shanks, which are inexpensive but need long cooking, I immediately think of this stew, which my Armenian-American friend Bob taught me how to make. I could cheerfully eat *fassoulia* night after night. It is so good. Sometimes I toss in a potato or two, peeled and diced, for the last hour of cooking. If I don't, I like to have some good bread for dunking in the juices.

2 to 4 lamb shanks, depending on their size (about 4 pounds total)

2 quarts canned green beans, about 2 pounds fresh green beans, or about 8 cups frozen green beans

1/2 cup olive oil

1 large onion, chopped

3 cloves garlic, smashed and minced

1 teaspoon salt

1/2 teaspoon freshly ground black pepper

1 pint canned tomatoes (any type) or 1 (141/2-ounce) can tomatoes

Water, tomato juice, or chicken broth, if needed

Preheat the oven to 325°F.

Drain the beans, if you are using canned. If you are using fresh green beans, wash and prepare the beans by removing their tops and tails, and then breaking the beans into 2-inch pieces. Tumble the beans into a heavy casserole with a tight-fitting lid.

Heat the oil in a large, heavy skillet over medium-high heat. Add the onion and garlic and cook, stirring occasionally, until the onion softens, 5 to 7 minutes. Transfer the mixture, with the oil, to casserole. Tip in the tomatoes with their juice and stir to combine.

Nestle the lamb shanks on top of the bean mixture. Sprinkle the salt and pepper over the lamb. Cover and bake for 2 hours, or until the meat is falling off the bone.

Remove the lamb shanks and set aside until cool enough to handle. Remove the bones and gristle and discard; coarsely chop the meat. Return the meat to the casserole with the beans; stir to combine. Serve immediately, or cover and return to the oven to cook longer (adding a little water if the mixture looks dry), if that suits your schedule better. *Fassoulia* can cook for a long, long time (24 hours or more) and only gets better.

HOW TO CAN GREEN BEANS

Green beans must be pressure-canned. You will need $1^1/_2$ to $2^1/_2$ pounds of green beans to fill two pints or one quart jar. Wash the beans and discard any rusted or diseased beans. Remove the tops and tails and snap the beans into 2-inch pieces. Prepare the pressure canner, jars, and lids according to the directions on pages 253 and 254.

Pack the green beans tightly into the prepared jars, adding optional salt ($^1/_2$ teaspoon per pint, 1 teaspoon per quart) and leaving a generous 1-inch headspace. Pour boiling water into the jars to cover the beans, leaving 1 inch headspace. Remove any bubbles and add more water, if necessary, to achieve 1 inch headspace. Seal. Process the beans at 10 pounds pressure for 20 minutes for pints or quarts, according to the directions on page 254. Store in a cool, dry place for up to 1 year.

jambalaya

MAKES 4 SERVINGS

Cajun-Creole jambalaya is a regular on my kitchen rotation because it's a no-fuss, easy-prep dinner that pleases everyone. I usually make it with smoked sausage alone, but if you have leftover roast chicken, pork, or beef, or some shrimp on hand, add a cup of any to them to make it even better. Shrimp (peeled or unpeeled) can go into the jambalaya frozen; add it in the last 10 to 15 minutes of cooking time so it doesn't overcook and toughen.

1/4 cup olive oil

1 onion, chopped

1 green bell pepper, chopped

2 ribs celery, chopped

2 cloves garlic, smashed and minced

1 pound smoked sausage, cut into 1/2-inch thick slices

1 cup long-grain white rice

1 pint diced tomatoes with roasted green chiles, or 1 (14 1/2-ounce) can Rotel tomatoes (do not drain)

2 cups chicken broth

1 teaspoon dried oregano, crumbled

1 teaspoon dried basil, crumbled

1/2 teaspoon dried thyme, crumbled

1/2 teaspoon freshly ground black pepper

1/4 teaspoon salt

1 bay leaf, broken in half

Add the oil to a large, heavy skillet over medium heat; heat for 1 minute. Add the onion, bell pepper, celery, and garlic and cook, stirring, until the onion is softened and translucent, 5 to 10 minutes.

Add the smoked sausage and cook, stirring, until the sausage begins to brown slightly, about 5 minutes. Add the rice, stir to combine, and cook, stirring, until the rice is well coated with oil and becomes slightly translucent, about 5 minutes.

Pour in the tomatoes and stir to combine. Add the chicken broth, oregano, basil, thyme, pepper, salt, and bay leaf; stir to combine. Bring the mixture to a boil; cover and decrease the heat to the lowest setting.

Cook for 25 minutes. Uncover and stir. If the rice has not absorbed all the liquid, continue to cook for another 5 minutes, or until it has. Remove the bay leaf halves. Serve immediately.

FALL

12

On the traitorous sumac, seeking warmth, and the plentiful pantry

ONE MORNING WHEN I SLEEPILY OPENED the kitchen door to let Boon and Guffy out, I saw that the wind had pasted a cherry-red sumac leaf against the screen.

I think of sumac as fall's sentinel. Its leaves color long before the maples, oaks, hickories, and elms begin their brilliant display, and the sumac's blazing crimson initiates autumn's bittersweet sadness in me. Sure, we have plenty of warm days ahead yet. Sure, autumn has its own beauties, especially here in Michigan, where fall skies are as often azure as gray, and crisp sunny days draw me outside. Yet the traitorous sumac tells me that fall has arrived, whatever the calendar says, and winter's challenges are on the horizon.

I was especially nervous about winter that year. The pantry shelves, both upstairs and down, were neatly filled with ranks of preserved fruits and vegetables, the freezer was stocked with meat, so I knew I wouldn't go hungry. Wally continued to bring me bag after bag of his garden's riches. Every time I looked at those shelves, I felt safe and secure. Yet there was something weighing on my mind.

The forty-year-old oil furnace, original to the house, became balky just at the end of winter the previous year, and the repairman said he was not sure how long he could keep it limping on. I needed to marshal the money to fill the fuel-oil tank—nearly five hundred dollars a pop—and I was not sure how I was going to do that. If the furnace conked, it would put Pippin at risk. While Boon and Guffy and I could pile into the bed, snug under layers of comforters, I could do nothing to protect my beloved parrot without heat. Even swaddling his cage in heavy blankets might not be enough. Moreover, if bad weather knocked out the power in winter, as it had done in the past, the oil furnace would be essentially useless. With no electricity to power its motor and its fans, it becomes an inert basement behemoth. And, of course, I had no idea how I would come up with the money—three or four thousand dollars—to replace the furnace, should it fail.

I decided to confer with my friend John Parker. John works with my neighbor Jim, and John and I had arrived at our own friendship. I like to cook for John—he's what my mother used to call "a happy eater," someone who appreciates good food and isn't painfully picky. Evenings spent playing cards or just talking after dinner have been good for both of us, I think. John told me that he has renovated more than one house and has been kind enough to do some small repairs for me—he fixed a drippy pipe under the kitchen sink and hung ceiling fans in both kitchen and bedroom—so I trusted his judgment.

"Well, first, of course, you need to get that oil tank filled," he advised me. "But you might consider a small wood-burning stove, just in case."

"Could you help me put that in? I mean, do it properly, safely, and correctly?"

"Sure," John said. "That would be a fun project. Do your research and find the stove—your house is so small that you'll need to make sure you don't put in one that's too big, that will run you out of the living room—and then we'll figure out how much the project will cost."

The next few weeks were busy as I scrambled for some freelance work that would provide me with the money I needed to fill the fuel-oil tank and invested time in researching wood stove possibilities. John and I conferred frequently. Eventually, on his recommendation, I settled on one of two stoves. I invited John to go with me to Caledonia, to the store that sells the little Jøtul stove I was especially interested in. We looked at the smallest one, then the next size larger, and discussed the matter with the store's owners, Jim and Lynne. All agreed that the smallest one was the right choice for me, that the next size larger stove would be too big and would make the living room far too warm, even with its damper at the lowest setting. With an estimate in hand, I knew exactly how much I'd need to get the stove and its necessary fittings. The store's owner said he would install the stove for one thousand dollars, so I knew exactly how much money John's willing help would save me. It was time to scramble again, fitting in the last of the season's food preservation between freelance assignments that would pay for the little stove and the building of the safe hearth it would stand on.

Over dinner one night, John and I planned the project. We could do it in two steps, he said. First, we would build the elevated hearth and install the fireproof backer board it needs for safety, then face the backer board and hearth with cultured rock and cap the hearth with a thick granite slab I found as scrap from a local stonecutter. Then, the following weekend, we would install the stove itself. It's really a small project, John said.

I thought, "It may be to you, but to me, it's huge." I could never do this by myself; ask me to devise a recipe or invent a knitting project, and I'm good to go, but the technicalities involved in this project terrified me. A recipe or a knitting project don't have the power to burn the house down if they're not properly executed.

John arrived at around noon on Saturday, coffee in hand, and before long, he was cutting away the wood paneling where the stove would stand and screwing panels of the fireproof backer board to the studs. "Look," John said, pointing to one of the studs, where someone's name was scrawled in pencil, beside the year 1943. "That must be when the cottage was built." I handed John a pencil so he could add his signature and the year—2009—alongside.

By the end of the weekend, the elevated hearth was ready. John had designed it to be open on one side, to provide storage underneath for kindling and other materials for fire-starting.

Neighbor Jim told me that he had bought firewood in the past from a guy named Coondog—his name is really Kenny, but everyone calls him Coondog because he used to train raccoon- and bear-hunting dogs in the Upper Peninsula. Armed with Coondog's telephone number, I arranged for a cord of firewood. A few days later, Coondog's battered pickup pulled down the drive. He had cut the oak and cherry to the short length I needed for my itty-bitty wood stove, split it, and was soon stacking it. I knew that one cord of wood would not see me through the heating season. Coondog just laughed when I told him I would have to wait to order more until I could pay for it. "You call me when you need it," he said. "We'll worry about payment later. I know you'll pay me when you can."

John and I began the following weekend with a visit to the store to pick up the stove and its many, mysterious fittings—double-walled stovepipes, chimney cap, a collar for the ceiling inside, flashing to fit around the stovepipe on the roof. John and Jim put their heads together and conferred about the installation, which involved arcane language and ideas I didn't fully understand. Later, on the drive home, I mentioned this to John. He laughed and said, "It's like baking cookies. You just need to have a good recipe, one that you understand. You know how to read a recipe; I know how to install a woodstove. We all have different skills."

By Sunday late afternoon, miraculously, the woodstove was installed. John lit the small fire that the stove's maker recommended for its first burn, and we stood back and marveled at its simple, elegant beauty, watching the flames dance behind the glass door. Everything about the project, from the stove's matte-black cast-iron body to the rock-faced hearth with its inch-thick granite slab, delighted me. "Each day for the next few days, you'll want to build a slightly larger fire," John told me, "so the stove can break in properly. You'll be ready for as big a fire as you need long before the bad weather comes."

A few days later, Wally was at the door with several bags of late tomatoes, peppers, onions, zucchini, carrots, cabbages, and potatoes. "This is about the last of the garden," he told me. "I see all the firewood outside. You put in a woodstove?"

I was proud as I showed him the stove, and I thought he was impressed with its compact simplicity. What he couldn't know, of course, was how thoroughly the woodstove had eased my fears about the coming winter.

"What will you do with all this stuff?" he asked as we returned to the kitchen, pointing to the bags of vegetables he'd brought me.

"Well, sauerkraut with the cabbage, of course. Salsas, probably, with the rest of the stuff. I'll can or freeze some of the carrots, dehydrate most of them. The potatoes will store in the basement. It's cool and dark there, just right for them."

"Yuck! Sauerkraut!" Wally said, and we both grinned, although for different reasons. I love sauerkraut, even the most awful commercial kind, but homemade sauerkraut, properly fermented, is mild and toothsome, with a welcome crisp crunch that winter menus often lack. My mom used to bake country-style spareribs on a bed of sauerkraut, and it was one of my favorite meals as a child. At least now I knew that Wally won't want any of my sauerkraut.

"What kind of salsa?" Wally said. "I've been making some, too."

"I think I'm going to do a batch of fire-roasted stuff this time," I said. "Char the tomatoes, onions, and peppers on the grill. It will make the flavors very 'deep,' very complex."

Wally looked at me expectantly.

"Yes, dear," I said, laughing. "I will definitely make enough to share with you."

As I walked up the hill with Wally, the breeze scattered the fast-falling leaves and plastered another crimson sumac leaf on the thigh of my jeans. With winter's arrival no longer worrisome, with my woodstove installed and my larder filled, the sumac leaf no longer looked traitorous to me. Instead I could appreciate its brilliant color and deep hue. It was a thing of the simplest, deepest beauty.

Later, tucking the leaf into a corner of the mirror on the dresser in my bedroom, I realized the lovely sumac leaf would remind me that preparing for the worst, in its own right, delivers a sense of freedom and safety. Foresight and planning to be able to meet one's needs—whether by a pantry rich in wholesome food or by a woodstove bright with dancing flame—creates confidence in the future. It was a mighty lesson, to be contained in such a small package.

zucchini bread

MAKES 2 LOAVES

Zucchini bread is the classic way to use up one of the garden's most prolific vegetables. When I come into a surplus, I bake a couple of batches of this bread, wrap the cooled loaves well, and stash them in the freezer, where they will keep for months and months. If I still have extra zucchini to deal with, I often grate it all in my food processor and freeze it in the 2-cup amounts that this recipe requires. Those oversized zucchinis that escaped the gardener's notice are fine for grating. Thaw the frozen zucchini before using.

3 cups self-rising flour

1 tablespoon ground cinnamon

1 teaspoon grated nutmeg

$^1/_2$ teaspoon ground cloves

$^1/_2$ teaspoon salt

3 large eggs

$^1/_2$ cup vegetable oil

$^1/_2$ cup whole milk

$2^1/_4$ cups sugar

1 tablespoon vanilla extract

2 cups grated zucchini

1 cup chopped walnuts, pecans, or other nuts

Preheat the oven to 325°F. Thoroughly grease and flour two 9 by 5-inch loaf pans.

Sift the flour, cinnamon, nutmeg, cloves, and salt into a bowl. Set aside.

Beat the eggs, oil, milk, sugar, and vanilla in a large bowl until thoroughly combined. Add the sifted ingredients to the egg mixture and stir to combine thoroughly. Stir in the zucchini and nuts until well combined. Divide the batter among the prepared pans.

Bake for 45 to 60 minutes, until a tester inserted in the center comes out clean. Cool in pans on a wire rack for 20 minutes. Remove the breads from the pans and cool completely before slicing.

zucchini "planks"

MAKES ABOUT 1¹/₂ POUNDS

For this recipe, choose zucchini that are about 8 inches long. Use the zucchini planks to wrap around bits of cheese or ham as an hors d'oeuvre, or chop them to toss in pasta and salads. These are not long keepers, so you should plan to use them within 10 days.

---

3 pounds zucchini, each about 8 inches long, about 8 in total

Extra-virgin olive oil, for brushing and to cover

4 cloves garlic, smashed and minced

3 tablespoons mixed minced fresh herbs (parsley, basil, oregano, thyme, rosemary, savory, or any combination)

About 1 teaspoon coarse salt, such as kosher salt

¹/₂ teaspoon freshly ground black pepper

Remove the tops and tails from the zucchini, then cut the zucchini lengthwise into slices about ¹/₄ inch thick. Prepare a medium-hot fire in a grill.

Brush the zucchini slices on one side with olive oil and place the slices, oiled side down, on the grill. Grill for 1 to 2 minutes, until they have nice grill marks on the bottoms. Brush the tops with oil, turn the slices, and grill the second sides, 1 to 2 minutes longer. Remove the zucchini from the grill and allow to cool.

Make a layer of slices in a deep casserole dish with a close-fitting lid. Scatter about one-quarter of the minced garlic and herbs over the slices in the dish and sprinkle with some of the salt and pepper. Continue to layer the zucchini slices, topping each layer with the minced herbs, salt, and pepper, and ending with herbs. When all the zucchini has been layered into the dish, pour over enough olive oil to cover the zucchini. Cover tightly; refrigerate for at least 1 day and up to 10 days.

SEVERAL CARROT SALADS

EACH MAKES ABOUT 4 SERVINGS

If you tire of carrots steamed, boiled, or roasted, try one of these bright, crisp salads. You'll think about carrots in an entirely different way. Mediterranean cooks seem to intuitively think of carrots as a salad vegetable, so several of these ideas show their influence. Look for rose water and orange-flower water at Middle Eastern markets or in specialty food stores. Tightly capped, they keep indefinitely.

- To 2 cups of grated carrots, add 3 tablespoons extra-virgin olive oil, 3 smashed and minced cloves of garlic, 1 teaspoon ground cumin, the juice of half a lemon, and salt and pepper to taste. Toss with a fork to blend; then cover and let stand at room temperature for at least 1 hour and up to 8 hours before serving.

- To 2 cups of grated carrots, add 2 smashed and minced cloves of garlic, 1 tablespoon minced fresh mint, 2 tablespoons extra-virgin olive oil, and salt to taste. Toss with a fork to blend; then cover and let stand at room temperature for at least 1 hour and up to 8 hours before serving.

- To 2 cups of grated carrots, add 2 tablespoons honey and 1 tablespoon rose water. Toss with a fork to blend; then cover and let stand at room temperature for at least 1 hour and up to 8 hours before serving.

- To 2 cups of grated carrots, add 2 tablespoons fresh orange juice, 1 tablespoon orange-flower water, $1/2$ teaspoon ground cinnamon, and a bit of salt. Toss with a fork to blend; then cover and let stand at room temperature for at least 1 hour and up to 8 hours before serving.

- This was a Michigan standby at church suppers and athletic banquets when I was growing up. It's way better than it sounds. To 2 cups grated carrots, add 12 saltine crackers, crushed; $1/2$ onion, grated, and its juices; and salt and pepper to taste. Moisten with just enough mayonnaise to bind. Refrigerate, covered, for at least 1 hour and up to 8 hours before serving.

- Even my small farmers' markets now have vendors selling Asian vegetables, such as daikon, the Japanese white radish. But if you can't find daikon, you can make this with turnips, regular radishes, or even jicama. To 2 cups grated carrots, add 1 cup grated daikon, turnip, radishes, or jicama. Prepare a dressing by combining 1/2 cup white vinegar, 1/2 cup water, 3 tablespoons sugar, 1 teaspoon grated fresh ginger, and 1 star anise in a small nonreactive saucepan. Bring to a boil, stirring to dissolve the sugar, and let cool. Fish out the star anise and discard. Pour the dressing over the vegetables. Refrigerate, covered, for at least 1 hour and up to 8 hours before serving.

CANNING, DEHYDRATING, AND FREEZING CARROTS

- Carrots must be pressure canned. I usually put them up by the raw-pack method. Prepare the pressure canner, jars, and lids according to the directions on pages 253 and 254. Wash the carrots, then drain and peel them. Slice or dice large carrots, or leave small carrots whole. Pack raw carrots into hot jars, leaving a generous 1-inch headspace; add salt ($^1/_2$ teaspoon per pint, or 1 teaspoon per quart); pour boiling water over carrots and remove any air bubbles. Seal. Process at 10 pounds pressure for 25 minutes for pints or 30 minutes for quart jars, according to the directions on page 254. Store in a cool, dry place for up to 1 year.

- Dehydrated carrots are perfect for soups and stews, where the braising liquid will rehydrate them in cooking. They'll lose a little of their vitamin A, but their bright color will be welcome in winter meals. I neither treat with sulfite nor wash them in a cornstarch-water mixture, as many guides recommend. Wash the carrots, then drain and peel them. Slice crosswise or diagonally into slices no thicker than $^3/_8$ inch, or cut into $^3/_8$-inch dice. Steam-blanch by placing the carrots in a steamer basket set over boiling water for 3 to 4 minutes, or until their color has brightened noticeably. Drain.

  To dry in a dehydrator, place the carrots in a single layer on dryer trays and dry at 140°F for 2 to 3 hours. Decrease the temperature to 130°F and continue to dry until the carrots are very tough and brittle, 12 to 24 hours.

  To dry in an oven, set the oven to the lowest temperature setting. Arrange the carrots in a single layer on rimmed baking sheets or jelly roll pans. Place the baking sheets in the oven, prop the door open with a wooden spoon, and dry the carrots until tough and brittle, 12 to 24 hours.

Either way, let the carrots cool completely before packing in jars with tight-fitting lids for storage at room temperature. They will keep indefinitely.

- Freezing carrots is simple, but like all vegetables, they benefit from blanching—cooking for a few minutes in boiling water—just until their color brightens because doing so destroys enzymes that will degrade their quality over time. Wash the carrots, then drain and peel them. Slice or dice the carrots; blanch in boiling water for 2 minutes, or until their color has brightened noticeably. Plunge the carrots into an ice-water bath to cool. Drain the carrots thoroughly; pack into zip-top bags or freezer containers in meal-sized portions. They will keep for up to 6 months.

how to make sauerkraut

Making sauerkraut is not difficult, but it will require a few minutes' work every day or two for a couple of weeks. The lactic fermentation of sauerkraut is a little odiferous—I happen to like the smell—so you may prefer to let the kraut ferment in the garage or basement. I use a German-made Harsch Gairtopf sauerkraut crock, designed so its lid rests in a gutter filled with water (which allows gases to escape but does not permit contaminants to enter), but you can make sauerkraut in a stoneware crock or a food-grade plastic bucket, if that's what you have on hand. These directions are written for fermenting in an open vessel. Follow the directions with your crock if you buy something new.

25 pounds green cabbage, about 5 large heads, outer leaves discarded, each cabbage quartered and cored

1 cup pickling or canning salt, plus more if needed

In a food processor with a slicing attachment, or using a cabbage-cutting board, mandoline, or sharp knife, cut the cabbage into shreds of about $1/_{16}$-inch thickness. Remove any large pieces; shred them by hand if you wish (or eat them yourself, or give them to your parrot).

In a large stone crock or food-grade plastic bucket, combine a layer of shredded cabbage about 2 inches thick with 3 tablespoons of the salt. Let stand for 15 minutes or until the cabbage wilts slightly. Use your hands to press down on the cabbage, until the cabbage is slightly bruised and the juices rise to the surface. Repeat until all the cabbage and salt is used, leaving at least 4 inches space between the cabbage and the rim of the container. Sprinkle any remaining salt over the last layer of cabbage. If the cabbage has not released enough juice to cover the cabbage, make a brine of $4^1/_2$ teaspoons salt to each 2 quarts of water. Bring it to a boil and stir to dissolve salt. Let this brine cool to room temperature, then pour it over the cabbage to cover.

Place a large inverted plate that fits inside the crock or bucket directly onto the cabbage and weigh it down with 2 or 3 quart-size jars filled with water and capped. The cabbage should be 1 to 2 inches below the surface of the brine. Cover the container with a clean, heavy towel. Let it stand in a cool room (70° to 75°F). Check it every day and skim off any scum that has formed.

During fermentation, gas bubbles will form. When the bubbling ceases, fermentation is complete. The temperature of the fermentation space will determine how long it will take—cooler temperatures mean longer fermentation. The sauerkraut could be ready in as little as 2 weeks or as long as 4.

When you are certain fermentation has finished, you are ready to can the sauerkraut. You can do this by the raw-pack or the hot-pack method. I find raw-pack easier because it doesn't involve working with hot kraut.

- For raw pack: Prepare a boiling water bath canner, jars, and lids, according to the directions on page 253. Pack the raw sauerkraut, with brine, into the hot jars, leaving 1/2 inch of headspace. Remove any air bubbles and adjust headspace, if necessary, by adding more brine. Seal. Process pints for 20 minutes, quarts for 25 minutes, according to the directions on page 253. Store in a cool, dry place for up to 1 year.

- For hot pack: Prepare a boiling water bath canner, jars, and lids, according to the directions on page 253. In a large stainless steel saucepan or pot, bring the sauerkraut and brine to a simmer over medium-high heat. Do not boil. Pack the hot sauerkraut and brine into jars, leaving 1/2 inch of headspace. Remove any air bubbles and add more brine, if necessary, to adjust headspace. Seal. Process pints for 10 minutes, quarts for 15 minutes, according to the directions on page 253. Store in a cool, dry place for up to 1 year.

13

On cider, cornmeal, and comfort

ALTHOUGH YOU'D MORE FREQUENTLY find me studying the constellations at 2:00 a.m. than greeting the rising sun at dawn, in early fall I become a natural morning person. Something in the crisp daybreak wakes me effortlessly. When night's cool air collided with the lake's warm waters, the resultant morning mists, quavering visibly, were often dense enough that I couldn't see my own dock. It was ineffably beautiful, and I typically took my coffee standing on the deck, to better appreciate the view, relaxing into the scene's glory.

Hunters' pickup trucks stood in all the pullouts that dot the dirt roads winding through the Barry State Game Area. Some were bowmen, taking advantage of the early deer season, but most were gunners, scouting the best spot for their tree stands and blinds. Many, if not most, of the hunters are responsible sportsmen who want only to bag a little meat for the family's freezer, and I'm lucky to know several. While I have no quarrel with hunters or their sport, it's hard to miss the empty whiskey bottles and boxes of beer cans scattered about many of the campsites where they've pitched their tents or parked their campers. It takes just one jittery, still-drunk or hungover hunter with a gun and buck fever to wreak havoc: in 2008, a man standing in his own yard not two miles from my house was killed by a stray bullet fired from a drunken hunter's gun a quarter-mile away. So I stuck to the road on my walks, even with the fluorescent yellow vest I wore to signal that I am not a deer. It seemed prudent, as well, to leave Boon at home, and I missed his lolling-tongued happy company. I tried to squelch my resentment that the hunters take over the woods from early October to January—a time when a walk in the woods seems especially appealing—but I frequently failed.

The peppery, dusty, sharp scents of summer had given way to the earthier odors of leaf mold and goldenrod. Where goldenrod grows, though, so does ragweed, which meant my fall allergies roared in. I sometimes punctuated the day with a dozen or more mind-fogging sneezes in a row.

Still, despite the hunters and the allergies and the cooling nights, autumn is perhaps my favorite season. I adore its golden streaming light, so different from the high summer's harsh brilliance, and the way that light sets the coloring leaves afire. The trees' beauty is redoubled by their reflection in the glassy lake. I love, too, the braises and long-simmered dishes for which fall's chilly temperatures create an appetite.

Of all the glories that autumn has to offer, however, the biggest and foremost in my mind is apples. I'm in love with apples, in love especially with the names of the older varieties: Sheepnose, Wolf River, Macoun, Seek-No-Further, Cox's Orange Pippin—poetical names that whisper of older times and simpler values. Hundreds of apple varieties still grow all over the country—apples meant for sauce, or pies, or eating out of hand; apples meant for long-keeping or for making into cider; apples meant for drying, or for pairing with cheeses. But commercial apple growers seem to concentrate on only a few. It seems pitiful to me that even a well-stocked supermarket carries just a handful of varieties, and those the same no matter where you live: the trusty Empire, the insipid Red and Golden Delicious, the bright-tart Granny Smith, and, these days, the ubiquitous, sugary Galas, Honey Crisps, and Fujis.

Farmers' markets and farm stands often offer a wider variety—especially the Northern Spies and Romes that I like for pies, occasionally Baldwins and russeted Pippins with their rough skin—but every year, more orchards fall to developers who build subdivisions where the humble rows of apple trees once rooted.

If you buy apples at any season other than the late summer and fall when they ripen, you're buying apples from cold storage, a process in which growers store their harvest in controlled-atmosphere closed bins, where piped-in nitrogen replaces the oxygen that apples need to ripen and rot. It is a system that has made it possible for apple growers to spread their income over the year, which is a good thing, I reckon; yet, even under the best of circumstances, I find those controlled-atmosphere apples are often mealy and dissatisfying.

A better solution, perhaps, than buying out-of-season apples might be what people used to do, back when I was young. Nearly every mudroom and glassed-in sunporch in the houses I visited boasted a couple of bushels of apples, and we ravenous kids coming in from school were encouraged to help ourselves. The apples would be gone just about the time everyone tired of eating them, sometime after the New Year; and then we would go without until the following fall. Because I live alone, I don't need bushel after bushel, but I will buy a half bushel each of a couple of varieties—both for cooking and for eating out-of-hand—to set in my cool, dark basement. They will store there comfortably, along with the rest of my home-canned pantry items.

Michigan has always been among the premier apple-growing states, of course; the moderating effect of the Great Lakes creates a climate that suits apples to a T, with enough deep snow to protect the trees from dry, cold winter winds, and enough dormancy days to encourage the trees to set a good crop. Washington State grows more apples, but Michigan grows more varieties of apples, something of which I am unjustly proud. I felt that pride even as a kid. I remember dressing as Johnny Appleseed for Halloween when I was about ten, going out to trick-or-treat with one of my mom's Revere copper-clad saucepans on my head and wearing a burlap feed sack tied with rope at my waist. So perhaps my apple-love is but another part of my sense of place.

The apple harvest naturally means cider, too, another glory of the season. So when Jim told me that Bowens Mills, a privately owned historic grist mill in nearby Yankee Springs, had a cider festival coming up and wondered if I'd like to go with him, I said yes with alacrity.

Cider might be the most truly American of all drinks. The colonists started their day with mugs of cider, probably the lightly alcoholic "hard," or fermented, type, drawing on their traditions in England and elsewhere. It may have been a good choice, given that safe, potable water was sometimes scarce, and that fermented beverages may destroy intestinal bugs. English ciders remain my favorite, although I also love the peculiar French ciders, which often have a whiff of the barnyard about them. I even like domestic hard ciders, such as Woodchuck and Hornsby, although they have been dumbed down for mass consumption by upping the sugar to make them sticky-sweet.

It's sweet cider we think of, though, when we think of cider and doughnuts and pumpkin patches. Nowadays, thanks to our panicky attitudes about food, sweet cider must be pasteurized before sale in many states after an E. coli outbreak in raw cider a few years ago—remember that? A cider maker used apples contaminated by cow manure in his cider and it sickened some people. So many states rushed to require that cider be pasteurized.

The United States Department of Agriculture oversees food labeling and has created thousands of "standards of identity" for the foods we eat. The standards of identity are meant to ensure that the ice cream we buy actually has cream in it, or that the Velveeta on sale last week must be labeled "cheese food product," because it isn't really cheese. So if you have ever wondered what the difference is between apple juice and cider, well, this is it: nothing. The standard of identity for apple juice says it must be pasteurized. In the loopy world of government regulation, today, cider must also be pasteurized. Therefore, apple juice and cider—both often sold with sodium benzoate added to further reduce the chances of bacterial contamination—are the same thing. The cider we all look forward to drinking each fall is now nothing much different from the Treetop or Welch's frozen concentrate in cans you can pick up year-round. Unless, perhaps, we informally agree that cider is usually fresh-pressed, generally within a couple of days of its sale, and typically unfiltered. The government sees no such distinction.

I hadn't visited Bowens Mills before and was pleased to see a parking lot full of cars when we arrived. At one side of the lot, men unloaded horses from their trailers—draft types, butternut-brown Belgians with flaxen manes and tails, dappled gray Percherons, and chestnut and bay Clydesdales with their flashing white stockings and hooves as big as dinner plates—to ready for the pulling contest. Children scampered hither and yon like the bees drawn to the cider press, and parents pushing strollers clogged the paths. I could hear the fiddles and banjos of a bluegrass band off in the distance. I could see that vendors had set up tables, and one of the concessionaires offered what smelled like very good barbecue.

Jim and I wandered around a bit, and then, seeing that he was going to spend some time looking at the muzzle-loading rifles offered at one booth, I excused myself to step over to the horse pull. I couldn't care less about a tractor pull or anything else that involves machines and motors and engines, but if an animal is involved, especially one that wants to work, I will stop dead in my tracks to observe. I could have watched those extraordinary horses pull for hours—their dancing anticipation as they backed to the loaded sled, their straining muscles as they dug for purchase before leaning into the collar to pull, their pride and dignity and grace as they were unhitched—and sat happily in the sun, completely contented and at peace, until Jim found me, a new rifle in his hand.

We set off to watch the cider press, powered by the musical stream rushing over moss-covered rocks, crush and juice the mountains of apples stacked in wooden crates nearby. I asked the cider-maker what type of apples he was using and, recognizing all the varieties he named as dessert apples, knew his cider would be sweet and good. Not terribly complex—the best ciders mix sweet, sharp, bitter, and tart varieties, whereas he was using just sweet varieties—but it would be cool and delectable, and taste of fall.

"Think I'm going to buy a couple of gallons of that cider, Jim, and make hard cider," I said. At this, Jim's ears perked up.

"Teach me how?" he said.

"Sure. It won't be the finest hard cider in the world, but it'll taste good. We'll both like it, I think."

The cider-maker told us that gallon jugs of his cider were available in the mill's gift shop, so we headed that way.

A temporary cooler housed gallons of cider, so it was easy to snag a few. Tucked on a shelf to the right of the cooler were two-pound bags of coarse cornmeal, each dressed in a little faux burlap sack. Although the bags were labeled "Bowens Mills," I wasn't sure if they were simply souvenirs or products of the mill.

I turned to the woman staffing the cash register. "Do you grind this cornmeal? Here?"

"Yes," she said. "We grind it every week or so." She handed me a brochure that detailed the mill's history—built in 1836 as a sawmill, with the addition of a grist mill around 1864, Bowens Mills started making cider in 1902—and I saw that the brochure mentioned that the old French stone millstones had been renovated and redressed to make them operable.

I don't use a great deal of cornmeal, probably less than ten pounds a year. But I do like to keep some on hand for cornbread and muffins, for polenta and its kinfolk, and to use to add a little gritty body to waffles, pancakes, and breads. When I lived in the Deep South, I never cultivated a passion for grits at breakfast—no self-respecting Michigan girl would choose grits over hash browns! But a little study showed me that grits is coarse cornmeal is polenta. They're all essentially the same thing, although I think technically some have the germ of the corn sifted out, some don't. (Note that there are two kinds of grits: hominy grits and regular grits, and I am referring to regular grits.) The stone-ground stuff that Bowens Mills had on offer was whole-grain, with germ and everything. All the better, to my mind. After confirming that the gift store was open all year and that it always had cornmeal in stock, I picked up two 2-pound bags to add to my purchase.

With cornmeal stashed in the pantry, I literally have a world of dishes at hand. Naturally, you and I both think of cornbread first, because it is the most familiar. Cornbread is so easy to make that I can't figure the appeal of mixes: Stir together one cup each cornmeal and self-rising flour, two beaten eggs, three tablespoons vegetable oil or melted butter, two tablespoons of sugar if you're not a breast-pounding Southerner, and enough buttermilk or milk to make a stiff batter; bake at 350°F until golden, preferably in a well-greased ten-inch cast-iron skillet. When I bake a batch of cornbread, I usually plan to use the leftovers for cornbread dressing to go with pork chops or chicken within a couple of days.

Good coarse cornmeal can also lead to polenta, which is plain old Midwestern cornmeal mush or Southern grits in a dressier, slightly more exotic guise—and which is treated as a much-loved peasant food in its native Italy. Although I sometimes make polenta to serve with spaghetti sauce, more generally I treat it as a side dish and dress it with butter and cheese to make it creamy and rich. Every few months I get hungry for polenta with blue cheese, and on those occasions, that and a salad are all I need for dinner.

When I was a kid, my mother used to occasionally make a loaf pan of cornmeal mush, from which she cut slices to fry in butter and serve with maple syrup at breakfast. She acquired that appetite at the table of her Iowa-born mother, and while I liked it well enough, it never became a favorite of mine. But just thinking about it made me want to step into the kitchen to make a batch in my mother's memory.

I have seen tubes of already cooked polenta at the grocery store, and they are pricey. Yet again, making polenta from scratch literally costs pennies instead of dollars, and polenta is so simple to make that I can't see why anyone would buy the manufactured stuff, which I find unpleasantly rubbery. Make regular grits, polenta, and mush all the same way: one-half cup cornmeal to one-half cup cold water; stir together to prevent lumps, then slowly add two cups boiling water and cook over very low heat, stirring almost constantly, until the mixture is thick and bubbly and tastes cooked, usually within twenty minutes (although longer won't hurt it). Add a pinch of salt while it simmers. If it's polenta, top it with pasta sauce or stir in butter and the cheese of your choice and serve it as a side dish. If it's to be mush, pour the hot stuff into a buttered loaf pan and refrigerate, uncovered, until it firms up enough to slice and fry. And if it's going to be grits, serve with butter and sugar or salt and pepper at breakfast, perhaps with a little redeye gravy, if you happen to have it handy.

There's another polenta/mush/grits kind of thing that I like very, very much. Oddly enough, the small Michigan village in which I grew up is home to La Vatra, the United States headquarters of the Romanian Orthodox Church. My parents often took us to the annual festival at La Vatra's lovely tree-shaded grounds on Greytower Road outside the village, and I think my mother's hunger for the polenta-like *mamaliga* was the main reason we went. *Mamaliga* is the Romanian national dish, and the ladies' auxiliary at La Vatra always served it in one form or another, with *mamaliga cu branza*, or *mamaliga* baked with cheese and sour cream, the most common offering. Eventually, my mother inveigled some of the women to teach her to make *mamaliga*, and we all learned to love it. Now I had the beginnings of my own *mamaliga cu branza*.

Collecting our goodies, Jim and I called it a day and headed back to the lake. We agreed to meet the next day to set our hard cider to working, and I assured him that I had plenty of yeast and equipment to handle his and my batch both. I snitched a glass of frothy cider from one of my gallons and carried it out to the deck to enjoy as the October day readied itself for bed. The spectacular blushing oranges, reds, and pinks of the sky above the ridgeline to the west told me that the next day would be every bit as fine as that day had been. Jim has a sweet tooth, I remembered; I could make a batch of buttermilk doughnuts tonight, cut them out, and refrigerate them overnight, to fry just before he arrived the next morning so they'd still be warm when he came in.

They would please him, I thought, every bit as much as this day of curiosity and contentment, cider, and cornmeal, had pleased me.

how to make hard cider

You may have had the experience of having your cider turn fizzy over time; if so, you've already made hard cider. But for consistent results, it's best to destroy the wild yeasts—which may or may not provide something that tastes good—and replace them with wine or beer yeasts. Your local home-brew shop or winemaking supplier (I like midwestsupplies.com, since I have no local brew shop) can advise you on yeast selection, as well as supply you with caps or corks and air locks. Make sure your equipment is spotlessly clean before you begin. Add up to 1 cup of sugar or honey if you'd like the alcohol content to be a smidgen higher. Technically, hard cider fermented with honey is called *cyser*. I highly recommend Ken Schramm's book, *The Compleat Meadmaker,* for more information on *cyser* and other fermented beverages. For equipment, you will need a glass gallon jug with a tight-fitting lid, a water air lock, and 5 clean wine bottles.

---

1 gallon cider

Up to 1 cup sugar or honey (optional)

1 (5-gram) envelope wine or beer yeast

Pour the cider into a large stockpot and heat over medium heat until it is steaming. Reduce the heat to low and simmer the cider for 30 minutes. Do not boil; boiling sets the pectin in the juice and will leave your cider hazy. Remove from the heat and let cool to room temperature.

Transfer the cider to a clean gallon-size glass jug. Add the sugar or honey, if using. Cover the jug with a lid and shake well, for 3 to 5 minutes, to aerate it (and to dissolve the sweetener).

Add the yeast, recap the jug, and shake for an additional 3 minutes. Remove the cap, install the air lock, and place the jug someplace cool (60° to 70°F) and relatively dark. Let stand, undisturbed, for 2 to 3 months, or until bubbles no longer surface in the air lock. Be sure to check the air lock every few days to see if it needs more water added, to keep unwanted bacterial contamination at bay.

When you are confident that fermentation has ended, siphon the cider into clean wine bottles using a length of plastic or rubber tubing and avoiding the dregs at the bottom of the fermenting vessel. Cap or cork securely; store the bottles in a cool, dark place for at least 6 months before drinking.

joe's ancient orange-cinnamon-clove mead

MAKES 1 GALLON, ABOUT 5 (750-ML) WINE BOTTLES

Joe Mattioli, whom I've never met, is responsible for starting me and many others in making mead, hard cider, and wine, and I want to give him the credit he's due. His instructions, which I found at gotmead.com and in many other places around the Web, gave me the confidence to make my first mead, and it's the one I use to teach first-timers the basics of home winemaking. It finishes in about 2 months, requires no complicated steps, and is ready to drink at bottling time. Make this easy mead in early October so it will be ready to drink with your Thanksgiving turkey. I've recast Joe's recipe to follow contemporary recipe style. The only special equipment you need to get started is an empty glass gallon jug with a tight-fitting cap (a gallon of cheap wine will give you both the jug and an excuse to invite some friends over to empty it) and a water air lock, available from home-brewing stores or from an online source like midwestsupplies.com. Follow the directions exactly for your first batch and save the experimentation for later batches. I have found that the Fleischmann's yeast he recommends will yield a wine that finishes very sweet; if you want a drier mead, use Red Star yeast instead, or reduce the honey to 3 pounds (not both). Make sure your yeast is not expired. Don't make any other substitutions, though, or neither Joe nor I are responsible for your failure.

3¹/₂ pounds honey	1 or 2 whole cloves
4 cups hot tap water	Tiny pinch of grated nutmeg and/or ground allspice (optional)
1 large orange	
1 small handful of raisins (about 25 raisins)	Cold water
1 (3-inch) cinnamon stick	1 teaspoon Fleischmann's or Red Star active dry yeast (not fast-rising yeast)

Dissolve the honey in the hot water. Pour the mixture into a clean 1-gallon glass jug with a tight-fitting lid.

Wash the orange well to remove any pesticides from the skin, then cut it into 8 wedges. Push the wedges into the glass jug. Add the raisins, cinnamon stick, clove(s), and nutmeg; fill the jug to its shoulder with cold water. Put the lid on the jug and shake hard for 3 to 5 minutes. Set the jug aside and let the liquid come to room temperature.

Add the yeast to the jug, cover, and swirl gently to mix the yeast. It doesn't need to be thoroughly incorporated; the yeast is happy to go to work for you.

Remove the jug lid and install the water air lock. Put the jar in a dark place if your curiosity can bear having it out of sight (mine usually can't). The yeast will begin to work very quickly, within an hour.

After the major foaming stops in a few days, add a little additional water to raise the level to the neck of the jug. Reinstall the water air lock and put the jar someplace dark and warm (70° to 75°F) where it can stand undisturbed for 2 months. Don't shake the jug or mess with it in any way; leave it alone and untouched. Keep an eye on the air lock to be sure it always has water to provide a barrier from airborne contaminants, though.

The mead is ready to bottle and drink when it clears; sometimes the orange wedges sink to the bottom, sometimes they don't. If the liquid is clear, it's ready to bottle.

Wash and dry five empty wine bottles. Carefully siphon off the mead into the bottles using a length of plastic or rubber tubing, avoiding the sediment at the bottom of the jug. Cork or seal the bottles carefully. Discard the sediment in the fermenting jug and wash it thoroughly so it will be ready for the next batch. The mead is now ready to drink. Like all meads, this will improve with age and can store for years without harm. Lay the bottles on their sides in a cool, dark place for longer storage.

honey-oat bread

MAKES ONE 9 BY 5-INCH LOAF

This is my go-to bread, the recipe I make most frequently. It's sturdy enough to stand up to sandwiches, but also makes good toast, and is savory enough, despite the honey, to complement any meal. A loaf baked in a 9 by 5-inch pan will just fit into a gallon-size zip-top plastic bag (you might have to eat a couple of slices first to shorten the loaf, poor you!) and because the honey attracts moisture, the bread will keep for up to a week stored that way. It's always long gone before it can go stale, at least in my house.

$1^1/_4$ cups whole milk, plus more as needed

1 teaspoon sugar

2 teaspoons active dry yeast

3 cups all-purpose flour, plus more for kneading

1 cup rolled oats (not instant), plus more for sprinkling if using the egg wash

3 tablespoons honey

2 tablespoons salted butter, melted and cooled

$1^1/_2$ teaspoons salt

EGG WASH (OPTIONAL)

1 large egg

In a small saucepan over medium heat, scald the milk by cooking until steam begins to rise from it. Remove from the heat and let cool to about body temperature. Stir in the sugar and yeast; let stand for 10 minutes, or until yeast mixture is creamy and bubbly.

Combine the flour and rolled oats in a large mixing bowl. Add the honey, butter, and salt. Stir to combine.

Pour in the milk mixture. Stir to combine, adding more room-temperature milk if necessary to achieve a stiff dough. Tip the dough out onto a floured surface and, with floured hands, knead the dough until it is smooth and elastic, about 10 minutes. Gather the dough into a ball, tucking the ends under the ball's bottom.

Wash the bowl in which you mixed the dough, dry it, and oil it lightly with a neutral-tasting oil, such as canola or soybean. Put the dough in the bowl, seam side up, and twirl it around so the top of the dough is lightly greased.

Flip the dough ball over so the seam is on the bottom. Cover the bowl and let the dough rise in a warm place for 1 hour, or until doubled in bulk.

Lightly oil a 9 by 5-inch loaf pan. Punch down the dough with your fist. Tip the dough out onto a floured surface and knead well. It should not be sticky at this point; sprinkle the ball with flour lightly if it is. Shape the dough into a loaf and place it in the prepared pan seam side down. Lightly oil the top of the loaf and cover it with a clean kitchen towel. Let rise for 45 to 60 minutes, or until doubled in size.

Preheat the oven to 350°F.

Bake the bread for 35 to 40 minutes, until it sounds hollow when thumped with a finger. If you wish to use the optional egg wash, in a small bowl, lightly beat the egg with 2 tablespoons water. Bake the loaf for 20 minutes, remove from the oven, brush with egg wash, and scatter additional oats over the top of the loaf. Return it to the oven to continue baking.

Let cool on a wire rack for 10 minutes, then remove the loaf from the pan and continue to let cool. The cooled loaf will keep sealed in a gallon-size zip-top bag for up to a week.

buttermilk doughnuts with cider glaze

MAKES ABOUT 1¹/₂ DOZEN DOUGHNUTS

These are cake-style doughnuts, not raised doughnuts leavened with yeast. They are light and fluffy, yet still humble and homey. A cider-sweet glaze seems just right for the season. Use a candy thermometer to monitor the frying oil's temperature; the doughnuts will be greasy if the temperature drops below 375°F, and they will burn before they cook through if the temperature goes much higher.

DOUGHNUTS

4 ¹/₄ cups all-purpose flour, plus more for dusting

1 tablespoon baking powder

¹/₂ teaspoon baking soda

³/₄ teaspoon salt

¹/₂ teaspoon ground cinnamon

¹/₄ teaspoon ground cloves

¹/₄ teaspoon ground allspice

¹/₄ teaspoon grated nutmeg

2 large eggs, plus 1 large egg yolk

³/₄ cup granulated sugar

1 teaspoon vanilla extract

1 cup buttermilk (or 1 cup milk soured with 1 tablespoon vinegar)

3 tablespoons salted butter, melted

Neutral vegetable oil, such as canola or soybean, for frying

GLAZE

1¹/₂ cups confectioners' sugar

2 to 4 tablespoons cider

In a large bowl, combine the flour, baking powder, baking soda, salt, cinnamon, cloves, allspice, and nutmeg. Whisk to lighten and combine well.

In the bowl of a stand mixer, or in a large bowl using a hand mixer, beat the eggs and egg yolk with the granulated sugar and vanilla until light and fluffy, 2 to 3 minutes.

In a large measuring cup, stir together the buttermilk and butter.

Alternately beat the dry ingredients and buttermilk mixture into the egg mixture, one-third at a time, until all of the ingredients are combined and a soft, sticky dough forms.

Fill a deep fryer or a large pot with oil to a depth of at least 3 inches, and heat the oil to 350°F over medium-low to medium heat.

Meanwhile, with floured hands, transfer the dough to a generously floured board and gently roll out until the dough is $1/2$ inch thick. Using a 3-inch biscuit cutter, cut the dough into rounds, spacing the rounds as close as possible. Poke a hole in the center of each round with the handle of a wooden spoon, wiggling the spoon to widen the hole. Collect the scraps and roll out to form another batch of doughnuts (Note: the second batch may be a little tougher than the first as the dough has been worked.) If you have scraps left over after rolling out the dough the second time, discard them.

When the oil is ready, working in batches, place the doughnuts in the oil, being careful not to crowd them. Fry the doughnuts, turning them once, until puffed and golden, $1^{1}/_{2}$ to 2 minutes on each side. Remove the doughnuts and place on a wire rack to drain. Before adding the next batch, give the oil a few minutes to return to frying temperature.

When all the doughnuts are cooked, on the wire rack, and slightly cooled, ice them with cider glaze. To make the cider glaze, in a bowl, combine the confectioners' sugar and 2 tablespoons of the cider. Whisk to blend. Add additional cider as needed to reach a thick glaze consistency. Pour the glaze into a measuring cup and drizzle it over the doughnuts.

Doughnuts are best the day they are made. For longer storage, place the doughnuts on a rimmed baking sheet, freeze until solid, and transfer to zip-top plastic bags before storing in freezer. To serve, warm the frozen doughnuts for a minute or two in the microwave.

cider-braised pork loin with apples and onions

MAKES 6 TO 8 SERVINGS

Do we like pork with apple-y flavors because pork was traditionally slaughtered in the fall, when apples also ripen? Or because ciders and apples simply complement pork's rich sweetness? Either way, pork with anything apple is a guaranteed delight. Choose an apple variety that holds its shape in cooking, such as Granny Smith, Gala, Jonathan or Jonagold, or Braeburn. If you have leftover pork, it makes a fine sandwich.

+-+

8 cups cider

3 large apples

1 (3- to 5-pound) bone-in pork loin

2 onions, sliced

1 teaspoon dried thyme

$^1/_2$ teaspoon salt

$^1/_4$ teaspoon freshly ground black pepper

$^1/_4$ cup cornstarch

Preheat the oven to 350°F.

Pour the cider into a medium saucepan and bring to a boil over high heat. Boil the cider until it reduces in volume by half, about 15 minutes. Remove from the heat.

Core the apples, but do not peel. Cut the apples into eighths. Put the pork in a Dutch oven or heavy pot. Surround the pork with the apples and onions. Sprinkle everything with the thyme, salt, and pepper. Pour the reduced cider over all.

Bake the pork, uncovered, for 1 to 1$^1/_2$ hours, basting once or twice with the cider, until the pork reaches an internal temperature of 155°F on a meat thermometer inserted into the center of the roast. Transfer the pork, apples, and onions to a platter, cover, and keep warm.

Place the Dutch oven over medium-high heat and bring the juices to a boil. In a bowl, dissolve the cornstarch in a little cold water and whisk the mixture into the juices in the pot. Cook, stirring constantly, until the mixture thickens, about 5 minutes. Slice the roast and serve immediately, passing the sauce at the table.

baked Indian pudding

MAKES 6 SERVINGS

Humble Indian pudding is a hearty dessert that's right for cooler-season menus. It can slide into the oven alongside a roast or braise, and offers some nutrition that ice cream or cake certainly can't offer. I like the leftovers for breakfast, warmed in the microwave and dressed with milk.

- -

1/3 cup yellow cornmeal

1/2 teaspoon salt

1/2 teaspoon ground ginger

1/2 teaspoon ground cinnamon

3 1/2 cups milk

1/2 cup blackstrap molasses or sorghum syrup

1/8 teaspoon baking soda

1/2 cup strong brewed coffee, at room temperature

2 tablespoons salted butter

Ice cream or whipped cream, for serving

Preheat the oven to 300°F. Grease a 2-quart baking dish. Fill a large saucepan with about 2 inches of water.

In a large heatproof bowl that fits securely on top of the saucepan, combine the cornmeal, salt, ginger, and cinnamon.

Scald 2 cups of the milk by heating in a second saucepan over medium heat until it steams; add it slowly to the cornmeal mixture, stirring constantly. Add the molasses and baking soda, mixing thoroughly. Add the remaining 1 1/2 cups milk, the coffee, and the butter; stir well.

Set the bowl over the saucepan containing the water. Place the pan over medium heat, and cook the cornmeal-milk mixture, stirring occasionally, until it has thickened slightly, about 15 minutes. Pour into the prepared baking dish.

Bake, uncovered, for about 2 hours and 10 minutes, or until a knife inserted 1 inch from the center comes out clean. Serve warm with ice cream or whipped cream.

mamaliga cu branza (romanian polenta with cheese and sour cream)

MAKES ABOUT 6 SERVINGS

Mamaliga is a dish with a great deal of cultural significance to Romanians, and I make no claim to authenticity for this version because I am not Romanian. It is the way my mother, who loved it, learned to make it from the good women of La Vatra, however, and the way we ate it in my house. If my mother couldn't find feta or brick cheese, she sometimes used other kinds of cheese, including Cheddar or Colby, and she often included diced roasted chiles in the middle layer as well. If you have leftovers, try frying slices in a bit of butter until browned for breakfast.

1/2 cup coarse-ground cornmeal

1/2 cup cold water

1/2 teaspoon salt

2 cups boiling water

1 cup crumbled feta, brick, or other dry, semifirm cheese, plus extra for serving

1 cup sour cream

Preheat the oven to 350°F. Generously butter a deep 2-quart casserole or 9 by 5-inch loaf pan.

In a large, deep saucepan, combine the cornmeal, cold water, and salt. Stir to combine with a wooden spoon. Place the saucepan over medium heat. Little by little, add the boiling water to the cornmeal, stirring constantly, until all the boiling water is incorporated and the mixture is smooth. Cook, stirring constantly, until the mixture comes to a boil, 3 to 5 minutes. Decrease the heat to its lowest setting; cover the pan and cook, stirring frequently, for 20 to 30 minutes, or until the mixture is thick and no longer tastes "raw."

Pour half of the cornmeal mixture into the buttered casserole. Scatter the cheese over the cornmeal mixture. Pour the remaining cornmeal mixture over the cheese; spread the sour cream over the second layer of the cornmeal mixture.

Bake, uncovered, for 30 to 40 minutes, or until the mixture is bubbly. Serve hot, passing additional cheese at the table.

14

On pumpkins, pears, and woolly bears

GUFFY FOUND HIMSELF A WOOLLY BEAR one day and spent a while batting the poor caterpillar about before I saw him and rescued it. I don't think Guff hurt it, really; the caterpillar had made itself into a tight, snug little ball, and I believe Guffy was just prodding it to make it move. When I took the caterpillar away, the cat cleaned his mitts and strolled off. But I bent to look at the little caterpillar closely.

I still find myself ruminating over what kind of winter the woolly bears say we will have each fall when I see them inching along on the road or in the yard. Woolly bears are active in the fall because they're stoking their systems with the last nutrition they can find before they overwinter—the woolly bear makes its own natural antifreeze to help it survive the long, cold months. Sometime early in the spring, it will mutate into a moth, live through the summer to reproduce, and then die. The woolly bear is the caterpillar form of the Isabella tiger moth, and scientists say that the width of its central band is determined by one or more biological factors: when the caterpillar hatched, whether it grew in dry or moist weather, perhaps even how old it is. They've learned that woolly bears hatched from the same batch of eggs will vary in the width of their central stripe. That's what the scientists say, and I believe them. Yet even though I don't put much stock in it, I still look to see what the woolly bear of the moment has to say. The folklore is that a wide brown central band means a mild winter, while a narrow band means a tough one.

Guffy's catch sported a little bitty skinny brown band, boding a bad winter. I paid more attention to the mad scurrying of the squirrels as they gathered the acorns that bombarded my house with the sound of small-arms fire. The squirrels were unusually fat and glossy and sleek as they prepared for the coming cold. If a bad winter lay ahead, I was about as ready as I was going to get.

By doing a little bit of canning, freezing, and dehydrating each week over the long summer, I had amassed a stockpile of fruits and vegetables to see me through. Careful shopping had filled my freezer with versatile cuts of meat, mostly roasts and whole chickens. The freezer's corners bulged with bags and containers of strawberries, raspberries, cherries, cooked beans, and other goodies.

I was still gathering food, though, because the last crops of summer—the winter squashes, potatoes, onions, apples, and pears—keep well in a root cellar. In my case, the root cellar is my cool, dark half basement. All winter long, it stays at a constant temperature of about 38°F, making it a perfect place to store fruits and vegetables that don't need refrigeration to preserve them. A garage can also serve as a root cellar, as can a pit dug in the ground. The old technique of root cellaring—whether in a cellar like mine, or in a barn or outbuilding—was another way that those who went before us extended the use of the fruits of the harvest, but we've largely lost touch with those old ways.

Instead, now we just go to the grocery store and buy what we need each week. And then, according to a lot of statistics, we let a third to a half of it spoil before we use it. That just seems wrong to me, that terrible waste of food.

So I calculated my needs and figured out I'll want about a dozen acorn squashes and a few butternut squashes and pie, or sugar, pumpkins. I laid in a half-bushel each of apples for cooking and apples for eating out-of-hand, and the same of pears. Wally invited me to come to his house to dig potatoes, so I have a bushel of a couple of kinds of baking potatoes and one of boilers. He also gave me onions—small white and yellow ones—so I had enough of those to keep me going for a while.

One thing I really missed was sweet potatoes. When I lived in the Deep South, we bought a bushel of sweet potatoes each fall and enjoyed them all winter, baked, mashed or, rarely, candied. But sweet potatoes—yams are a totally different vegetable that happen to have a similar sweetness—don't grow real well here in the Great Lakes region, and I haven't seen any at the market. To replace sweet potatoes, both nutritionally and culinarily, I lean on winter squash and pie pumpkins for the bright color, beta carotene, and vitamins that are common to both. And I cut myself a little slack: if I get super-hungry for sweet potatoes, of course, I can pick up one or two at the store.

By the time Thanksgiving rolled around, my weekly grocery bill dropped considerably, from forty dollars to about fifteen. Looking ahead, I could see that all I'd need to buy each week was a gallon of milk, plus whatever odd ingredient I might need for something I planned to cook; a can of chipotles, say, or a little tuna, or some refill of a spice.

So I used the remainder of my weekly grocery budget to replenish stocks of staples that don't go bad—sugar and spices go on sale as the holidays arrive, so it's a good time to restock on those. Citrus comes into season in the winter, so I refill my jar of preserved lemons and perhaps make some marmalade. I watched the grocery store circulars for good prices on items such as mustard and ketchup, dried beans and flours, and canned goods, such as salmon and tuna.

It took me a little while to retrain my mind—longer to do that than to put all the food by for winter, actually. I used to think of my pantry like a checking account. Each week, I'd make some deposits (by shopping), and each week I'd make some debits (by using up what I bought). My goal, in those days, was to keep the balance pretty much even between the two.

But lately I've realized that filling a pantry requires a different kind of thinking. I've been carefully building a big savings account, and now the goal was to spend it all by eating up what I've put by, to empty the account. So my new challenge was to learn a way of thinking that spread that "spending" over the winter, ending with an almost empty pantry by the time the first new crops began to arrive in spring. It's not rationing, exactly; it's much closer to budgeting. It was certainly a big change, however, from my old mindset of pantry-as-checking account.

I needed to do that because, of course, the goal of having food was to eat it. I may have extended the usable life of the foods I've put by for weeks or months, but eventually even those good foods lose their quality and their value. So I had to get past the idea that I was "saving" the food that I preserved for "someday," and accustom myself to using it up. That's why I put it there in the first place: to use it up.

The jars of preserves, canned vegetables, and dehydrated fruits and vegetables in the cellar were safe from pests and vermin, such as mice and the odd chipmunk that found its way into my house from time to time. (Although Guffy's arrival seemed to have changed the chipmunks' minds about the desirability of my cellar as a condo.) Safe also was the food in the freezer.

But the fruits and vegetables I planned to store at cellar temperature needed a small amount of special attention. Apples, for example, release ethylene gas as they ripen, which causes other produce to spoil, so they had to be either individually wrapped in newspaper or stored in a covered crate. The pears got the same treatment. Carrots can be stored washed and cleaned or just as they came from the garden, but the crate or bucket they are stored in should be covered with newspaper and elevated off the ground. The winter squashes and pumpkins should be rubbed with vegetable oil to slow mold and to keep air from encouraging them to rot, and it's a good idea to set them on layers of newspaper. They store better on the wire shelving in the slightly warmer, less damp bathroom than down cellar. Almost any root vegetable, from beets to turnips, can be preserved in a tub of barely moist sand, as long as the tub is kept closely covered. I tied the onions in the legs of pantyhose, with a knot separating each pair of onions, and hung the odd-looking thing from the rafters. They keep well as long as they don't touch each other. I'd prefer to braid some heads of garlic into a long strand to hang nearby, but the growers who offered garlic seemed never to sell it with the stalks attached. So instead, I stored my winter's supply in a lidded shoebox with holes punched in the sides.

There are many ways to preserve vegetables right in the garden, although these become kind of a moot point for me since I can't grow anything except herbs in my shady yard. Parsnips, kale, Brussels sprouts, cabbage, and many kinds of greens can be left in the garden all winter, especially if protected with layers of straw against the worst weather. My chickens especially like kale, so I planted a row of decorative kale in the raised stone-faced flowerbed next to the steps; if I could just keep the deer out of it, I could treat them—and me!—to fresh kale all winter. Still, the growers who announced that they'll sell at the new winter market in Kalamazoo will know these techniques, and they'll also know how to grow lettuces and other hardy greens in cold-frames and hoop houses.

If any of the fruits and vegetables I've root-cellared start to look iffy, I cook them right away, and if I have more to deal with than I can use at that moment, I can preserve them in various ways. If the pumpkins or squashes start to get squishy, I cut away the bad parts and either can their flesh in chunks or make pumpkin puree for the freezer to use in future pies (it's not safe to can pumpkin puree because its density means it can never reach safe temperatures all the way through to the center).

If the apples begin to slip away, I can a batch of pie filling, or applesauce, or apple butter, or spiced apple rings. Fading pears can go into relish or be canned as halves or slices; pears, too, make a good fruit butter. My goal was to eat all the food I set by and not waste any of it, and if, to do that, I needed to help it last by doing another level of preservation, I was fine with that.

The work that filled my days all summer long drew to its natural end as the growing season closed. Like Guffy's little woolly bear, I could draw my small world tightly around me, to feel safe and secure against almost every threat.

apple or pear butter

MAKES ABOUT 8 HALF-PINT JARS OR 4 PINT JARS

Making fruit butters used to mean constant attention and careful stirring to keep the thick fruit puree from burning. Now I just tumble fruit, unpeeled but cored and quartered, into my slow cooker and let it simmer until it has the texture I want. The classic test for fruit butter is this: spoon a bit onto a chilled saucer, and if the fruit butter holds its shape and no liquid forms a rim around it, it's done. If you don't have cider handy to add to the apples while cooking, apple juice is fine, but water will also work. Choose apples that don't hold their shape in cooking for apple butter; McIntoshes are a good choice.

◆-◆

6 pounds apples or pears, unpeeled, cored, and quartered

2 cups cider

3 cups sugar

2 teaspoons ground cinnamon

1 teaspoon ground cloves

1 teaspoon grated nutmeg

2 tablespoons salted butter

Combine the apples, cider, sugar, cinnamon, cloves, nutmeg, and butter in a large slow cooker and set the slow cooker to high heat. Cover and cook for 30 minutes. Stir to make sure the sugar is dissolved and re-cover, this time setting the lid ajar so the liquid can evaporate.

Cook, stirring again after 2 hours and again after 4 hours, until the fruit has softened completely, 6 to 8 hours. Use a handheld potato masher or immersion blender to puree the fruit. Re-cover with the lid ajar, and continue to cook until the mixture holds its shape on a spoon and no juices form a rim when you place a spoonful on a chilled plate. This may take as few as 8 hours or as many as 12 hours total.

Prepare the boiling water canner, jars, and lids, according to the directions on page 253. Spoon the fruit butter into the jars, leaving 1/4 inch of headspace. Seal. Process for 10 minutes, according to the instructions on page 253. Store in a cool, dry place for up to a year.

how to can pumpkin or winter squash

MAKES 1 QUART JAR FOR EACH 2^1/$_2$ POUNDS PUMPKIN
OR SQUASH FLESH

It's not safe to can pumpkin or squash puree, but canned pumpkin and squash
are easy to puree when you need to use them. A quart of pumpkin chunks,
mashed into puree, is about equal to a 15-ounce can of pumpkin puree, which
is the right amount for a pie, a pot of soup, or a batch of muffins. Look for
pie pumpkins, sometimes called sugar pumpkins, for canning. Canned winter
squash can substitute for pumpkin in all those places, although its flavor will
be slightly different, of course. Note that both must be pressure canned.

Wash the pumpkin or squash, cut it in half, and scoop out the seeds. Cut
the halves into smaller pieces and remove the rind. Cut the flesh into 1-inch
chunks. Weigh the pumpkin or squash; prepare 1 quart jar for each 2^1/$_2$ pounds.

Prepare the pressure canner, jars, and lids, according to the directions on
pages 253 and 254.

In a large stainless steel saucepan or stockpot, combine the pumpkin or
squash with boiling water to cover. Bring to a boil over medium-high heat
and boil for 2 minutes, or until the chunks are heated through but not soft.
Drain, discarding the cooking liquid.

Pack the hot pumpkin or squash into hot jars, leaving a generous 1-inch
headspace. (You may wish to add 1 teaspoon uniodized salt to each quart; I
usually don't.) Pour fresh boiling water over the pumpkin or squash, remove
any bubbles, and add additional boiling water as needed to leave a 1-inch
headspace. Seal. Process at 10 pounds pressure for 1^1/$_2$ hours, according to
the directions on page 254. Store in a cool, dry place for up to a year.

thai-style pumpkin soup

MAKES ABOUT 4 SERVINGS

Colder weather makes me long for thick, rich soups. This inauthentic Thai soup features the peanut and ginger flavors of its more authentic cousins, but uses ingredients that I'm likely to have on hand. When fresh ginger is available at a good price, I buy it, "grate" it unpeeled in the food processor or blender, and freeze dollops of it in teaspoon-sized mounds on a rimmed baking sheet before transferring them to a zip-top freezer bag. In this soup, you may add it frozen if you have done likewise.

4 cups chicken broth

1 quart jar pumpkin chunks, drained, or 4 cups raw pumpkin chunks

2 teaspoons grated fresh ginger or 1 teaspoon ground ginger

3 cloves garlic, smashed and minced

1/2 teaspoon crushed red pepper flakes

1/4 cup creamy peanut butter

2 tablespoons rice vinegar

2 tablespoons finely chopped scallion, white and tender green parts

1/4 cup finely chopped fresh cilantro

1/3 cup whole milk

In a large saucepan, combine the chicken broth, pumpkin, ginger, garlic, and crushed red pepper. Bring to a boil over medium-high heat, stirring occasionally. Decrease the heat to low; cover and simmer until the pumpkin is very tender, 20 to 30 minutes. Remove the pumpkin chunks; allow the cooking liquid to continue to simmer.

Working in batches with a blender or food processor, or using an immersion blender, puree the pumpkin with a little of the cooking liquid to make a smooth, thick paste. Return the pumpkin to the saucepan; whisk to blend.

Stir in the peanut butter, vinegar, scallion, and 1 tablespoon of the cilantro. Cook, stirring occasionally, until the soup returns to a boil, 5 to 8 minutes. Stir in the milk.

Serve immediately, sprinkling each serving with a little of the remaining 3 tablespoons cilantro.

pumpkin muffins

MAKES 1 DOZEN REGULAR-SIZED MUFFINS
OR 6 "TEXAS"-SIZED MUFFINS

Pumpkin puree not only helps keep these muffins moist, it also adds fiber and nutrition, in the form of vitamin A and beta carotene. I don't often have buttermilk on hand, so I sour the milk by adding a teaspoon of vinegar and letting it stand for a few minutes at room temperature. If you have buttermilk, however, use it here. The key to tender, tall muffins is to mix them quickly, with a very light hand; it's okay if streaks remain in the batter before baking.

2 cups all-purpose flour

2/3 cup packed brown sugar

1/3 cup granulated sugar

1 tablespoon baking powder

1 teaspoon salt

1 1/2 teaspoons ground cinnamon

1/4 teaspoon baking soda

1/4 teaspoon ground ginger

1/4 teaspoon ground cloves

1/4 teaspoon grated nutmeg

1/3 cup whole milk

1 teaspoon cider vinegar

1/2 cup (1 stick) salted butter, melted

1/2 cup pumpkin puree

2 large eggs, lightly beaten

Preheat the oven to 400°F. Grease a regular 12-cup muffin tin or a 6-cup jumbo muffin tin, or line the cups with paper liners.

Combine the flour, brown sugar, granulated sugar, baking powder, salt, cinnamon, baking soda, ginger, cloves, and nutmeg in a large bowl.

Sour the milk in a small bowl by adding the vinegar; let stand at room temperature for 2 minutes.

Combine the butter, pumpkin, eggs, and soured milk in a bowl. Add to flour mixture; stir just until moistened. Spoon into the prepared muffin cups, filling each cup about three-quarters full.

Bake regular-size muffins for 15 to 20 minutes and jumbo-sized muffins for 20 to 25 minutes, or until a tester inserted in the center of one of the muffins comes out clean. Cool in the pan on a wire rack for 5 minutes; remove to a wire rack and let cool completely.

winter squash risotto

MAKES 6 SERVINGS

Risotto suits me in any season, but this one, with butternut squash, is especially good in the fall. Try changing the cheese to vary it; add bits of roasted chicken, ham, or pork to turn it into a main dish. Even without the meat, however, a bowl of this makes a very happy supper for me.

◆-◆

8 cups chicken broth

1 butternut squash (about 1 pound)

A fistful of sage leaves, about 24, or 1 tablespoon dried sage, crumbled

Coarse salt, such as kosher salt

Freshly ground black pepper

¹/₄ cup (¹/₂ stick) salted butter

1 onion, minced

2 cups Arborio rice

¹/₂ cup dry white wine

¹/₂ cup shredded or finely cubed Fontina or Havarti cheese

In a medium saucepan over medium heat, heat 1 cup of the broth. Peel and halve the squash, remove any seeds and fiber, and dice the flesh into very small cubes. Add the squash, sage leaves (reserve a few for garnish if you're using fresh sage), and a pinch each of salt and pepper to the broth in the pan. Bring to a simmer and cook, uncovered, until the squash is tender but not mushy, 5 to 10 minutes. Remove the squash and cover to keep warm; add the remaining broth to the pan and continue to simmer.

In a large, heavy-bottomed saucepan, melt 2 tablespoons of the butter over low heat. Add the onion and cook until translucent, about 5 minutes. Add the rice and a pinch of salt and cook for 3 minutes, stirring often, until rice has turned slightly translucent, with an opaque pearly "eye" in each grain. Increase the heat to medium and add the white wine. Once the wine has been absorbed, add enough hot broth to cover the rice. Stir well and decrease the heat to medium-low.

Gently simmer the rice, stirring occasionally, until the broth is absorbed. Add another 1/2 to 3/4 cup warm broth, and stir occasionally until the newly added broth is absorbed. Repeat the process until all the broth has been absorbed by the rice, and the rice is tender. This could take up to 30 minutes.

When the rice is mostly tender, add the cooked squash, cheese, and the remaining 1 tablespoon butter. Cook until the cheese is melted and the squash is heated through, 3 to 5 minutes. Add salt and pepper to taste. Serve hot, garnishing with the reserved sage leaves.

15

On Thanksgiving and the local table

DRENCHING CHILLY RAINS drove the last of the leaves from the trees. The days were gray and wet, the skies an unrelenting pewter, and night came earlier after we turned the clocks back with the end of daylight savings time. By the end of the month, it was full dark by 5:00 p.m. The first snow fell before my birthday in late October, but the one that stuck, the one that whitened the ground, happened mid-November. The winter solstice, when the days would once again begin to lengthen, seemed impossibly far away to me. I completely understood why the druids celebrated the solstice as the most important day of the year. November is easily the hardest month.

Its one bright spot is Thanksgiving. Quite happily, I spent it alone.

Several people extended invitations, for which I was most grateful. I begged off on each one, though, pleading a previous commitment. I did have a previous commitment: to myself.

Years ago, my career in newspapering took me far from family, and the holidays often found me in new places where I knew few people. In combination with that, as a junior member of the staff with the least seniority, I frequently had to work on Thanksgiving Day, or on the Friday afterwards, which made it impossible for me to travel home.

So I decided back then to begin my own rituals around Thanksgiving. It became important to me to develop a strategy that made me anticipate a day alone, rather than dread it.

The first thing I decided: There had to be a carefully planned and prepared full meal, just for me. It might or might not include turkey—I'm not a big fan of turkey at the best of times, and even a small bird is a mighty lot of meat for a solo person (although the extra certainly can be frozen). It had to be a complete meal, with a thoughtfully dressed table, some hors d'oeuvres to tease me, a main dish and sides, and dessert. The best bottle of wine I could afford needed to stand at the ready.

I also decided to really, truly give thanks, by pausing to look back over the preceding year and studying its gifts. I elected to be grateful even for its challenges, because we often don't grow without a push. The second half of giving thanks was to look forward, to consider the coming year and to mull over how what I learned in the year preceding could help me live better in the next one. I also gave thought to my family and friends, to remember and celebrate the lives of those I loved so much who were already gone, and to remind myself of the depth of my love for those I was lucky enough to still have.

The third part of my Thanksgiving Day ritual was to begin rereading one of my three favorite books, each dealing with an overarching theme of the human condition. I would not finish the book on Thanksgiving Day itself; but I must begin reading it on that day.

The first of the three books is John Gunther's 1949 masterpiece, *Death Be Not Proud*, which takes its title from the John Donne poem of the same name, of course. It details the last fifteen months of the life of Gunther's seventeen-year-old son, Johnny, who died of brain cancer. By all accounts, young Johnny was much beloved for his intelligence, grace, and selflessness. His family took its joy from each day that he survived, and found sustenance in the way that he lived his last days with intelligence and verve. His father's courageous, painfully honest book immortalized the boy, and thereby defeated the Death that tried to steal him. The book's essential message, clearly, is that we choose how to live our lives, however briefly we may have them. Young Johnny Gunther insists that I live bravely and well, whatever may come into my life.

The second is James Agee's *Let Us Now Praise Famous Men*, published in 1941. Agee's collaboration with photographer Walker Evans documented the lives of three sharecropper families in rural Alabama during the Great Depression. In the United States of the time, families like these, their desperate poverty and terrible living conditions, were virtually invisible. Agee's prose blends straightforward journalism with passages of literary beauty and poetic lyricism, and Evans' starkly moving photographs force readers to contend, face-to-face, with those they might prefer to ignore. The book was published to critical acclaim and stands as an American classic. I heed Agee's plea that the reader look past the heartrending poverty to see the humanity and grandeur, the dignity, of these lives—and, by extension, of every human life.

The last book is Ross Lockridge, Jr.'s 1948 novel, *Raintree County*. The sprawling novel is frankly Midwestern and details John Shawnessy's life from his beginnings in rural Indiana through the Civil War and afterwards. Lockridge wrestles with the ideas of our need for heroes and the attempt to become one, the mythology of a great man predestined to appear, and the value of a quest, however quixotic. The book is by turns lyric and ribald, funny and sad, moving and mundane. It is, in short, all the things that life should be, and I never tire of the reminder.

I can't remember which book I chose that first year, but I remember vividly where I lived and what I ate. In a small central Massachusetts town, I treated myself to a bottle of buttery French Meursault and enjoyed the first glass with a small plate of the little tidbits the French call "amuse-bouches": a couple of cherry tomatoes filled with a piping of Boursin cheese, a skinny slice of tinned foie gras pâté, and a bit of a baguette with a shattering crust. Later, I sat down to a roast Cornish hen, its cavity stuffed with lemon and garlic; steamed green beans; buttery baked-and-mashed acorn squash; more of the baguette, and, in a nod to more traditional Thanksgiving observances, the cranberry-orange relish my mother used to make. Dessert that year was chocolate-orange mousse, rich with heavy cream and egg. I think no one could fear the future after eating like that.

These past many years, I haven't been alone on Thanksgiving. While those accompanied Thanksgivings had their pleasures, I don't remember any of them well enough to tell one from the other. Yet I can remember, with perfect clarity, each of my solo Thanksgivings. So I really looked forward to resurrecting my old custom.

This year, I settled on *Let Us Now Praise Famous Men*. I filled the house with classical music on Thanksgiving Day, rose early, and did a little of everything I love to do: cook, read, knit, spin at my wheel, go for a walk with Boon, play with Pippin and Guffy, study the lake.

I roasted a small turkey, just because I want to give some custom to Otto's Turkey Farm, Tom and Jeri Otto's business in Middleville. I have spent little of my money with them this year. Everything else on the menu also came from within fifty miles of my cottage: the cider to brine the turkey; the meats for the homemade pâté; the Brussels sprouts; the cranberries; the mashed potatoes; the dressing made with my homemade bread, dried cherries, and Don Geukes' pork sausage; the pumpkin for the pie. Because I have winnowed my grocery spending down to just a few dollars, I spent a little extra on a good bottle of wine; these days I lean toward a crisp, bright white—an Albariño perhaps, or a Viognier.

After dinner, while I cheerfully cleaned up my messy kitchen, I gave Boon and Pip and Guffy each a bit of turkey, my nod to their Thanksgiving. I carried the vegetable trimmings and my kitchen scraps out to the chickens for theirs.

I mentally composed my list of things to be grateful for this year, and it's a long one already. I have old friends far and new friends near; I have much-beloved animals to amuse and pester me. Even the year's challenges looked like blessings from where I sat that day. I believed they would be instructive as I considered what lies ahead.

HOW TO CIDER-BRINE A TURKEY

MAKES ONE 12- TO 14-POUND BRINED TURKEY

Brining keeps a turkey moist and juicy, yet doesn't make it salty. Don't use the drippings for gravy, though; they will taste of the brine. The hardest part of brining is making room in the refrigerator for the turkey.

8 cups apple cider

2/3 cup coarse salt, such as kosher salt

1 cup firmly packed brown sugar

1 whole orange, chopped

1 cup chopped onion

1 cup chopped carrot

1 cup chopped celery

2 bay leaves

1 inch fresh ginger, sliced

2 teaspoons black peppercorns

1 teaspoon whole cloves

4 cups cold water

1 (12- to 14-pound) turkey, thawed if frozen

Combine the cider, salt, brown sugar, orange, onion, carrot, celery, bay leaves, ginger, peppercorns, and cloves in a large stockpot. Bring to a boil over medium-high heat and cook, stirring occasionally, until the sugar and salt dissolve, about 5 minutes. Remove from the heat, add the cold water, and let cool to room temperature.

Wash the turkey inside and out and remove the giblets and neck, reserving them for gravy or stuffing, if desired.

Put the turkey in a pot large enough to hold the turkey and the brine. Or, use a large food-safe plastic bag resting in a pot or roasting pan, which will make the bird easy to move.

Pour the brine over the turkey, making sure both cavities of the turkey are filled as well. Cover or tightly close the bag and refrigerate for at least 12 hours and up to 24 hours. If you are using a bag, rotate the turkey a few times.

Before roasting, remove the turkey from the brine and rinse with cold water. Pat dry with paper towels and proceed with your favorite roasting method. Discard the brine.

sage dressing with cherries, apples, and sausage

MAKES 12 TO 14 SERVINGS

When my brother and I were very young, my mother would sit us down on the couch the night before Thanksgiving with a big roasting pan and a couple of loaves of bread. "Earn your keep," she'd say, pouring herself another martini. Our job was to tear the slices of bread into chunky pieces so it could stale on the counter overnight for her dressing the next day. We were so proud at dinner, when everyone raved about "our" dressing. Even the littlest ones can pitch in to help with preparation. Why deprive them of that by buying stuffing mix? I prefer to bake the dressing in a separate pan for the last hour of the turkey's roasting time, rather than putting it in the bird.

2 loaves rustic white bread, sliced

1/4 cup (1/2 stick) salted butter

1 large onion, chopped

2 ribs celery, chopped

1 pound bulk fresh pork sausage

3 large apples, unpeeled, cored, and chopped

1/2 cup dried cherries

1/2 cup chopped walnuts

1 tablespoon dried sage, crumbled

1 to 2 cups chicken broth

On Thanksgiving eve, tear the bread into chunks about 1-inch in size. Spread the bread out on a rimmed baking sheet; leave the bread on the counter or in the oven overnight to stale.

On Thanksgiving day, butter a 4-quart casserole or baking dish.

Melt the butter in a large heavy skillet over medium heat. Add the onion and celery; cook, stirring occasionally, until the onion is golden and softened, about 10 minutes. Transfer the onion and celery to a very large bowl.

Into the same skillet, crumble the pork sausage. Cook the sausage, stirring to break up large chunks, until it is well-browned and no pink remains, about 10 minutes. Drain the sausage and add to the bowl; discard the drippings.

continued

Add the stale bread, apples, cherries, walnuts, and sage to the bowl; stir to combine. Moisten the bread mixture with enough chicken broth to get it to hold together but not be soggy. Transfer the dressing to the prepared casserole and refrigerate if you are not baking immediately.

Bake the dressing, covered, at 350°F for 1 hour and then serve.

blasted Brussels sprouts

MAKES 12 TO 14 SERVINGS

Pity the poor Brussels sprout. A lot of people who think they dislike sprouts have only had them overcooked, mushy, and watery. This method has converted a number of my guests, because the high heat of the broiler caramelizes some of the sprouts' sugars, making them toothsome and crisp.

3 pounds Brussels sprouts

2 tablespoons olive oil

Coarse salt, such as kosher salt

Clean the Brussels sprouts by removing any damaged outer leaves and trimming away the stem end. Cut them in half from the top to the base.

Put the sprouts in a large bowl. Pour the oil over them, sprinkle with 1 teaspoon salt, and toss to make sure every sprout is dressed in oil. Tumble the sprouts onto a rimmed baking sheet.

Move an oven rack to its closest position to the broiler and heat the broiler.

Broil the Brussels sprouts, shaking the pan every couple of minutes, until they begin to char slightly, about 10 minutes. Sprinkle with additional salt to taste and serve immediately.

butternut squash with honey, sherry vinegar, and chipotles

MAKES 12 TO 14 SERVINGS

The sweet-hot-tart dressing for the squash is an unexpected treat at the Thanksgiving table, where everything else seems to taste only of butter and cream. It's certainly much more interesting than canned candied yams with marshmallows on top, although I know that dish has its fans.

3 butternut squash, about 1 pound each

1/2 cup honey

1/4 cup sherry vinegar

2 chiles from a can of chipotles in adobo, with whatever sauce clings to them

Preheat the oven to 350°F. Butter a 2-quart baking dish with a lid.

Cut the squash in half and scoop out the seeds and fibers. Cut each half into quarters; peel and then chop the squash into pieces about 1 inch square. Put the squash in the prepared baking dish.

In a food processor or blender, combine the honey, vinegar, and chiles. Process until well-blended. Pour the mixture over the squash, stirring to combine. Cover the baking dish.

Bake for 1 hour, or until squash is tender when pierced with a knife. Mash coarsely with a potato masher—you want large pieces still left—and stir to combine the juices with the puree. Serve hot.

16

On making something from nothing, or the value of kitchen wizardry

IT WAS SO VILE HERE the first week in December that going out hadn't even crossed my mind. With temperatures in the low forties, a steady, biting wind blown in from Canada, and rain, the chickens steadfastly refused to come out of their coop. Boon took one horrified look outside, turned to look at me as if to say, "Why did you do this?" and backed rapidly away from the door. Guffy rushed to the door when I opened it for Boon, sniffed the dank air, and fled back to his secret spot, hidden under the comforter on the bed. The woods were silent, as the hunters retreated to warmth and comfort. Even the small birds that normally came to my feeders had tucked themselves into the lee sides of spruces and tamaracks to hide from the relentless wind, fluffing up their feathers to provide their own down coats. It seemed more important to them to stay warm and dry than to be well-fed, at least for the day.

On Friday, my friend Mary, the poultry expert and postal carrier, trudged down the hill to deliver a large, unexpected box. Turns out my old friend Beverly in Texas surprised me with a gift of a half-dozen varieties of teas and the kind of imported confectionary treats that I hadn't seen in a long, long time. Tucked in among the other goodies were several skeins of yarn, including two lovely multicolored space-dyed skeins of sock yarn, to feed the passion we now share. That sock yarn sang softly to me.

So we stayed in. Coondog's well-seasoned firewood crackled in the woodstove, providing the company of a lively fire and companionable coziness. Boon, having recovered from his horror at the weather outside, groaned as he settled his old bones near the warmth of the stove. In the kitchen, Pippin nattered away on his play stand, terrorizing the wooden blocks on the toy hanging above it with such vigor that the attached bell rang like a frantic fire alarm. In the bedroom, the lump that was Guffy under the comforter purred so loudly I heard him as I passed through en route to the bathroom.

I was too lazy, snug with the socks I'd just cast on, trying once again to teach myself how to knit a pair from the toes up instead of from the cuff down, to wish to spend much time in the kitchen. Beverly told me this toe-up construction is easier, but I'd yet to be able to figure it out. Still, I wanted to learn the method because we hand-spinners like being able to quit at the cuff when we run out of hand-spun yarn, rather than having to poke around in our yarn stash to work the foot in something else.

I thought about what to make for dinner as I knit the stitches around the four toothpick-thin, size two double-pointed needles, paging through my mental recipe box. It seemed like every dish that sounded good required one or two key ingredients I knew I lacked. Of course, the freezer, the pantry, and the cupboards held plenty of food, but complex dishes require lots of prep and special ingredients. One idea, for example, included chipotles, but I knew I'd run out. Another idea would have been just right, but I used the last of the ground ginger the previous week in gingerbread. No, I thought, it was time to put on my kitchen wizard hat.

One of the biggest changes I've noticed in the ways that people cook over the last couple of decades has been a shift in cooks' comfort level in substituting ingredients in recipes. Doing so requires some knowledge of how a recipe works, of course, and it seems like many of today's less confident cooks lack that knowledge. Once again, I thought of my mother and praised her for the cooking skills she taught me as a child. She not only taught me the fundamentals of cooking, she taught me the fine points, too: which herbs blend neatly together to enhance a dish, how to calculate which size pot or pan is just the right size.

And she taught me how to make something from nothing. In her case, charged with providing meals for five hungry children and a hard-working husband—even when money was tight or nonexistent—being able to do so was often a necessity. Armed with a few staples and a great wealth of both imagination and knowledge, she could make dinner seem interesting even when its foundations were scanty. She did this by keeping a well-stocked pantry.

In my case, my pantry always holds the ingredients for a couple of my favorite it's-too-nasty-to-go-out dishes. These staples include a couple of cans of wild-caught salmon, double-strength homemade chicken broth, home-canned tomatoes, cooked-and-frozen beans in various hues, lentils, bacon, Colby or Cheddar, and Parmigiano-Reggiano cheese. Thanks to the chickens, I always have eggs. One area of my pantry holds the flavoring ingredients I need for Asian-style dishes—soy sauce, sesame oil, fish sauce, and so on. Another area holds specialty ingredients for Middle Eastern–influenced dishes—orange-flower water and rose water, for example. Yet another area is dedicated to Mexican specialties—chipotles in adobo, roasted diced green chiles, enchilada sauces, and so forth. I want onions—both globe and scallions—on hand at all times, together with several kinds of rice, pastas and other noodles, and potatoes. Having my pantry arranged in this way makes it easy to see what I have most of and, sometimes more importantly, what I lack.

Naturally, the spice rack is home to the families of herbs and spices I need to send a basic dish in one direction or another: oregano, basil, and rosemary for an Italian influence; thyme, marjoram, and savory for something French; cumin and chile powders for Latino dishes; ginger for both the Asian dishes and—with cinnamon, cloves, nutmeg, and allspice—for the Moroccan dishes I love.

If I haven't the ingredients on hand for egg drop soup, for example, it's easy to shift gears to *tortellini en brodo*, which is basically a bowl of chicken broth with dried filled pasta poached in it, if my pantry is well stocked. If I'm hungry for enchiladas but out of enchilada sauce, a dish of *migas*—eggs scrambled with torn corn tortillas, served with some of my homemade salsa—can scratch that itch.

But I chiefly find on crummy days that my taste runs to the simplest foods, the kind of things that people eat everyday in other cultures. These dishes typically don't require lots of special ingredients, because they are street food—meals that are easy to prepare, using simple methods, with food that is almost always on hand. Because they are so simple, having just a few ingredients on hand means I always can think up something tasty to prepare for myself. So on that crummy day, as I was knitting along, I was trying to decide between *mujadara*, the Middle Eastern lentil-and-rice bowl of comfort, and *gallo pinto*, the Costa Rican black bean and rice dish that reminds me of my friend Christian. Or would salmon loaf, so blandly American and so typically Gram Mather, be better?

Hard to say. Faced with such indecision, I decided to let my appetite perk along a bit longer, knowing it would reveal its secret hunger in its own time. As I considered that, I suddenly realized that the toe-up sock I was working on had gone terribly wrong. I was going to have to rip it out and start all over. My inner knitting geek cussed. People have been knitting socks from the toe up for centuries in every culture, literally. It can't be as difficult as my hands seemed to want to make it.

Fortunately, dinner wouldn't be difficult at all, once I figured out where my hunger was leading me. It was just a question of deciding which culture I wanted to visit that night.

ginger fried rice

MAKES 1 SERVING

This recipe is to serve one person, and is adapted from one of Mark Bittman's. If you'd like to serve more, up to four portions, just do the math and have at it. I usually have fresh ginger on hand because whenever I buy a "hand" of ginger, I use what I need and put the remainder, unpeeled, in a jar with enough sherry to cover it in the refrigerator. It keeps almost indefinitely that way, and the gingery sherry is a good addition to marinades and stir-fries. Alternatively, you can puree fresh ginger in a food processor or blender and then freeze it (see page 182). If you've done that and want to use that ginger in this recipe, stir it into the skillet along with the rice and let it cook for a minute before transferring the rice to a bowl.

2 tablespoons peanut oil or other vegetable oil

2 cloves garlic, smashed and minced

1 teaspoon minced fresh ginger

Salt

1 leek, white and light green parts only, sliced, or 3 scallions, white and tender green parts, thinly sliced

1 cup day-old cooked rice, preferably basmati, at room temperature

1 large egg

1 teaspoon toasted sesame oil

1 teaspoon soy sauce

Heat 1 tablespoon of the oil in a large, heavy skillet over medium heat. Add the garlic and ginger and cook, stirring occasionally, until crisp and brown, 3 to 5 minutes. With a slotted spoon, transfer to paper towels and salt lightly.

Decrease the heat to medium-low and add the leek or scallions. Cook, stirring occasionally, until very tender but not browned, about 10 minutes for the leek, or about 3 minutes for the scallions. Season lightly with salt.

Increase the heat to medium and add the rice. Cook, stirring well, until heated through, about 5 minutes. Season to taste with salt. Transfer to a bowl and keep warm.

In a small nonstick skillet, heat the remaining 1 tablespoon of oil over medium heat. Fry the egg, sunny-side up, until the edges are set but the yolk is still runny, 5 to 7 minutes.

Top the bowl of rice with the egg and drizzle with the sesame oil and soy sauce. Sprinkle the crisped garlic and ginger over everything and serve. Mixing the fried egg with the hot rice will create a rich, yet delicate sauce.

salmon loaf

If you keep a couple of cans of red or pink salmon stashed in the cupboard, you almost always have the rest of the ingredients you need on hand to make salmon loaf. I like the leftovers in sandwiches. Sometimes I make salmon patties instead of a loaf by shaping the salmon mixture into $1/4$-cup patties. Chilling the patties, covered with plastic wrap, for an hour or so before you cook them helps them hold their shape better. Cook the patties in a non-stick or cast-iron skillet over medium heat with $1/8$ inch of oil until they are browned on both sides.

---

3 slices whole wheat bread, crusts removed

2 (14³/₄-ounce) cans red or pink salmon, drained

1 onion, minced

2 large eggs

2 tablespoons capers, drained (optional)

$1/2$ teaspoon dried dill

$1/2$ teaspoon salt

$1/4$ teaspoon freshly ground black pepper

Preheat the oven to 375°F. Grease a 9 by 5-inch loaf pan by spraying it with vegetable cooking spray.

Tear the bread into pieces and whiz the pieces in a food processor or blender to make coarse crumbs.

Using a fork or your hands, combine the salmon, onion, bread crumbs, eggs, capers, dill, salt, and pepper in a mixing bowl. Pack the mixture into the prepared loaf pan.

Bake, uncovered, for 1¹/₄ hours, or until a skewer or knife inserted in the middle comes out clean. If the loaf seems to be browning too quickly, cover it lightly with aluminum foil toward the end of the cooking time.

Let the loaf rest in the pan for 10 minutes. Turn out loaf onto a serving platter and let cool 10 minutes longer before serving.

spaghetti alla carbonara

MAKES 2 SERVINGS

Because I almost always have some of Geukes's delicious smoked bacon on hand, whether in strips or as ends and pieces, I know this dish is perennially a possibility. The hot bacon drippings and the heat of the cooked pasta cook the egg, turning it into a silky sauce for the pasta. Many carbonara dishes call for a lick of heavy cream, but that seems like gilding the lily to me, so I've never made it that way. I keep portions small for this dish because it is rich; it wants a big salad, dressed with a bright, tart vinaigrette, alongside.

4 strips bacon

1 large egg, at room temperature

$^1/_2$ cup freshly grated Parmigiano-Reggiano cheese, plus more for serving

8 ounces spaghetti, spaghettini, or linguine

Salt and freshly ground black pepper

Cook the bacon in a large, heavy skillet over medium heat, turning frequently, until it is well browned and crisp, 8 to 10 minutes. Remove the bacon from the skillet, reserving the drippings and keeping them warm; drain the bacon briefly on a paper towel and chop. Set the bacon aside.

In a small bowl, combine the egg and cheese with a fork. Beat until the mixture is well combined.

Cook the pasta according to package directions, omitting any fat and salt. Drain the pasta and, working quickly, transfer the pasta to a large bowl. Stir in 1 tablespoon of the warm bacon drippings; toss to combine. Stir in the egg mixture and toss until well combined; sprinkle with a bit of salt—the bacon may provide enough salt—and plenty of pepper. Toss again to combine.

Divide the spaghetti between two bowls. Scatter half the chopped bacon over the top of each bowl. Garnish with additional grated cheese and serve.

cheese soufflé with greens

MAKES 4 SERVINGS

Soufflés are easier to make than their reputation might lead you to believe, and they are a classic French way to use up odd bits of meat, cheese, or vegetables leftover from other dishes. Because of their finicky reputation, soufflés impress everyone when you pull one, puffed and golden, from the oven. They are a little light as an entrée by themselves, however, so I usually serve this as a second course after a bowl of hearty soup. Doing so solves another problem with soufflés: they can't wait. Serving soup first "captures" the guests and keeps them at the table. Slide the soufflé into the oven just before you serve the soup, and it will be ready about the time you finish and have removed the soup bowls from the table.

$1/2$ cup grated Parmesan cheese or fine breadcrumbs, for the baking dish

$1/4$ cup ($1/2$ stick) salted butter

$1/4$ cup all-purpose flour

2 cups whole milk

4 large eggs, separated, at room temperature

1 cup shredded sharp Colby or Cheddar cheese

1 cup chopped cooked greens, such as kale, collards, mustard greens, or turnip greens

$1/2$ teaspoon salt

Freshly ground black pepper

$1/4$ teaspoon grated nutmeg

Preheat the oven to 350°F. Butter a 2-quart baking dish, then dust the inside with bread crumbs or grated Parmesan cheese. Fashion a collar for the baking dish from aluminum foil; affix it to the baking dish (I use a paper clip to secure the ends, and just crimp the bottom edge around the baking dish) and butter it and dust the inside of it, too, with bread crumbs or grated cheese. Set aside.

In a small saucepan over medium heat, melt the butter. Whisk in the flour. Cook, stirring frequently, until the mixture starts to just color to a very pale blondish brown, about 2 minutes. Stir in $1/2$ cup of the milk; whisk constantly until the mixture is smooth. Whisk in the remaining milk, bring to a simmer, and cook, stirring constantly, until the sauce is smooth and thick, about 5 minutes.

Decrease the heat to low. Place the egg yolks in a bowl. Whisk a small amount, perhaps a 1/4 cup, of the hot milk mixture into the egg yolks, then add the yolk mixture into the milk mixture in the saucepan, whisking well. (You are "tempering" the egg yolks so they won't curdle in the sauce.) Stir in the cheese; continue to cook, stirring occasionally, until the cheese is melted. Stir in the greens. Season with the salt, pepper to taste, and the nutmeg. Keep the mixture over low heat while you whip the egg whites.

Using a balloon whisk or hand mixer, in a bowl, beat the whites to stiff peaks that hold their shape when you lift the whisk or beater. Add about one-quarter of the milk–egg yolk mixture to the beaten whites and, with a rubber spatula, fold to combine using a scooping motion; turn the bowl one-quarter turn after each stroke. You don't want to mix so thoroughly that you remove all the air that you just troubled yourself to beat into the egg whites. This should take three to five strokes.

Add the remaining milk–egg yolk mixture to the beaten egg whites and fold to combine. It's okay if white streaks remain; you simply want to incorporate the two mixtures with a few quick licks. Pour the mixture into the prepared baking dish.

Bake for 30 to 35 minutes, or until the soufflé is puffed and golden brown. Remove the collar and serve immediately. Use the tines of two forks, held back to back, to split the soufflé into serving portions without deflating it, inserting the forks and then pulling them gently apart. Use a spoon to scoop the portions out.

gallo pinto

MAKES 2 SERVINGS

When I worked at the *Chicago Tribune*, I was lucky enough to take a Berlitz Spanish class with a charming Costa Rican named Christian. He told us about *gallo pinto*, the national dish of Costa Rica. Its name means "spotted rooster" in Spanish, a reference to the black beans dotting the white rice. It's quick and delicious, and good for breakfast, lunch, or dinner. You can make this a little heartier by serving a fried egg atop each portion—in that case, Christian said, it's *gallo pinto casada* or "married gallo pinto." The Costa Ricans like a savory vegetable-based sauce called Salsa Lizano with this; I order it online and a bottle keeps forever at room temperature. If you don't have it, substitute A.1. Steak Sauce, although the flavor will be different.

3 tablespoons olive oil

1 onion, diced

2 cloves garlic, smashed and minced

1/2 green or red bell pepper, diced (optional)

2 cups cooked long-grain rice

2 cups cooked black beans

Salt

Salsa Lizano or A.1. Steak Sauce

1/4 cup chopped fresh cilantro

Fried egg (optional)

Heat the oil in a large, heavy skillet over medium heat. Add the onion, garlic, and pepper; cook, stirring frequently, until the onion is golden and translucent, about 10 minutes.

Stir in the rice and beans; continue to cook, stirring frequently, until the mixture is heated through, about 5 minutes. If it begins to stick, add just a little water.

Season to taste with salt and Salsa Lizano; the dish should be quite brown, so be generous. Remove from the heat. Stir in the cilantro. Serve immediately, with or without a fried egg on top.

mujadara

MAKES 2 TO 4 SERVINGS

Variations of this simple, earthy lentil-and-rice dish are found throughout the Middle East. Every version relies on slow, deep caramelization of the onions, so take your time on that step. The onions should be dark, dark brown; it's okay if some are even burned a little. Serve with a salad of chopped romaine dressed with olive oil and lemon juice and offer plain yogurt, drained to thicken (see page 93), as a garnish.

◆━●━━◆━●━━◆━●━━◆━●━━◆━●━━◆━●━━◆━●━━◆━●━━◆━●━━◆━●━━◆

$^1/_4$ cup olive oil

2 large onions (about $1^1/_2$ pounds), thinly sliced

1 teaspoon sugar

1 teaspoon ground cumin

1 cup brown or green lentils

$^1/_2$ cup basmati rice

1 teaspoon salt

Chopped fresh flat-leaf parsley, for garnish (optional)

Heat the oil in a large, heavy skillet over medium heat. Add the onions, sugar, and cumin, and cook, stirring occasionally, until the onions are deeply caramelized, 30 to 60 minutes. Don't try to rush this step.

Meanwhile, check the lentils for bits of dirt or stone. Wash them in a sieve, then put the lentils in a saucepan, add water to cover by an inch, and bring to a boil over medium-high heat. Decrease the heat to a simmer, cover the saucepan, and cook, undisturbed, for 20 minutes, or until the lentils are tender but still hold their shape. Drain the lentils and set them aside.

When the onions are ready, stir in the rice. Add the cooked lentils, 2 cups water, and the salt. Stir to mix well and bring to a boil. Decrease the heat to keep the liquid at a slow simmer, cover, and cook for about 20 minutes. Remove the lid and give the mixture a gentle stir. If there is still some liquid visible, replace the lid, and keep cooking until the liquid is fully absorbed. If there is no obvious liquid, take a taste. If the rice is tender, the *mujadara* is ready. If the rice is not yet ready, add another splash of water, replace the lid, and cook until the liquid is absorbed and the rice is cooked. The *mujadara* is ready to eat when the rice is tender and there is no liquid left in the pan.

Scatter chopped parsley over each serving.

WINTER

17

On chilly winds and homey contentment

I SPENT MOST OF THE WEEK after Thanksgiving getting the house ready for winter, and it proved to be just in the nick of time. The prevailing wind switched from west to northwest, and changed its nature from balmy breeze to cruel nose-nipper. With the leaves off all the trees, I could see the deer come down to drink across the lake at Circle Pines's beach, picking their way daintily with their clever small hooves. The lake wasn't frozen yet, but its leaden waters echoed the overcast sky. Everything was damp and gray in the moment between fall's rich color and winter's severe elegance.

We'd had some spitting snows, but the flakes were small and mingy and did not stick. It rained a lot, too, which meant that Wally and his wondrous-if-noisy leaf blower had been unable to tidy things up. I'd done some desultory raking, although the shin-deep carpet of leaves that covered my yard from the top of the hill down to the lake defeated me. So I concentrated my efforts on picking up sticks to use as kindling, and there were armload after armload of them.

Winterizing the house had been enough work, anyway.

I uprooted the dead geraniums from the flower boxes and planters and covered their sphagnum moss with a few pine boughs, to provide a bit of color at the kitchen window and to keep the moss from blowing away. The last of the tattered tender herbs went onto the compost heap, and the dish gardens and planters from around the yard went into the shed. On the deck, the Adirondack chairs and their table went under a tarp, as did the dining table and chairs, though the latter will probably need to be replaced next spring.

The collection of candles, little oil lamps, and mosquito repellers moved downstairs, and the extra chairs were collapsed and leaned against the side of the house.

The hummingbird feeders came down, to be washed and stored in the basement, replaced by the hanging suet feeders and a cool little stick-on tray feeder that I attached at the kitchen window overlooking the back patio. I knew the pestilential squirrels would soon discover it and look me in the eye as they perched there, stealing all the best bits meant for the birds. But squirrels have to eat too, I guessed.

The wood pile serves as a windbreak for the chicken yard, but I also took the precaution of banking a couple of bales of straw against the outside of the coop, cleaned its inside, and laid down a thick layer of fresh straw for the gals to snuggle into when the winds howl.

The windows all needed to be washed, inside and out, before I put up the heat-shrink plastic film that conserves heat in the house and cuts down on drafts. That took me two long days, but I wanted the windows clear and clean to admit as much light as possible.

I spent a while trimming the wick and inspecting the mantle and chimney of the Aladdin kerosene lamp John gave me for my birthday. The lamp had certainly come in handy, as late storms caused the power to blink out, but my friendly feelings toward it came from the heat it produced as much as its soft and beautiful light. The first thing I did on chilly mornings was light the Aladdin. Even on its lowest setting, it warmed the kitchen by ten degrees in about thirty minutes, so by the time the fire was built in the woodstove and I was ready for coffee, the kitchen felt cozy.

Once everything had been taken care of, I settled down to think about which comfort food dishes would suit me best in the next few days.

There's plenty of evidence to show that we humans have a kind of hibernation urge as winter draws in, although our clock-ruled lives and indoor jobs don't acknowledge it. One reason why we suddenly want the carbohydrate-heavy pleasures of mashed potatoes and big bowls of pasta is that they lull us into sleepiness, and sleep is what we all want to do at this time of year.

I think it's best to frankly acknowledge those seasonal appetites and lean into them rather than fight them. While I won't permit myself huge portions and heavy desserts, I do change my cooking style to meet the season head-on, because I think the changing weather demands something different from our bodies than summer's heat insisted upon. So summer's speedy sautés and flash grillings gave way to long-simmered soups and brothy braises. Nutrition experts tell us, again and again, that a calorie is a calorie, that it doesn't matter whether the calories come from a steamed chicken breast and vegetables or a fast-food hamburger (their complaint with the burger is that it is not "nutrition-dense," and is full of empty calories). I think, though, that this position fails to acknowledge the role that emotion plays in our appetites. I remain unconvinced that a bowl of salad provides the same comfort on a crummy wet day that a bowl of stew does.

I guess we all define "comfort food" a little differently, though. For me, the definition involves the dishes that my mother cooked when I was a kid, but she cooked some dishes that only lately have I come to realize never appeared on the tables of my friends' homes. They ate meatloaf, pot roast, and spaghetti with ground beef in red sauce. We ate oxtail stew, steak-and-kidney pie, and braised beef short ribs. I don't mean to suggest that one is better than the other, mind you. I mean to say that the foods you ate as a child will be the ones that comfort you as an adult. If you're raising children now, you might pause for a moment to consider that. Are your children going to become adults who think chicken McNuggets are the most comforting thing in the world?

I can still remember arriving home from high school one day, drenched to the skin by a nasty November rain, to find my mother, hand on hip, standing at the stove browning oxtails. "Oxtail stew!" I said gleefully, because the rich, thick stew is one of my favorites. "Go hop in a hot bath," my mother said, "and get warmed up. But make it a quick one. I need you to peel the potatoes and carrots." A bit later, swathed in warm, dry clothes, I was happy to lend her a hand and watched with interest as she taught me how to make the dish. Someone once asked me if I resented helping my mother in the kitchen when I was growing up. The question perplexed me. Its underlying assumption is that cooking is unpleasant. Why on earth would I resent learning a new skill? Even as a kid, I knew that, in my family at least, cooking wasn't an odious chore. It was fun, and led to something good to share with others.

Comfort food for me also tends to mean seasoning with a heavier hand, and reaching for the warm spices of allspice, nutmeg, ginger, cinnamon, and cloves more frequently. I'm much more likely to bake a batch of gingerbread than one of cookies in early winter, for example, because I not only want the gingerbread, I want the warming scent of its spices to fill my home. The aroma will linger for days.

Having done all the needful things to ready the house for the coming winter, I had time to relax, to reach for my knitting needles or spinning wheel or that book I'd been meaning to dive into. No longer busy with the work of putting food by, I could settle in and enjoy the leisure I earned in those long summer days of hissing kettles and canning jars. By recalibrating my life to a more natural rhythm, I found an instinctive understanding of the old agrarian ways, when winters were slower and more peaceful. Winter was the season of reflection, I had come to see.

So come, December snows, and blow, December winds. I fear you no more.

beef and onions braised in beer

MAKES 6 TO 8 SERVINGS

This and the next two recipes use essentially the same ingredients and methods, but taste remarkably different. This is a humbler version of the classic Belgian dish *carbonnade à la flamande,* and the quality of the stew depends on using good beer. I buy a growler of good dark beer from my local brew pub when I have it in mind to make this dish. If you make with a typical American pilsner-style beer, it will be insipid and unsatisfying. If you don't have a brew pub nearby, seek out Guinness Stout or another strong, dark beer. Like most braised dishes, it's good the first day and even better the second.

2 tablespoons olive oil, plus more as needed

3 pounds onions, halved lengthwise and sliced lengthwise 1/4 inch thick

1 (41/2- to 5-pound) boneless beef chuck roast

Salt and freshly ground black pepper

1 bay leaf

1 teaspoon dry thyme, crumbled

2 (12-ounce) bottles dark beer

2 tablespoons red wine vinegar

2 to 4 tablespoons brown sugar

1/4 cup cornstarch

1/4 cup cold water

Hot cooked wide egg noodles, drained and buttered, for serving

Preheat the oven to 350°F.

Heat the oil in a large, heavy skillet over medium heat. Add the onions and cook, stirring, until onions are golden, about 10 minutes. Transfer the onions with a slotted spoon to a large Dutch oven or casserole with a tight-fitting lid.

Trim all visible fat and gristle from the chuck roast, then cut it into 3-inch-long strips about 1 inch wide by 1/2 inch thick, or into 1-inch cubes. Brown the beef in the same skillet on all sides, adding more oil if needed. Transfer the beef to the Dutch oven. Season the beef and onions with a sprinkling of salt and pepper.

continued

Break the bay leaf in half and tuck the halves into the beef-onion mixture. Scatter the crumbled thyme over the beef and onions. Pour the beer over the beef and onions. Cover the Dutch oven.

Bake until the beef is very tender, 3 to 3½ hours. Put the Dutch oven on the stove top and, over low heat, stir in the vinegar and 2 tablespoons of the brown sugar. Taste the sauce; you may want to add more brown sugar. The flavor should not be sweet, but instead a balance of sweet and tangy.

Increase the heat to medium-high. In a small bowl, dissolve the cornstarch in the water; stir this into the beef-onion mixture and bring just to a boil. Decrease the heat and simmer, stirring constantly, until the sauce thickens, 3 to 5 minutes.

Remove the bay leaf halves. Serve hot over the buttered noodles.

oxtail stew

MAKES 4 SERVINGS

For many years, oxtails were hard to find, and expensive when you could find them. Now I see them regularly in even the smallest markets, and they are quite inexpensive at Geukes Market. If you've never cooked them, this recipe is an excellent way to start. The large amount of bone lends a silky richness to the stew that can't be matched by using chunks of beef. Like all stews, this is good the day you make it, but it's really best if you can refrigerate it overnight and reheat to serve the next day.

1 cup all-purpose flour

Salt and freshly ground black pepper

3 pounds oxtails

2 tablespoons olive oil

2 cloves garlic, smashed and minced

1 large onion, halved lengthwise and sliced lengthwise 1/4 inch thick

1/2 cup red wine

2 cups diced tomatoes with juice

1 cup beef broth

2 bay leaves

1 teaspoon dried thyme, crumbled

1/2 teaspoon dried rosemary, crumbled

1 pound carrots, peeled and chopped into large chunks

3 pounds potatoes, peeled and chopped into large chunks

Put the flour in a heavy-duty zip-top bag and season it generously with salt and pepper. Working in batches, add the oxtails to the bag and shake to coat thoroughly with flour on all sides. Transfer the floured oxtails to a plate. Discard the flour.

Heat the oil in a large stockpot or Dutch oven over medium-high heat. Working in batches, add the oxtails and brown on all sides, about 3 minutes per side. Transfer the oxtails to a plate and set aside.

Add the garlic and onion to the stockpot and cook, stirring frequently, until the onion is softened and translucent, about 5 minutes. Add the wine

continued

and stir to scrape up any browned bits. Cook until the wine has almost all evaporated, about 5 minutes.

Return the oxtails to the pot. Add the tomatoes and enough beef broth to cover. Break the bay leaves in half and tuck them into the pot. Bring to a boil, decrease the heat to a simmer, cover, and cook for 2 to 2^1/$_2$ hours, or until the meat is nearly tender.

Add the carrots and potatoes. Cover and simmer for 45 to 60 minutes longer, until the meat is tender and the vegetables are cooked through. Remove the bay leaves and serve immediately.

braised beef short ribs

MAKES 6 TO 8 SERVINGS

Short ribs are almost always inexpensive, so they are a boon to the budget-minded cook. While delicious, they are very fatty, so if possible, plan to cook this dish and refrigerate it overnight so you can skim off the fat before reheating. You may find it too rich if you don't.

1/2 cup plus 3 tablespoons all-purpose flour

Salt and freshly ground black pepper

3 pounds beef short ribs

2 tablespoons vegetable oil

2 onions, halved lengthwise and sliced lengthwise 1/4 inch thick

2 cloves garlic, smashed and minced

1/2 cup dry red wine

2 cups canned diced tomatoes with juice or crushed tomatoes

2 cups beef broth

1 bay leaf

4 potatoes, peeled and cubed

4 carrots, peeled and chopped

Put 1/2 cup of the flour in a heavy-duty zip-top plastic bag and season generously with salt and pepper. Working in batches, add the short ribs and shake to flour completely. Transfer the floured short ribs to a plate. Discard the flour.

Heat the oil in a large stockpot or Dutch oven over medium-high heat. Working in batches, add the beef and brown well on all sides. Transfer the short ribs to a plate and set aside.

Add the onions and garlic to the pot. Cook, stirring, until the onions are softened and translucent, about 5 minutes. Add the wine and cook, stirring to scrape up any browned bits. Cook until the wine has almost all evaporated, about 5 minutes.

Return the short ribs to the pot. Add the tomatoes, broth, and bay leaf. Bring to a boil, cover, and decrease the heat to a simmer, cover, and cook for 1 1/2 to 2 hours, or until the meat is falling off the bone.

continued

Add the potatoes and carrots. Cover and simmer for 30 to 60 minutes longer, until the vegetables are tender. Transfer the meat and vegetables to a serving platter, cover, and keep warm.

You should have about 2 cups of liquid remaining in the pot. In a small bowl, dissolve the remaining 3 tablespoons flour in 3 tablespoons water. Add this to the pot and bring to a boil over medium-high heat. Decrease the heat and simmer, stirring constantly, until thickened. Remove the bay leaf. Pass the gravy at the table.

wolverine gingerbread

MAKES 1 LOAF

Years ago, I read Marion Cunningham's recipe for Moosehead Gingerbread, lively with dry mustard and pepper as well as the more usual spices, and fell in love with it immediately. I like a slice for breakfast, toasted and spread with butter or yogurt cheese. Over the years, I've tinkered with the recipe, trying out different additions to vary the heat that the mustard and black pepper contribute. Sorghum syrup is made locally here in Michigan, but substitute molasses, preferably blackstrap, if you can't find it. This is my current version.

+-+

1/2 cup (1 stick) salted butter, at room temperature

1/2 cup firmly packed dark brown sugar

2 large eggs

1 cup sorghum syrup

2 1/2 cups all-purpose flour

2 teaspoons baking soda

1/2 teaspoon salt

1 tablespoon unsweetened cocoa powder

2 teaspoons ground ginger

1 teaspoon ground cinnamon

1 teaspoon ground red pepper (cayenne)

1 teaspoon ground cloves

1 cup hot strong brewed coffee

Preheat the oven to 350°F. Generously butter a 9 by 5-inch loaf pan. Lay a sheet of parchment paper into the pan so that it overhangs the long sides.

In the bowl of a stand mixer or a large bowl with a hand mixer, beat the butter and brown sugar until very light and fluffy, about 3 minutes. Add the eggs, one at a time, beating after each addition. Beat in the sorghum syrup.

Sift together the flour, baking soda, salt, cocoa, ginger, cinnamon, red pepper, and cloves onto a piece of waxed paper. Add to the sorghum mixture alternately with the hot coffee, ending with the dry ingredients. Mix thoroughly. Pour into the prepared loaf pan.

Bake for 45 to 60 minutes, until a tester inserted at the center comes out with only a crumb or two adhering. Let cool on a wire rack for 10 minutes, then turn out of the pan and let cool completely.

18

On blizzards and dried beans

A MAJOR STORM BLEW THROUGH in late December, with sleety rain starting Monday, heavy snow starting Tuesday night that continued through Thursday, and a final icing of snow on Friday. We already had snow on the ground, but it hadn't come all at once. It was the first big storm for the chickens, and I was worried about them.

Since the old furnace (original to the house and dating from the 1940s) started acting up last spring, I had fretted about how the little woodstove John helped me install would do in keeping the house warm and safe for the animals and me should the furnace fail. Was it big enough to heat the house? Would its warmth be enough to keep the pipes from freezing? The coming storm would test its mettle as well as my own.

I spent Tuesday carrying in armload after armload of wood, until the floor beneath the big picture window in the living room was stacked sill high from one end of the window to the other with wood of all sizes. To get the "splits," as Coondog calls them, the smaller pieces that are best for firing the stove in the morning on the previous night's embers, I used a small maul and a diamond-shaped wedge to break big pieces of wood into smaller ones. Before long, the work warmed me enough that my heavy cap and double-thick mittens were too much. I labored with a bare head and hands, my hair damp with sweat, despite temperatures below freezing. I was grateful for the lull between sleety rain and heavy snow that let me get the wood in.

Boon and Guffy kept me company at the woodpile, the dog alert for the intruders he apparently feared may arrive at any moment, the kitten capering in the first snow he'd ever seen, snow so deep it nearly covered him. They watched with curiosity as I checked and filled the bird feeders, because I knew that the small wild things, too, counted on me for sustenance against the storm. Both the dog and the cat eagerly returned to the house when the work was done and settled into twitching dreams near the woodstove. When I closed the kitchen door for the final time late Tuesday afternoon, Pippin, hanging upside down on his spiral of rope suspended from the kitchen ceiling, said, "You stay!"

"Gladly," I said, leaning in to plant a kiss on his beak. "I'm not going anywhere now."

The snow began Tuesday just as night fell.

And so we all settled in to wait out the storm. The last thing I did before turning in on Tuesday night was to put a couple of cups of dried navy beans to soak.

When I woke Wednesday morning, the snow lay thick and deep on the ground, and it was easy to see that it would snow heavily all day long. My legs, hips, and butt ached from dozens of trips up and down the steps to the woodpile the day before. My arms and shoulders, unused to swinging the heavy maul, burned pleasurably to remind me that they'd worked hard, too. Checking on the chickens, I found them happy and content, with plenty of unfrozen water and lots of feed. Late Wednesday afternoon, I shoveled the snow from the steps, knowing I'd have to do it again the next day, and used my snowshoes to tramp a path up my hillside driveway from my steps up to the mailbox. I knew the car, parked at the bottom of the hill in snow now topping its hubcaps, wouldn't go anywhere until the storm passed.

The storm raged outside, the wind whipping snow past my windows so furiously that I sometimes could not see the neighbors' houses. A pot of bean soup, rich with Don Geukes's smoky ham hocks and some of Wally's onions and carrots, and fragrant with summer savory from my dish garden, filled the house with a lovely aroma. When the power blinked off, just as I feared it might, I simply moved the soup pot to the top of the woodstove to continue cooking and settled into the little rocker beside the stove with a book. When the power was restored, perhaps two hours later, the simmering soup hadn't missed a beat. A bowl of thick, sturdy soup, sided by a couple of pavers of fresh-baked bread and butter, made a fine supper on such a blustery night.

As a true daughter of Michigan, I'm a bean lover. One could argue that beans built Michigan: not only in the growing of the crops, but in their eating. Michigan's earliest settlers and the woodsmen who logged off the land saw beans on the table almost every day, sometimes at all three meals. Michigan is second only to North Dakota in dried-bean production, averaging 14 percent of the country's total from 2006 to 2008, according to the USDA. While most of the Wolverine State's crop is black beans and navy beans, Michigan farmers also grow cranberry, kidney, small red, and pinto beans. In fact, many years ago, a New Orleans chef told me that there would be no red beans and rice— one of the Big Easy's iconic dishes—without Michigan's small red beans.

These days, Americans eat just under six and a half pounds of dried beans per person a year, with pintos first at about two and three-quarters pound per person and navy beans second, at just under a pound. At least that's what the USDA reported for 2006. That definitely seems low to me; I'm sure I eat more than that each year. My mom loved bean soup, and from fall to spring, we had some kind of bean soup for dinner about once a week. She almost always cooked dried beans, although I sometimes use canned or frozen beans as a time-saver. Whenever I cook dried beans, I double the batch and freeze half of the beans in recipe-sized containers.

But dried beans are easy to cook and don't even need to be soaked if you have the time to simmer them. My recipes don't call for presoaking the beans, because I have the luxury of working from home and can supervise their cooking. However, presoaking will save an hour or more in the beans' cooking time, which can make it possible for you to have beans from scratch after work. If you don't have time to cook them unsoaked, "speed soak" them by covering the beans with water up to the depth of your index finger's second knuckle, bringing them to a boil, cooking covered for ten minutes, and then removing the pot from heat and letting the beans stand for an hour. Then drain, rinse, and begin your recipe with fresh water. Or, just soak the beans in cold water overnight, draining and rinsing before you begin to cook. You can also speed up the cooking of dried beans by using a pressure cooker. Be sure you follow the instructions, though; dried beans create a lot of foam in the pressure cooker, so you mustn't overload it.

Most of the sugars in the beans that give some people tummy problems— oligosaccharides, to be scientific—vanish down the drain with the soaking water. Fiber-rich beans can also create issues for those who don't eat a high-fiber diet. The cure for that? Eat more beans. Your digestive system will adapt quickly. In fact, if beans give you trouble, it's a telltale sign that you're not eating as much fiber as you should.

Cover them while they cook if you want them to be creamy and mashable; leave them uncovered while they cook if you want them to stay whole, adding more boiling water to the beans as needed. If your water is very hard, as mine is, the beans may never get truly soft; for that reason, I usually use filtered water to cook beans. Tomatoes' acidity prevents beans from softening, and I generally salt toward the end of cooking time.

A pound of dried beans cooks into about six cups, which should serve six to eight in a side dish such as baked beans, or in a salad. In soup, I usually figure two pounds to serve that many, because there's little else in the soup to stretch the beans' volume.

Beans are so nutritious and so cheap that I could eat them every day for a month and eat incredibly well, without boredom and with excellent nutrition. They're high in protein, fiber, and lots of other good nutrients. Almost every culture has good bean recipes, because beans grow easily in most locales, and a pot of beans will fill a lot of bellies cheaply and well. And for me, because of the good bean soups I ate at my mother's table growing up, nothing says safety like a steaming bowl of beans. The soup I ate for supper during the blizzard soothed me, both my belly and my spirit, as the storm howled around the eaves.

On Saturday, the skies cleared and the sun emerged for a while, making diamonds dance on the brilliant snow. More than half the wood I'd carried into the house against the storm remained. I opened the door of the chicken coop, and the chickens emerged, chattering madly, into the sun and snow, glad to get out after two days of being literally cooped up. This time, when I stepped into the snowshoes, it was for the sheer pleasure of being outside. Boon and I set out for the old road that winds up the hillside, no longer open to traffic. I let him set the pace, tramping behind him for half an hour or so, but we turned back when his old injured knee had enough and he began to limp. Still, he, too, was glad to be uncooped, and he danced and wriggled with joy as we returned to the house.

We had weathered our first serious storm without problems. The little woodstove proved trusty and reliable, keeping all of us, as well as the pipes, snugly warm. I knew that my mind had shifted, once and for all, from the right-now mentality I'd had formerly to the be-prepared attitude I had so long wanted to acquire. And I knew at last that I could care for myself—and all those who depend on me—in the worst that winter had to offer, through the very hardest times.

frijoles de olla

MAKES 6 TO 8 SERVINGS

"Pot beans," as *frijoles de olla* translates into English, are incredibly versatile. A pot of stew-y beans on hand—whether frozen or just cooked—can turn into homemade refried beans, form the foundation of a chili, be mashed into a base for bean dip, or used to fill burritos, the Mexican equivalent of a peanut butter-and-jelly sandwich. I like a big bowl of these hot from the pot, served with cornbread or warmed tortillas and long-cooked pot greens on the side. Remember some chopped onion to garnish the beans.

1 pound (about 2¹/₂ cups) dried beans (red, navy, pinto, black, adzuki, speckled—what have you)

2 tablespoons bacon drippings

1 onion, chopped, plus more for serving (optional)

2 cloves garlic, smashed and minced

1 bay leaf, broken in half

Boiling water, as needed

Salt

Salsa, to serve (optional)

Sort the beans by spilling them onto a baking sheet and removing any debris and broken beans. Transfer the beans to a colander and rinse them under cold running water.

Pour the beans into a deep, heavy 4- to 6-quart pot, such as a cast-iron Dutch oven, with a lid. Add 10 cups cold water, then remove any beans that float. Add the bacon drippings, onion, garlic, and bay leaf. Bring the beans to a rolling boil over high heat, then decrease the heat to low so the beans are at a very gentle simmer. Cover the pot, leaving the lid a bit ajar, and cook the beans until they are thoroughly tender, about 2 hours. Add boiling water to the pot as needed to keep the level of the liquid covering the beans at its starting level.

When the beans are completely tender, season with salt to taste and cook for 15 minutes longer. Remove the bay leaf. Eat as is, with salsa and additional chopped onion, or continue to the recipe opposite for refried beans.

REFRIED BEANS

¹/₄ cup bacon drippings or vegetable oil

Salt

Crumbled goat cheese, yogurt cheese, freshly chopped onion, and salsa, for serving

To make refried beans, drain the beans in a colander placed over a bowl to catch the broth. Heat the bacon drippings in a large, heavy skillet over medium heat. Add the drained beans, a couple of a spoon-fuls at a time, mashing each addition of beans with a wooden spoon or, my preference, a potato masher. When all the beans are mashed, stir in enough broth to give the beans the consistency of mashed potatoes—creamy, but with some larger bits. Taste and add salt if necessary. Serve with crumbled goat cheese, or a dollop of yogurt cheese, freshly chopped onion, and salsa, or use as a filling for burritos or enchiladas or as a bean dip.

red beans and rice

MAKES 6 SERVINGS

I never eat red beans and rice without remembering a wonderful, long-lost bar-restaurant in Jackson, Mississippi named George Street Grocery. It was like a community living room, and I could always count on finding friends within. The novelist John Grisham was a regular there back when he was still a young Mississippi lawyer serving as a state representative, before he became famous. Red beans and rice was a staple on George Street's menu, and with a generous serving of pan-grilled smoked sausage, bread and butter, and a couple of crisp scallions, it made a satisfying and inexpensive supper. It still does.

BEANS

1 pound dried small red beans

4 ounces bacon or smoked ham, chopped, or 1 smoked ham hock

Vegetable oil, if needed

1 onion, diced

2 cloves garlic, smashed and minced

6 cups chicken broth

2 teaspoons dried thyme, crumbled

1 teaspoon dried oregano, crumbled

1 bay leaf, broken in half

Salt

TO SERVE

1¹/₂ pounds smoked sausage, such as kielbasa or andouille

6 cups hot cooked white rice

1 bunch scallions, trimmed, white and tender green parts

Warm bread and butter

Hot sauce

Sort the beans by spilling them onto a baking sheet and removing any debris and broken beans. Transfer the beans to a colander and rinse the beans under cold running water. Set the beans aside.

Heat a deep, heavy 4- to 6-quart pot with a lid, such as a cast-iron Dutch oven, over medium heat. Add the bacon or ham and cook to render the fat, about 10 minutes; you may need to add a bit of additional oil if the ham is lean or if you use a ham hock—you want about 3 tablespoons of fat in all.

(If using a ham hock, you'll be adding it a little later.) Remove the bacon or ham and reserve.

Add the onion and cook, stirring frequently, until golden and tender, about 10 minutes. Add the garlic and cook for 1 to 2 minutes longer, until the garlic is golden and fragrant.

Add the rinsed beans and chicken broth to the pot. Add the ham hock here, if that's what you're using. Bring to a rolling boil, then decrease the heat to keep the beans at a simmer. Add the reserved bacon or ham, thyme, oregano, and bay leaf. Cover the pot, leaving the lid slightly ajar, and cook, stirring occasionally, until beans are completely tender, about 2 hours. Remove the bay leaf halves.

Scoop about half of the beans out of the pot and drain in a colander set over a bowl to catch the broth. Mash the drained beans coarsely with a potato masher or wooden spoon, then return the beans and any broth from them to the pot. You should have a thick, gravy-like base studded with tender whole beans. If the mixture seems too thin or wet to suit you, continue to cook the beans, uncovered, stirring occasionally, until its consistency pleases you. Season to taste with salt. Keep warm.

To serve, heat a large, heavy skillet over medium-high heat. Cut the smoked sausage into six serving-sized lengths, then split each piece in half lengthwise. Lay the sausage, cut side down, in the skillet. Turn and cook for an additional 3 minutes. Remove the sausage from the skillet.

Place a cup of cooked rice on each plate or in a deep bowl. Ladle about a cup of the bean mixture over each portion. Garnish each serving with two pieces of sausage. Serve the scallions on the side, with warm bread and butter, and hot sauce to add as desired.

don marquis's baked beans

MAKES ABOUT 6 SERVINGS AS A MAIN DISH

Don Marquis (1878–1937) was a newspaper columnist for the *New York Sun*. Poet, playwright, and novelist, his Archy and Mehitabel poems are perhaps his best-known works. In *The Almost Perfect State*, Marquis wrote a paean to the baked bean. His recipe goes on for several pages and is a wonderful read; it's easy to find in an Internet search. In the name of contemporary recipe style, I've redrafted it. I've included the baking soda he says to use in soaking the beans—some old-time cooks thought it helped the beans soften in cooking, others say it gives a soapy flavor to the beans. You may omit it if you wish.

1 pound small white beans

3 tablespoons baking soda

1 pound salt pork, sliced

1 bay leaf

1 cup dark sulphured molasses

1/2 onion, sliced

2 tablespoons Dijon-style mustard

Freshly ground black pepper

Boiling water, if needed

Lemon juice or vinegar, for serving

Sort the beans by spilling them onto a baking sheet and removing any debris and broken beans. Transfer the beans to a colander and rinse the beans under cold running water.

Pour the beans into a deep, heavy 4- to 6-quart pot with a lid, such as a cast-iron Dutch oven. Cover the beans with water to the depth of the second knuckle on your index finger, stir in the baking soda, and soak at room temperature for 12 hours or overnight.

The next day, drain and rinse the beans well. Return them to the pot, cover them again with cold water to the depth of your second knuckle and add about one-quarter of the salt pork to the pot. Bring to a rolling boil over high heat, then decrease the heat to a simmer and cook, uncovered, for 2 hours or until the beans are tender and little liquid remains. Discard the salt pork in the pot; it has served its purpose.

Preheat the oven to 325°F. In a tall, deep earthenware pot or casserole with a lid, make a layer of beans "four fingers deep," as Marquis says—use about a third of the beans. Poke the bay leaf into the beans.

Cover the layer of beans with a few slices of the remaining salt pork. Drizzle with a thin layer of molasses. Make another layer of beans, tuck the onion slices into the beans, and dot the mustard on the onions. Cover with another layer of salt pork and another drizzle of molasses. Season this layer with a few grinds of black pepper. Continue to alternate layers of beans and salt pork, finishing with salt pork and molasses, and making the last layer of salt pork and molasses a little more generous than the others.

Bake the beans for 4 to 6 hours, covered, checking from time to time to make sure they do not need more liquid. If they do, add boiling water, no more than $1/2$ cup at a time; the goal is simply to keep the beans from sticking, not to make them soupy. Remove the bay leaf and serve, passing lemon juice or vinegar at the table.

navy bean soup

I make this recipe just for myself, freezing half or more in individual plastic containers that hold 2 cups, just enough for a fast lunch or simple supper. Some people, including me, like a little lemon juice or cider vinegar stirred into a bowl of bean soup, to brighten and sharpen the flavors.

2 pounds (about 5 cups) dried navy beans

1 1/2 pounds smoked ham hocks

1 onion, chopped

4 carrots, peeled and chopped

2 teaspoons dried summer savory or dried thyme

Salt and freshly ground black pepper

Sort the beans by spilling them onto a baking sheet and removing any debris and broken beans. Transfer the beans to a colander and rinse the beans with hot water until slightly whitened. Pour the beans into a large pot with a lid and add 2 quarts hot tap water. Bring to a boil over medium-high heat. Cover, decrease the heat to low, and simmer for 1 hour. Drain the beans by pouring into a colander in the sink; rinse with cold water. Return the beans to the pot.

Add the ham hocks, onion, carrots, and 2 quarts hot tap water; bring to a boil. Decrease the heat to simmer, cover, and cook for 3 hours. Remove the ham hocks and set aside to cool. Allow the soup to continue to simmer.

Remove the meat from the ham hocks. Dice the meat and return to the soup, discarding gristle and bones. Add the savory. Season with salt and pepper. Simmer the soup for 30 minutes longer, then serve.

19

On intoxicating aromas
and the world outside my door

WINTER CLOSED IN FULLY ON THE LAKE. The ice was thick enough to hold the ice fishermen's shanties; I saw those stout souls trudging to and fro, pulling the little sleds that held their fishing gear, kerosene heaters, augers for drilling through the ice, tip-up flags, and other supplies. Wally, who loves ice fishing, told me ice fishermen are happiest when the ice is at least two feet thick, without too much snow cover, although they rarely get ideal conditions. Still, I mistrusted the ice and would not venture out on it.

Earlier that winter, before the lake's ice had really gotten thick, I was working at the computer one afternoon. Looking out the window to compose my thoughts, I was horrified to see that Jim's gigantic yellow Labrador Retriever, Bob, had fallen through the ice at the end of the cove. Bob had his front feet up on a neighbor's dock, but couldn't jump high enough to pull himself out. I was out the door in a flash, pulling on my coat and hat as I ran to rescue him. At the dock, I could see that the dog had been in the water long enough for the water to freeze around him, poor dear. I don't know how I found the strength to haul the 120-pound Bob out of the water by his collar, but I did. Freed from the water, Bob stared at me for a second, gave himself a mighty shake, and, after a few wobbly steps on his ice-chilled legs, took off for home at a dead run. Jim told me later that Bob was quite content to lay near the fire for a day or two to recover.

But that had been, by far, the most exciting thing to happen in my new life in recent months. With only a handful of us in residence year-round at the lake, things were mighty quiet. Between snowstorms every couple of days and the miserable roads—although the county kept them well plowed, they quickly became icy and slick—I didn't go out much, and it was hard for people to get in to visit me. It was a good thing I liked to spend time alone.

Yet, I was not alone, not really. Thanks to the Internet, I could remain in close contact with my friends. I followed the postings on the Yahoo! group I belong to that is dedicated to local eating in southwest Michigan; the conversations there continued to be lively, if perhaps a bit more philosophical than they were in the summer, when everyone was busy. There's probably a group for your neighborhood, too, which you can find by typing "local food" in the search engine at groups.yahoo.com. The last time I looked, there were nearly 350 groups there. Look, too, at groups.google.com and groups.msn.com.

Because my grocery bills had dropped so drastically, I could afford to replenish the spices and other nonperishable specialty goods in my pantry through the Internet, too.

Herbs were easy for me to find, because I can grow the ones I use most frequently, as I've mentioned before. Technically, herbs are the leaves of an aromatic plant. Spices, though, are more problematic. Spices are the bark (like cinnamon), berries (like allspice and peppercorns), or other material from plants (like ginger root and nutmeg) that we use in cooking. And those, with the exception of juniper berries, don't grow in my neck of the woods.

So I had to cast farther afield to find them. Still, I applied a local mindset to their purchase.

Years ago, I learned about Talamanca peppercorns, for example. I make an annual order from the Brugger brothers, Bill and Dan, in Miami Beach, Florida. The Bruggers import their peppercorns from family farmers in Costa Rica, Honduras, and Ecuador. I prize the floral scent and bright flavor of Talamanca peppercorns and don't use any other kind. You can learn more about the Bruggers' efforts at talamancapepper.com.

I buy saffron—still the world's most expensive spice, which figures in a number of my favorite Moroccan recipes—from latienda.com, because they, too, source it from family farms. La Tienda sells only La Mancha saffron, the highest grade. A gram lasts me a year or more, because saffron's iodinelike, medicinal aroma and flavor means it is used in tiny quantities.

For other spices, I try to split my money between thespicehouse.com, based in Chicago, because I know its owners, and penzeys.com, because I like Bill Penzey very much. If I had an excellent local vendor of spices, I would certainly patronize the store; but I don't, so my spice orders must come from far away.

The Internet proved invaluable for locating other specialty ingredients as well. The orange-flower and rose waters I need for many of the Middle Eastern dishes I fancy have to be mail-ordered; so, too, does the Salsa Lizano I want for *gallo pinto*. Some kinds of beans and grains—like the light green flageolet beans for making cassoulet and farro, the Italian whole grain so good in winter dishes—were also impossible for me to find locally.

Coffee, too, came from far away. By shopping carefully, I found coffee beans that came from small farms, so I knew my money was supporting an individual rather than a corporation—and I also wanted to give the good small companies that import those coffees my business.

Still, I tried to keep these purchases at a minimum. I viewed them as special treats (with the exception of coffee, which, of course, is a daily pleasure). I calculated carefully what I actually needed, and made it a point not to overbuy. And certainly I spread these purchases over weeks and months.

Yet it was fun to see the intrepid Mary, my postal carrier, or one of the perennially cheerful UPS guys—they're all men on my route—bringing a box to my door. Every arrival was like a little Christmas and prompted a new round of cooking something exotic to celebrate their part in my life.

Outside my windows, my little lake slept for the winter. A quick glance might have suggested I was snowbound and isolated. But thanks to the Internet, the inside of my house smelled like Marrakech, or Provence, or Palma de Majorca, or Turin. Those bitter months were when I traveled—culinarily, at least.

seffa medfouna (saffron-braised chicken with steamed vermicelli)

MAKES 4 SERVINGS

This is an elaborate-looking classic Moroccan feast dish, but it is actually not difficult to prepare and needs no specialty ingredients, other than the saffron. You will need a double-boiler type pot with a steamer insert or a colander that can fit into a stockpot, and a close-fitting lid. The directions look long because they detail the four (or five) steamings of the vermicelli, which gives the pasta an entirely different texture than boiling would. The savory chicken and its sauce combine with the sweetened vermicelli to make an incredibly lush, complexly flavored dish that is totally foreign to most Americans. Your guests may be skeptical; mine usually are. But once they taste the dish, it disappears quickly.

VERMICELLI

1 pound dry vermicelli

1 teaspoon salt

2 tablespoons olive oil

1/2 cup raisins, soaked in 1 cup hot water

1/4 cup (1/2 stick) salted butter, melted

1/2 cup confectioners' sugar, plus more for serving

Ground cinnamon, to garnish

CHICKEN

1 whole 31/2- to 41/2-pound chicken, cut into eight pieces and skin removed

2 large sweet onions, chopped

1 tablespoon ground ginger

11/2 teaspoons freshly ground black pepper

2 (3-inch) cinnamon sticks

1 teaspoon saffron threads, crumbled

1 teaspoon ground turmeric

Salt

1/4 cup (1/2 stick) salted butter, melted

1/4 cup olive oil

1/4 cup chopped fresh cilantro

To make the vermicelli, break the vermicelli into pieces about 2 inches long. In a bowl, toss the vermicelli with the oil, making sure that all strands are coated. Fill the bottom of a large pot with a steamer insert about half full of water. Toss in a penny; if the penny stops clicking as the vermicelli steams, you will know you need to add water.

Tumble the vermicelli into the steamer insert or colander and fit the insert into the pot so that it does not touch the water below. Seal the joint where the steamer meets the pot with a damp dish towel or piece of cloth tied round the pot, if it does not form a tight join. Bring the water to a boil. Cover the pot. When you can see steam rising from the pot, begin timing and steam the vermicelli for 20 minutes. At the end of the steaming time, you will see some ends of the vermicelli poking straight up from the bed of vermicelli in the steamer.

Transfer the vermicelli to a large bowl and add 3/4 cup cold water. Using your fingers (it will be hot!) or a spoon, toss the vermicelli to let it absorb the water. Return the vermicelli to the steamer insert; cover and steam for 20 minutes. Again you will see the ends of the vermicelli poking up.

Again transfer the vermicelli to a large bowl. In a small bowl, combine the salt with 1 cup water; stir this into the vermicelli and stir until the water is absorbed. Return the vermicelli to the steamer insert; cover the pot, and steam once again for 20 minutes. Look for those ends poking up.

Yet again, transfer the vermicelli to a large bowl. Stir in the raisins and their liquid. Toss to mix. Return the vermicelli and raisins to the steamer insert, cover, and steam again for 20 minutes. Taste the vermicelli and, if it is not as tender as you wish, steam it for another 20 minutes after adding another 1/2 cup of water to the vermicelli.

To dress the vermicelli, toss it in a large bowl with the melted butter and confectioners' sugar. Keep warm until serving time (although the chicken should be done about the same time as the vermicelli).

To make the chicken, while the vermicelli steams, mix the chicken, onions, ginger, pepper, cinnamon, saffron, turmeric, 1 1/2 teaspoons salt, melted butter, and oil in a Dutch oven or heavy-bottomed pot. Cover and cook over medium heat, stirring occasionally, until the chicken is very tender and pulls easily off the bone, about 1 hour. Do not add water; watch that the chicken does not burn.

continued

Remove the chicken pieces and set aside to cool. Meanwhile, continue to cook the liquid in the Dutch oven to reduce it until it is almost all oil, about 20 minutes. Discard the cinnamon sticks and taste to correct seasoning with salt (the sauce should be a little salty and quite peppery).

Pull the chicken meat from the bones and chop the meat into bite-size pieces, discarding the bones. Return the chicken to the pot.

To serve, spread a layer of steamed vermicelli on a platter. Spoon the chicken and sauce into the center of the vermicelli. Scatter the chopped cilantro over the chicken. Cover the chicken and sauce with the remaining vermicelli, shaping it into a mound. Sift additional confectioners' sugar over the mound and draw vertical stripes from the top of the mound to the platter with ground cinnamon (this is most easily done by placing ground cinnamon in a spoon or a squeeze bottle and using the spoon or bottle to "draw" the stripes downward).

Moroccan food is traditionally eaten with the right hand only, without silverware, but you may provide your guests with spoons if you wish. Each diner digs into the mound from his place at the table, rather than serving himself on a separate plate.

red-cooked shredded beef with cellophane noodles

MAKES 4 SERVINGS

Red-cooking is the Chinese technique of braising meats in a soy sauce–based liquid. Cellophane noodles, sometimes called "bean threads," are made from mung beans and don't require cooking—just a 20-minute soak in hot water. The noodles are often sold in net bags, and inside the bag, there will be several "bundles." This recipe uses two bundles.

2^1/$_2$ pounds beef short ribs	2 (3-inch) cinnamon sticks
5 cups dry sherry	3 dried hot red chiles
^{1}/$_2$ cup sugar	3 whole star anise
^{1}/$_2$ cup soy sauce	1 teaspoon freshly ground black pepper
4 scallions, white and green parts, cut diagonally into 1-inch pieces	3 cups water
1^1/$_2$-inch piece fresh ginger, peeled and flattened with a cleaver	2 bundles cellophane noodles

Bring a large saucepan of water to a boil over high heat. Add the short ribs and cook for 1 minute to remove some of the surface fat. Drain in a colander.

Combine the sherry, sugar, soy sauce, scallions, ginger, cinnamon sticks, chiles, star anise, pepper, and water in a Dutch oven. Stir to mix. Add the short ribs, cover, and bring to a boil over high heat. Decrease the heat to medium low, cover, and simmer until the meat is fork-tender, about 2^1/$_2$ hours.

Using a slotted spoon, transfer the ribs to a chopping board. Cut the meat from the bones, transfer the meat to a bowl, and discard the bones. Remove the scallions, ginger, and whole spices from the sauce. Boil the sauce, uncovered, until it is syrupy, glossy, and reduced to 3/4 cup, about 15 minutes.

While the sauce reduces, put the cellophane noodles in a large bowl and cover with hot tap water. Let soak for 20 minutes, then drain and transfer to a serving bowl.

Return the short rib meat to the Dutch oven and heat through. Spoon the meat and sauce over the cellophane noodles and serve immediately.

cardamom-coffee toffee bars

MAKES 16 SQUARES

Toffee bars are hard to beat, and these are especially good with a cup of coffee. The coffee should be ground to a powder in a coffee grinder. If you prefer, you can use 1 teaspoon instant espresso granules.

$1/2$ cup (1 stick) salted butter, cut into pieces

$1/2$ cup firmly packed dark brown sugar

1 teaspoon vanilla extract

1 teaspoon very finely ground espresso-roast coffee grounds

$1/2$ teaspoon ground cardamom

$1/4$ teaspoon salt

1 cup all-purpose flour

6 ounces semisweet chocolate, chopped, or 1 cup semisweet chocolate baking chips

$1/2$ cup almonds, toasted and chopped

Preheat the oven to 350°F. Line the bottom and sides of an 8-inch square baking dish with aluminum foil, letting the foil overhang the edges of the dish.

Melt the butter in a saucepan. Remove from the heat; stir in the brown sugar, vanilla, coffee, and cardamom. Add the salt and flour and mix just until incorporated. Spread the mixture in the bottom of the prepared baking dish.

Bake for 20 to 25 minutes, or until the toffee bars are golden brown with well browned edges. Remove from the oven and immediately scatter the chopped chocolate over the hot toffee bars. Return the toffee bars to the oven for a minute or two, or just until the chocolate softens. Remove from the oven and use the back of a spoon to spread the chocolate evenly over the toffee bars. Sprinkle the chopped almonds over the chocolate. Place the pan on a wire rack and let cool.

When the chocolate has set, lift the toffee bars from the baking using the edges of the foil. Use a sharp knife to cut into squares.

Store in an airtight container. These will keep for several weeks at room temperature or in the refrigerator.

> *Note: To toast the almonds, place them on a baking sheet and bake in a 350°F oven for about 8 minutes, or until lightly browned. Cool the nuts completely before chopping.*

20

On deep snow, bitter nights, and newfound wealth

JOHN CALLED TO TELL ME that his brother, Ed, and his mother were visiting. "I've been telling them about you, and I'd like them to meet you," he said. "Could we come over for a while tomorrow night? We'll have Andrew, Johnny, and Angel, too."

I looked around my tiny, messy house, considering the impossibility of entertaining anyone the way I was used to doing. Back in the day, I could seat fourteen at my gleaming Danish teak table, with its elegant chairs and stunning glass-fronted sideboard. I remembered the many merry dinner parties I'd hosted at that table and at others before it, tables dressed in gleaming snowy linens and crisp starched napkins, with sparkling glasses for the wines that accompanied each course and flickering candles to lend intimacy and warmth. I remembered tables that sagged under the weight of platters of food crafted to please those I'd invited, menus plotted to offer both new and familiar flavors, to tease and tempt my guests into a memorable evening. Those parties meant huge shopping lists and hours of preparation—all of it work that I loved, because the anticipation of a thing is one part of its delight, just as remembering it is another.

Now, my shoulders sagged. I felt a twinge of embarrassment, a fleet piercing of shame, that I could no longer entertain in the way I wished. My dear friend John knows my house, of course. But how small, how very shabby, it looked, as I surveyed its minute confines.

I considered it for a minute. It's now or never, I thought. You either make your peace with your new life, or you choose to spend your days grieving what you once had. I drew a deep breath, girded my spirit, and gave John my carefully thought-out response.

"Of course!"

It had been bitter those last several days, with temperatures below zero night and day. The knee-deep snow muffled most sound, save the creaking of the brittle trees and the rattling of the last of the oak leaves among their branches in the night winds. My decade-old Subaru grumbled and groaned before it rumbled to a start in that weather. It was always a gamble whether the good car would make it up the slippery driveway hill to the road on the first shot or if it would require several slewing, sliding, cursing tries. The snow crunched and squeaked underfoot like spilled popcorn on a tavern floor, and even my warm homemade hat and mittens couldn't prevent the cold's icy fingers from bruising my cheeks and turning my hands into unusable lumps.

Despite old silk longjohns and flannel-lined jeans, a heavy sweater over a turtleneck, and thick wool hand-knit socks, even with the little woodstove gamely putting her all into BTUs, I was chilly all the time as the sly, sharp wind found its way into the corners of the house. Pippin raised his feathers into a warm, downy pouf as he played on his rope in the kitchen or he huddled, one foot pulled to his belly to keep his toes warm, in his living room cage, which was draped on three sides with a blanket to keep him from drafts. Guffy disappeared, only to be rediscovered snugly nestled under the clothes filling the hamper, just the tip of his raccoon-striped tail giving him away. Boon twitched in his dreams, remembering younger days and faster rabbits.

Outside, the chickens sought whatever thin sunlight they could find, their feathers fluffed into an airy nimbus that made them look twice their usual size, but they didn't not venture long outside their warm coop.

I hadn't been into town in two weeks. Money was impossibly tight at that moment.

Although John said his people would have eaten, I wanted to make some nibbles available, because guests instinctively reach for something to eat when they're nervous or feel awkward, as well as when they're happy and having fun. So I set out a basket of crusty homemade whole wheat bread with bowls of olive oil and dukkah, the Egyptian nut-spice-seed mixture, for dipping. Nearby, a plate held a wedge of extra-sharp Colby. A dish of peppery pecans offered a different kind of flavor to tease and surprise. It was easy to put together a blueberry tart from the berries in the freezer, and a bowl of sweetened yogurt stood beside it, together with plates and forks. I opened a bottle of cyser and one of mead and ranged glasses around the bottles. I ground freshly roasted coffee and set up the Chemex pot so it would be at the ready. Pip's play stand gleamed, and Pip himself, who knows the signs of readying for guests, chattered away merrily. He loves company, does our Pip.

I had tidied the house, but tidying could do nothing about the gouged and scarred flooring in the kitchen, nor about the sagging couch, the overcrowded bookshelves, the bleak and dismal bathroom. It just had to do.

As the purpled shadows lengthened and the sky darkened to winter's inky blackness, John and his kinfolk pulled into the drive.

John and his brother made a chair of their arms and carried their mother through the deep snow and down the steps like a queen seated on a throne crafted of love and affection. Andrew held the kitchen door and suddenly, in a rush of cold air and many voices, the Parkers arrived.

Like most people who visit my house for the first time, Ed went straight through the house to the deck that overlooks the lake. I sat down with Mrs. Parker and told her that she had raised her son, who has been such a good friend to me, kindly and well, which put a beaming a smile on her sweet face and brightened her eyes. The kids—Johnny, Andrew, and Angel, all young adults—gathered in the kitchen with Mrs. Parker and me, reaching into the nibbles on the table. They talked about, and to, Pippin, who regarded them curiously and bobbed his head in greeting. Boon went from person to person, tail wagging, nosing hands for pats. Guffy made himself scarce at first; then, growing bolder, leapt to the kitchen windowsill, from which he could survey everything in safety. He slitted his eyes in sleepy curiosity, and I could hear his rumbling purr over the uproar.

Voices crisscrossed, and everyone talked at once. "I've never been in a kitchen like this," Mrs. Parker kept saying, alluding perhaps to the industrial shelving along one wall that holds dehydrated fruits and vegetables, glass jars of tomatoes and preserves and relishes, pantry staples, and stray kitchen equipment. Everyone roared with laughter when I called Ed by the wrong name for the third time in a row, and their hilarity at my gaffe warmed my blushing cheeks as efficiently as the lofty comforter on my bed warms my body on long, cold nights.

And then, suddenly, it was ten o'clock, hours longer than my guests had intended to stay. My cheeks ached from laughing and only crumbs remained on the table. The rafters rang with merriment and delight, here on the snowbound banks of little Stewart Lake. Imagine! My tiny house: a beacon of warmth on such a bitter, bleak night! I realized that I'd been standing for the last hour or more, leaning against the same counter where I'd tried to collect my tired, heartbroken thoughts back in April. When I lit here on that late spring evening, frightened and lonely, I could not imagine how happy I would be just a few months later. It seemed a genuine miracle.

After a flurry of rustling coats, where's-my-scarfs?, bear hugs, and kissed cheeks, the Parkers made their way up the hill to the car. Their farewells rang in the still, star-spangled night, drifting down to the very merry me still standing in the open door to see them away. When at last I closed the kitchen door on the gathering, hot, happy tears flashed in my eyes. Boon sniffed at the door, then turned and took himself off to bed. A blinking Guffy, still purring, twined about my ankles, asking for a snack. Pippin laughed, a throaty chuckle, apparently remembering the raucous outbursts of the last few hours; eventually, after a stretch of wings and legs, he shook himself to resettle his feathers. "Wanna step up!" he said. "Time for bed!" How right you are, Pip, I thought. As usual, how very right you are.

In these last months, I have learned how to create meaning in my life in new and different ways. I discovered wells of strength and confidence I didn't know lay within me. I became deeply embedded in my new spot and found myself delighting in the challenges that each day brought, instead of meeting them with fear and confusion.

The good food that I found near my home strengthened and nourished me and, together with the work of my own hands, gave me a sense of pride, security, and peace that I have never known before. The search for it led me to new friends and new ways of thinking about myself and the world in which I live. It provided me with the luxury of having enough to share, even on the spur of the moment, when money was tight and the future uncertain.

My life is newly deep and full of riches. I hope yours is as well.

dukkah

MAKES ABOUT 1 CUP

Traditionally, this Egyptian blend is made with hazelnuts, but they are very hard for me to find. I've made *dukkah* with cashews, almonds, pistachios, pecans, walnuts, and peanuts—sometimes a mix of several, sometimes with just one nut starring. Serve it with chunks of crusty bread and good olive oil; dip a bit of bread in oil, then in the *dukkah,* and pop the bread into your mouth. If you have leftovers, try rolling chicken breasts in it before a quick sauté.

2/3 cup nuts (hazelnuts, unsalted cashews, almonds, pistachios, pecans, walnuts or peanuts, or a mix of several kinds)

1/2 cup sesame seeds

3 tablespoons coriander seeds

2 tablespoons cumin seeds

2 tablespoons freshly ground black pepper

2 teaspoons crushed red pepper flakes

1 teaspoon coarse salt, such as kosher salt

Preheat the oven to 350°F. Spread the nuts on a rimmed baking sheet and toast in the oven for about 5 minutes, or until fragrant. Remove from the oven and set aside to cool. If you are using hazelnuts, tip them onto a clean kitchen towel while still warm and rub vigorously to remove the skins.

In a dry heavy skillet over medium heat, toast the sesame seeds, stirring constantly, until light golden brown, 3 to 5 minutes. Pour into a bowl.

In the same skillet, toast the coriander and cumin seeds, stirring occasionally, until they begin to pop, 3 to 7 minutes. Transfer to a spice mill or coffee grinder kept for grinding spices and process until finely ground. Tip the coriander and cumin into the bowl with the sesame seeds.

Put the cooled nuts in a food processor, spice mill, or coffee grinder and process until they are finely chopped but not so long that they form a paste. It's okay if some of the pieces are larger. Stir into the bowl with the sesame seeds and spices. Season with the black pepper, crushed red pepper, and salt. Mix to blend well.

Kept in a sealed jar and refrigerated, the *dukkah* will keep for a month or more.

buttered pecans with chile and brown sugar

MAKES 1 CUP

With nuts on hand, you can always offer something intriguing to your guests. These sweet-hot spiced pecans come together quickly and easily; their fiery praline-like glaze is crackly and surprising. Walnuts and almonds also take well to this treatment.

1/4 cup (1/2 stick) salted butter

1/4 cup firmly packed brown sugar

2 teaspoons crushed red pepper flakes

1 cup pecan halves

In a large, heavy skillet over medium heat, melt the butter. Add the brown sugar and cook, stirring frequently, until the sugar has melted and the mixture is bubbling merrily, 10 to 15 minutes. Stir in the red pepper. Cook, stirring constantly, for 5 minutes. Stir in the pecans. Remove the mixture from the heat.

Line a jelly roll pan or rimmed baking sheet with waxed or parchment paper and spread the pecan halves on the pan. Drizzle any remaining butter-sugar mixture in the skillet over the pecan halves. Let cool, then transfer the pecans to an airtight container. They will keep for up to 8 weeks.

IDEAS FOR PENNILESS ENTERTAINING

Fun party food doesn't have to be complex—or expensive. I think it's most appealing when there are lots of different flavors and textures on offer, so I try to include something sweet, something fierce, something crunchy, something smooth, and so on. I've tried all these with great success.

- Popcorn with various seasoning mixes. Pop a big batch, butter it lightly (guests dislike greasy fingers), and divide it among several small bowls. Season each bowl differently: one with grated Parmesan cheese, one with chili powder, one with ranch dressing mix, one with cinnamon-sugar. Dot the bowls around your party space so that one bowl is within easy reach wherever you know guests will gather.

- Choose a creamy base (yogurt, slightly drained, or sour cream, mayonnaise, cream cheese, or yogurt cheese) and stir in finely chopped or grated herbs and vegetables—scallions, bell peppers, carrots, whatever you happen to have handy. Leave it as is for a spread or thin it with a little milk to make a dip. It will disappear quickly.

- A Mather family variation on the above idea, which we call "Ethel Dip" for the woman who brought it into our lives, is $1^1/_2$ cups mayonnaise; $1/_2$ cup grated sharp cheese; $1/_2$ green bell pepper, grated (and its juice); and a bundle of scallions, thinly sliced, both white and green parts. Seasoned with a dash of Tabasco and a dash of Worcestershire sauce, it always seems a crowd-pleaser. It wants toasted thin rounds of bread, please, alongside.

- This is another old family favorite that sounds odd but is really very good: Mash equal parts of braunschweiger or smoked liverwurst and cream cheese or yogurt cheese together until smooth; season with a little dry mustard and good curry powder, enough to make it quite flavorful. Again, serve with toasted thin rounds of bread. I have observed even loudly self-proclaimed liver haters return to it again and again.

lemon-ginger blueberry tart with sweetened yogurt cream

MAKES 8 SERVINGS

I usually make tarts instead of pies for several reasons. Their shallow depth balances the proportion of fruit to pastry, and their fluted edges look dressy. They cook more quickly, and cool more quickly, too. A tart pan with a removable bottom makes serving them easy. I love crystallized ginger, and always keep some on hand for snacking. Omit it if you wish. Clearjel is a kind of cornstarch that is modified to stand up to canning fruits and pie fillings and is available from King Arthur (kingarthurflour.com) and other specialty food stores. Regular cornstarch can substitute in this tart's filling.

Pastry for a single-crust 9-inch tart

1 bright-skinned lemon

1/2 cup granulated sugar

2 cups frozen blueberries, thawed

3 tablespoons Clearjel, or 2 tablespoons cornstarch dissolved in 2 tablespoons cold water

2 tablespoons crystallized ginger, finely chopped

1 cup yogurt

2 tablespoons brown sugar

Preheat the oven to 350°F.

Line a 9-inch tart pan with a removable bottom with the pastry, trimming away any excess. Set aside.

Using a paring knife or a vegetable peeler, cut a couple of thin ribbons of zest from the lemon and set them aside for the garnish.

Using a Microplane grater, grate the remaining yellow part from the lemon onto a piece of waxed paper. Set aside. Cut the lemon in half; juice one half. You should have about 2 tablespoons of juice. Refrigerate the remaining lemon half for another use.

In a large, heavy saucepan over medium heat, cook the lemon juice, granulated sugar, and blueberries, stirring occasionally, until the blueberries

continued

soften and begin to pop, 5 to 10 minutes. Following the directions on the Clearjel package, add Clearjel (or cornstarch mixed with water) and cook until the mixture thickens, about 5 minutes. Remove from the heat. Stir in the ginger and grated lemon zest. Let the mixture cool slightly.

Pour the blueberry mixture into the pastry-lined tart pan. Bake for 20 to 25 minutes, until the pastry is golden and the filling is bubbly.

While the tart bakes, spoon the yogurt into a sieve lined with a coffee filter or paper towel placed over a bowl. Drain the yogurt for 30 minutes. Transfer the yogurt to a bowl and whisk to lighten and aerate it slightly, about 2 minutes. Whisk in the brown sugar. Cover and refrigerate until serving time.

When the tart has cooled, garnish it with the ribbons of lemon zest and refrigerate until serving. Serve warm or chilled, and top each piece with a dollop of sweetened yogurt.

AFTERWORD

DO YOU WONDER if you could do what I have done? I have some tips to share if you'd like to include more local food in your diet.

The very first piece of advice is to start slow. Think of something you use frequently in your kitchen and try to find a local source for it. When you're comfortable with that change, adopt another. Better to build on successes, I think, than to rush in and fail.

It's much easier to can six or seven jars of tomatoes every week than it is to can a bushel of tomatoes in one session. It's also kinder to the budget to buy a little bit of extra produce each week instead of a great huge lot at a whack. Putting up that half-dozen jars can be done while you're still delighted with what you just brought home from the farmers' market. I typically spend less than two hours canning and doing food preservation each week, not counting processing times (which are largely unattended). So plan to build your pantry little by little.

Alternatively, gather a few friends or members of your family and work together in a canning bee, splitting the results. By all means, include the kids if they're old enough to work safely with knives—age eight and above, I would think. Kids can hull strawberries and slice them, measure sugar for jams, lay fruits and vegetables on baking sheets or dehydrator racks, and perform many of the other chores involved in putting food by. Teens can wash canning jars and even load and unload canners. You'll be teaching your children valuable skills if you include them in the work. And you'll find they are much more willing to eat foods that they helped you preserve.

Look for, and join, an Internet group that discusses local eating in your area. Most have databases of local growers and will help you learn what issues particularly affect the locavore cause in your neighborhood.

A number of websites have sprung up to support local eating devotees. I certainly like localharvest.org, which has a searchable database for different kinds of local food producers, from community-supported agriculture ventures to farmers' markets to cheesemakers. Another website, localdirt.com, is newer and still expanding as I write this; it allows you to order directly from a farmer for pickup at a farmers' market or at the farm. If you live in the Midwest, familyfarmed.org has links to local growers, as well as information about local eating in general.

Find farmers' markets in your area either by searching localharvest.org or calling your county's Extension Office. New markets start every year, and one excellent trend I've observed is that many are organized to be convenient to people who work during the day. Additionally, if your family uses food benefits of some type, more and more farmers' markets are setting up to accept such programs. Take advantage of that.

As you do more and more food preservation, you will find that you quite naturally shift into cooking more. If your kitchen skills aren't strong, consider taking a class to bolster them. Beyond cooking schools, local colleges, libraries, and other institutions often offer cooking classes that are reasonably priced, as well as cookbook collections to fuel your imagination. Cooking from scratch is not only cheaper than buying processed food, it also keeps you in touch with where your food comes from.

Be patient with yourself, and kind. Change is hard, even good change. Give yourself credit for deciding to be proactive instead of unmindful. And enjoy the journey!

ACKNOWLEDGMENTS

No writer works in a vacuum, and I'm especially blessed by a strong and vocal bunch of supporters and friends.

At a time in my life when I could barely keep panic at bay, Scott Martelle not only listened patiently, but insisted that I create worthwhile work as a way through my troubles. I would have dedicated this book to him, but he would have been mortified. So to Scott, Margaret, Michael, and Andrew: I am ever in your debt for your amazing love and friendship.

A group of fellow strikers from the Detroit newspaper strike of 1995–1997 proved their lasting bonds of brotherhood by pitching in with cold cash and warm comfort when I needed it most. So to Rob and Audrey McKenna Decker, Greg Bowens, Michelle Andonian, Marla Dickerson and Reed Johnson, Dia Pearce, Emily Everett, Lou Mleczko, Daymon and Margaret Trimer-Hartley, Bryan Gruley, Mike McBride, the Martelles, George Waldman, Sandra Davis, and a couple of anonymous donors: your generosity humbled me. Know that my door is always open.

Old friends and new ones rallied to my side as I launched a new life.

My longtime cheerleaders include Michael Knobler, Joe Gray and Chris Layton, Barry Fitzgerald, Bob Fila, Sam and JJ Prestridge, Herald Grandstaff, Bob Pawlosky, Jill Melton, Beverly Bundy, Mark and Michael Swift, and Steve and Wheaten Mather.

My gaming friends in the Guardian of All guild, including Elijah Decker, Lucas Munoz, Justin Abney, Paul Gunther, Brandon Tellez, Tiffini Hargett, Scott Boyer, Aaron Davis, Chris Mullins, Steven Troyer, Kim Mcneil, Aereal Firlan, Alexis Wellington, Jim Latimer, and Edwin Javier Esquilin, kept me on an even keel in troubled times and converted virtual friendships into real-life connections I treasure deeply.

In my own backyard, Delton District Library director Cheryl Bowers and assistant librarian Tana Harding provided me with hugs and warm welcomes every time I walked through the library's door. Wally Davis, John and

Andrew Parker, Mary Guy, Jim Waller, and Kenny Null generously made room for me in their busy lives.

Every author should have a literary agent as dynamically capable—and as supportive—as I have been blessed to find in Jane Dystel and Miriam Goderich of Dystel & Goderich Literary Management. Their enthusiasm for this project bolstered my own. So to Jane, my lasting gratitude for your just-right combination of powerful encouragement and hands-offness, and to Miriam, my appreciation for your insightful, thoughtful comments on the work-in-progress.

In Ten Speed Press, I've been fortunate to find a home with a publishing house that shared my vision for this book from the get-go. So to publisher Aaron Wehner, editor Sara Golski, designer Nancy Austin, publicist Kristin Casemore, copy editor Andrea Chesman, and all the other Ten Speedians who helped bring this book to its lovely completion and launched it into the world: Thank you, thank you, and thank you again.

I couldn't have done it without your help. I wish also to make it clear that responsibility for any mistakes in this book falls squarely on my shoulders.

APPENDIX: HOW TO CAN

WHETHER YOU ARE CANNING in a boiling water bath or pressure canner, the first step is preparing the canner, jars, and lids.

To prepare a boiling water bath canner: Fill the canner with 4 inches of water and place over high heat. Place the rack in the canner. Cover. At the same time, fill a tea kettle with water and bring it to a boil.

To prepare a pressure canner: Fill the canner with water to a depth of 3 inches. Add $1/2$ cup of white vinegar if your canner is made of cast aluminum; the vinegar will help prevent hard water deposits on the jars and reduce mineral deposits in the canner.

To prepare the jars: Wash them in hot, soapy water. If you will be processing the filled jars for less than 10 minutes, immerse the empty jars in a boiling water bath and boil for 10 minutes to sterilize. Place the sterilized or washed jars on a shallow towel-lined baking dish and keep in a preheated 200°F oven until you are ready to fill them.

To prepare the lids: Set them in hot water for at least 5 minutes. They do not have to be boiled. Screw bands need no special treatment.

FILLING THE JARS

Fill the jars according to the recipe directions, leaving the headspace called for in the recipe. The headspace is the space between the top of the contents and the rim of the jar. To remove any air bubbles, use a slender rubber spatula or a table knife to cut through the jar's contents. Wipe the rims clean with a clean dish towel. Apply the lids and screw bands, securing the screw bands so they are just fingertight—that is, as tight as you can get them by using your fingertips, not your hand or a wrench.

PROCESSING IN A BOILING WATER BATH

Transfer the filled hot jars to the boiling water bath canner and add boiling water from the tea kettle as needed to ensure that the jars are covered by at least 1 inch of water. Cover the canner, bring the water to a boil over high heat, and process the jars for the amount of time specified in the recipe, beginning to count the time when the water returns to a hard boil.

When the processing time is up, remove the lid from the canner and let stand for 10 minutes before removing the jars and placing on a towel-lined baking sheet or counter.

Listen for the "ping!" that tells you have a good seal. The jar lids will have depressions in their center if the seal is sound. Let the jars stand for at least 12 hours before moving them to storage. Remove the screw bands before storing.

PROCESSING IN A PRESSURE CANNER

Transfer the filled jars to the canner. Apply the lid; it's much easier to secure when the water inside is not boiling, but the water needs to be warm so the jars don't crack from sudden temperature change. Bring the water in the canner to a boil; allow to vent steam for 10 minutes. Apply the gauge at the specified amount of pressure (usually 10 pounds). Process for the amount of time specified in the recipes, beginning the timing when the gauge begins to rock, adjusting the heat as necessary to keep the gauge steady at 10 pounds (for dial gauges) or rocking 3 to 5 times each minute (for weighted gauges). If the pressure drops, stop timing and raise the heat; resume timing when the correct pressure is regained.

When the processing time is up, allow the pressure in the canner to reduce naturally; the canner's safety gauge will drop to its original position and no steam will escape when you remove the gauge. When the canner is completely depressurized, uncover the canner and let stand for 10 minutes.

Transfer the jars to a towel-lined baking sheet or counter. Listen for the "ping!" that tells you have a good seal. Look for the concave dip in the jar lids to show that a secure seal has been obtained. Let the jars stand for at least 12 hours before moving them to storage. Remove the screw bands before storing.

Consult your canner's directions for adjustments in timing and pressure if you live at high altitudes; they vary from manufacturer to manufacturer.

Take time to label each jar. Months after the work is done, it can be hard to tell crushed tomatoes from tomato sauce. I use $1^3/_4$ by-$2^1/_2$ inch self-stick mailing labels, running them sideways up the jar on half-pint jars and putting them on the lids of larger jars.

Watch for signs of spoilage in home-canned goods. Such signs include mold, lids that bulge, leaks, or off odors. Discard such jars immediately, without opening them whenever possible, and don't sniff the contents to see if they're safe! The organisms that cause spoilage can be inhaled. I have never had a problem with my home-canned goods, but there's no reason to take dangerous chances with your family's health.

MEASUREMENT CONVERSION CHARTS

VOLUME

U.S.	Imperial	Metric
1 tablespoon	$1/2$ fl oz	15 ml
2 tablespoons	1 fl oz	30 ml
$1/4$ cup	2 fl oz	60 ml
$1/3$ cup	3 fl oz	90 ml
$1/2$ cup	4 fl oz	120 ml
$2/3$ cup	5 fl oz ($1/4$ pint)	150 ml
$3/4$ cup	6 fl oz	180 ml
1 cup	8 fl oz ($1/3$ pint)	240 ml
$1 1/4$ cups	10 fl oz ($1/2$ pint)	300 ml
2 cups (1 pint)	16 fl oz ($2/3$ pint)	480 ml
$2 1/2$ cups	20 fl oz (1 pint)	600 ml
1 quart	32 fl oz ($1 2/3$ pints)	1 l

LENGTH

Inch	Metric
$1/4$ inch	6 mm
$1/2$ inch	1.25 cm
$3/4$ inch	2 cm
1 inch	2.5 cm
6 inches ($1/2$ foot)	15 cm
12 inches (1 foot)	30 cm

TEMPERATURE

Fahrenheit	Celsius / Gas Mark
250°F	120°C / gas mark $1/2$
275°F	135°C / gas mark 1
300°F	150°C / gas mark 2
325°F	160°C / gas mark 3
350°F	180 or 175°C / gas mark 4
375°F	190°C / gas mark 5
400°F	200°C / gas mark 6
425°F	220°C / gas mark 7
450°F	230°C / gas mark 8
475°F	245°C / gas mark 9
500°F	260°C

WEIGHT

U.S. / Imperial	Metric
$1/2$ oz	15 g
1 oz	30 g
2 oz	60 g
$1/4$ lb	115 g
$1/3$ lb	150 g
$1/2$ lb	225 g
$3/4$ lb	350 g
1 lb	450 g

ABOUT THE AUTHOR

ROBIN MATHER is a Michigan native and third-generation journalist whose passion for food and its sources has taken her around the country and the world. She is a two-time James Beard Award finalist for feature writing on food, and her work has been syndicated in newspapers and magazines across North America and abroad.

Mather was the food editor of the *Detroit News* from 1987 to 1995, a senior writer at *Cooking Light* magazine from 2000 to 2003, and most recently, a staff reporter for the food section of the *Chicago Tribune* from 2003 to 2009. She also started and ran a small goat dairy from 1995 to 2000 in Mississippi. Her first book, *A Garden of Unearthly Delights: Bioengineering and the Future of Food* (Dutton, 1995) was the first book about genetic modification of crop and livestock (and its consequences for the food supply) aimed at a broad market. She lives in a 650-square-foot cottage on a small lake in southwest Michigan, where she is eight miles from the nearest street light. Visit thefeastnearby.com.

INDEX